THE SIX TRIALS OF JESUS

Books by John W. Lawrence

The Seven Laws of the Harvest

The Six Trials of Jesus

THE SIX TRIALS OF JESUS

JOHN W. LAWRENCE

kregel
PUBLICATIONS

Grand Rapids, MI 49501

The Six Trials of Jesus by John W. Lawrence

Copyright © 1977 and 1996 by John W. Lawrence

Published in 1996 by Kregel Publications, a division of Kregel, Inc., P. O. Box 2607, Grand Rapids, MI 49501. Kregel Publications provides trusted, biblical publications for Christian growth and service. Your comments and suggestions are valued.

Cover painting: *Ecce Homo* by Antonio Ciseri (1821–1891), Galleria d'Arte Moderna, Florence
Cover design: Alan G. Hartman

Library of Congress Cataloging-in-Publication Data
Lawrence, John W., 1927–
   The six trials of Christ / John W. Lawrence.
      p.   cm.
   Originally published: 1977.
   1. Jesus Christ—Biography—Passion Week. 2. Jesus Christ—Trial. I. Title.
BT414.L38   1996   232.96—dc20   95-52495
                                                                              CIP

ISBN 0-8254-3152-2 (paperback)

2 3 4 5 Printing / Year 00 99 98

Table of Contents

Preface

You are about to take a journey that is entirely different from any you have ever taken before. Few have ever experienced what you are about to experience as you walk with Christ through a day of His life. Don't stop your walk with the Lord until you are standing there beside Him this particular night of human history, and feel something of His heart. He had told His disciples, "Come unto me, all ye that labour and are heavy laden, and I will give you rest" (Matt. 11:28). They had done that. But He had also said to them, "Take my yoke upon you, and learn of me; for I am meek and lowly in heart: and ye shall find rest unto your souls" (11:29). This the disciples had failed to do—at least during the time when the Lord walked with them on earth. They never had learned His heart. During the coming hours He will say to three of them, "My soul is exceeding sorrowful, even unto death. Tarry ye here, and watch with me" (26:38), but they will fall fast asleep. Yet what they failed to learn, they came to understand later on, and so can we as we re-live this day in His life.

There has never been another twenty-four-hour period like this before in all of time, and there shall never be another. Everything in Scripture moves either toward this one day in human history, or everything moves away from it. It stands as the *ne plus ultra* of time.

Something of the importance of this day can be seen by taking a moment to examine the extent to which Scripture covers it at length. For instance, in the four Gospels we have four chapters devoted to the first thirty years of Christ's life, while we have 85 chapters devoted to the last three and a half years He was on this earth. The emphasis is clearly placed by God on *the last three and a half years.*

Of the 85 chapters devoted to the three and a half year ministry of Christ, 56 chapters are given to the entire period up to the last week, while 29 chapters concern the last week alone. The emphasis is clearly on *the last week.*

Now of the 29 chapters that speak on the events of the last week, 13 of these chapters are devoted to the events of the last day which began at sundown and ends at sundown. With 13 chapters devoted to one day's events, and 16 chapters for the other six days, the emphasis is clearly upon *the last day.*

Matthew	Last week—8	Last day—2
Luke	6	2
Mark	6	2
John	9	7
	29	13

But let us carry this one step further. The events of the last day are given in a total of 579 verses in the four Gospels. Of these, 218 are devoted to the betrayal, arrest and the six trials, with the remaining 361 verses given to all the other events of the day which include the passover supper and teaching ministry of Christ in the Upper Room, the Lord's supper, the high priestly prayer of John 17, the prayers in Gethsemane, the carrying of the cross, the crucifixion, together with all the events of the cross, and finally the tomb and burial. Something of the emphasis on the arrest and trial can be observed also by considering the time involved. The betrayal had to take place between 2:00 and 2:30 A.M., and we shall discover that the trials were concluded by approximately 6:30 in the morning. This makes less than a *five hour period*, leaving 19 hours for all the other events of the day. If the entire day was covered as extensively as this period, twice as much would have been written in Scripture about this day.

Anyway one looks at it, these trials are the emphasis of the Holy Spirit's writing of Scripture in reference to the life of Christ. Yet even though this is true, very few have made an effort to write or speak upon them, and even less to thoroughly study them. Therefore let us make an effort to correct this. Take time with an open Bible to read all the Scriptures involved. It is not my comments about the Scripture that is important, but the Scriptures themselves. Take time to meditate upon these things. Re-live them in your life. Become familiar with everything that happened, and you will be richly rewarded.

Having concluded the study of these trials, we will endeavor to discover why so much space is devoted to them. The message is vital, and, futhermore, it is practical.

Chapter 1

A Prophet in Israel

Any study of the trials of the Lord Jesus Christ must commence long before the Lord is led bound from the Garden of Gethsemane, and taken first to Annas. The Lord had, over a period of six months, told His disciples in detail what would take place when they went their last time to Jerusalem. Evidently He had specific reasons for doing this. He not only sought psychologically to prepare them for His rejection and death, but also was showing He knew all things that would be happening at this time. His death was not going to be an accident, nor was He the victim of an angry, uncontrollable mob. Rather, all things determined beforehand were going to be fulfilled in Him. But even more than this, He had of necessity, to demonstrate that He was *the prophet* that was to come.

The Law of the Prophet

The law had given Israel the specific procedure whereby the nation was to identify a true prophet and also a false prophet. Every prophet had to give predictions concerning the immediate history of people. When these predictions came to pass, then the people could know conclusively that this was a true prophet of the Lord to whom they must give heed. If the predictions did not come to pass, the people were to stone this one as a false prophet. The passage is Deuteronomy 18.

"The Lord thy God will raise up unto thee a Prophet from the midst of thee, of thy brethren, like unto me; unto him ye shall hearken; according to all that thou desirest of the Lord thy God in Horeb in the day of the assembly, saying, Let me not hear again the voice of the Lord my God, neither let me see this great fire any more, that I die not. And the lord said unto me, They have well spoken that which they have spoken. I will raise them up a Prophet from among their brethren, like unto thee, and will put my words in his mouth; and he shall speak unto them all that I shall command him. And it shall come to pass, that whosoever will not hearken unto my words which he shall speak in my name, I will require it of him. But the prophet, which shall presume to speak a word in my name, which I have not commanded him to speak, or that shall speak in the name of other gods, even that prophet shall die. And if thou say in thine heart, How shall we know the word which the Lord hath not spoken? When a prophet speaketh in the name of the Lord, if the thing follow not, nor come to pass, that is the thing which the Lord hath not spoken, but the prophet hath spoken it presumptuously: thou shalt not be afraid of him" (vv. 15-22).

The people of Israel had not wanted God to speak to them personally at Mt. Sinai, but they wanted Moses to be a go-between where God could tell Moses all His words, and then Moses could relate them to the people. God condescended to this arrangement, but in doing so Moses becomes only the prefigure of another Prophet God would send to His people, Israel, with His very words. To Him they were to give heed. The Lord Jesus Christ was that Prophet, and John's Gospel emphasizes this truth.

While there was to come the true Prophet in Israel, false prophets could be a persistent problem. How was Israel to know the true from the false? God's solution was specific. A prophet had to give predictions concerning immediate events, and only when these occurred would the people know that this prophet was to be listened to concerning all the rest that he said. If they did not come to pass—and remember he had to have a 100% accuracy record, as nothing less would do—the people were not to fear such a one, but rather stone him as a false prophet since he was seeking to lead the people astray.

In speaking into the immediate situation, a prophet would often compound the details so as to make the fulfillment of his prediction an impossibility by mere chance. For instance, when King Sennacherib's forces came against the kingdom of Judah at Jerusalem to besiege it and destroy it, Hezekiah, the king, went before the Lord. The prophet at this time was Isaiah, and God sent him to Hezekiah with a message from the Lord. "Therefore thus saith the Lord concerning the king of Assyria, He shall not come into this city, nor shoot an arrow there, nor come before it with shield, nor cast a bank against it. By the way that he came, by the same shall he return, and shall not come into this city, saith the Lord" (II King 19:32-33). While this was all totally contrary to the very intent of the king and his army, and the reason for which they had come against Jerusalem, this is what literally happened. By this method, Israel knew that Isaiah was God's prophet.

The Predictions of the Lord Jesus Christ

The Lord Jesus Christ, ministering before the people in the office of prophet, and being the fulfillment of Moses' prediction of the prophet that was to come, is no exception to the law of the prophets. He had to speak into the historical situation, and these predictions must be literally and completely fulfilled. The predictions of Christ are so specific, detailed, and numerous, that no amount of mere chance could fulfill them. Most of these predictions concern the last day of the Lord's life, and since many are directly connected with the events of the six trials, it would be well to trace them through Matthew's Gospel, arranging the Scripture to reveal each time a new predictive element is added. Matthew 16:21, "From that time forth began Jesus to shew unto his disciples how that he must go

    (1)   unto Jerusalem

    (2)   and suffer

    (3)   many things

    (4)   of the elders

    (5)   and chief priests

    (6)   and scribes

    (7)   and be killed

    (8)   and raised again

    (9)   the third day."

Matthew 17:12, "Likewise shall also the Son of man

    (10) suffer of them (whatsoever they listed)."

         This gives an added detail. While the Lord had said before that He was going to suffer, and to suffer many things, He now adds that He will suffer of them whatever they desired to do.

Matthew 17:22, "The Son of Man

    (11) shall be betrayed into the hands of men."

         The fact is added that He will be betrayed.

Matthew 20:18, "Behold, we go up to Jerusalem; and the Son of man shall be betrayed

    (12) unto the chief priests

    (13) and unto the scribes

    (14) and they shall condemn him

    (15) to death

    (16) and they shall deliver him

    (17) to the Gentiles

    (18) to mock

    (19) and to scourge

    (20) and to crucify him

and the third day he shall rise again."

Matthew 26:2, "Ye know that after

    (21) two days is the feast of the passover, and the Son of man is betrayed to be crucified."

         There are only two days to go. But they said that this was the one day that they would not take Him (26:3-5). He is calling the plays, not them.

         As we approach the cross we find a strange agreement between heaven and hell. Both light and darkness are going to the same direction—His death. Both God and Satan are aiming at the crucifixion of Christ. Righteousness and sin are going to meet each other on the cross. He has told the very day.

In Matthew 26:20, the two days had passed, as the Jewish day begins at sundown. By the next sundown, Christ must be dead, or He is a false prophet and deserves to die.

Matthew 26:21, "Verily I say unto you, that

(22) one of you shall betray me."

He will be betrayed by one of His own disciples.

Matthew 26:29, "But I say unto you,

(23) I will not drink henceforth of this fruit of the vine, until that day when I drink it new with you in my Father's kingdom."

The Lord prophesies He will not drink another drink of this fruit of the vine in His remaining hours upon earth. Had He merely said that He would not drink again of "the fruit of the vine," it would have been wrong.

To fulfill an Old Testament prophecy (Psa. 69:21), He will say, "I thirst" (John 19:28), and at this time they will give Him vinegar to drink, which He receives (19:29-30; Matt. 27:48; Mark 15:36).

Matthew 26:31, "Then said Jesus unto them,

(24) All ye

(25) shall be offended

(26) because of me

(27) this night."

All His disciples depart.

Matthew 26:32, "But after I am risen again,

(28) I will go before you into Galilee."

Galilee will be the disciples' rallying place after His resurrection.

Matthew 26:34, "Jesus said unto him [Peter], Verily I say unto thee,

(29) that this night

(30) before the cock crow

(31) thou shalt deny me

(32) thrice."

It will be this night before it even begins to get light, and it will not be once nor twice but three times that Peter will deny the Lord.

While these prophecies do not exhaust those given by the Lord, they do show something of the magnitude of His prediction.

The Law of Compound Probabilities

According to the law of compound probabilities, the likelihood of all of these predictions being fulfilled, particularly when many of them were exactly contrary to the wishes of the people involved, makes us realize that none other than the "Prophet like unto Moses" was on earth. To Him we are to give heed, for, as God has said, "whosoever will not hearken unto my words which he shall speak in my name, I will require it of him" (Deut. 18:19). The Lord, speaking to the people of Israel, said, "If any man hear my words, and believe not, I judge him not: for I came not to judge the world, but to save the world. He that rejecteth me, and receiveth not my words, hath one that judgeth him: the word that I have spoken, the same shall judge him in the last day. For I have not spoken of myself; but the Father which sent me, he gave me a commandment, what I should say, and what I should speak. And I know that his commandment is life everlasting: whatsoever I speak therefore, even as the Father said unto me, so I speak" (John 12:47-50).

Jesus Christ not only prophesied into the immediate situation, and had these prophecies fulfilled, He also fulfilled all the Old Testament prophecies concerning His first coming. These total somewhere in the area of 300. A careful analysis, for instance, of Matthew 26 and 27 finds no less than 41 direct prophecies fulfilled, with another 59 allusions to other Scriptures in these two chapters alone. The law of compound probabilities makes the fulfillment of all of these predictions in the life of one person astronomical. It is as the Lord Himself had said, "Scripture cannot be broken" (John 10:35). It would be easier for the moon and the stars to cease to be than for one word of the eternal God to fail to be fulfilled. Of a truth, "There are many devices in a man's heart; nevertheless the counsel of the Lord, that shall stand" (Prov. 19:21).

The Lord Jesus Christ has demonstrated that He is Israel's Messiah, and it is to Him that we must give heed. As Peter said before the Sanhedrin, "This is the stone which was set at nought of you builders, which is become the head of the corner. Neither is there salvation in any other: for there is none other name under heaven given among men, whereby we must be saved" (Acts 4:11-12). He who came to be the Savior of the world is the rightful focus of our study.

Yet the wonder of it all will never be grasped until you realize He came into this world to be your Savior too (John 4:42). Oh, that He might be your personal Savior! Then may the Spirit of Christ be pleased to take the things concerning His person, and reveal them unto you as we study these six trials.

Chapter 2

The Experience in the Garden

The path leading to the six trials that the Lord Jesus Christ was to experience, led through a Garden. It was there He prayed earnestly, and received strengthening from heaven. It was there He asked three of His disciples to remain by His side, but they failed Him. On such sacred ground Judas came and betrayed Him with a kiss. And it was there He was arrested and led away bound to begin the ordeal of that night.

It is only right, in the study of the six trials, to travel first with the Lord through this Garden. Yet there is no portion of Scripture that I feel we know less about than the Garden of Gethsemane. This is not only my own personal feeling, but the attitude of nearly everyone who has dealt with the subject. The more it is studied, the less one fully understands the depth of this experience through which our Lord went. Although it is a different experience from Calvary, yet we indeed stand on very sacred ground, and need, spiritually, to take off our shoes as we approach this Garden.

The record of events is given in Matthew, Mark and Luke. We will give Matthew's account in full, and then refer to specific details that Mark or Luke might add.

"Then cometh Jesus with them unto a place called Gethsemane, and saith unto the disciples, Sit ye here, while I go and pray yonder. And He took with him Peter and the two sons of Zebedee, and began to be sorrowful and very heavy. Then saith he unto them, My soul is exceeding sorrowful, even unto death: tarry ye here, and watch with me. And he went a little farther, and fell on his face, and prayed, saying, O my Father, if it be possible, let this cup pass from me: nevertheless not as I will, but as thou wilt. And he cometh unto the disciples, and findeth them asleep, and saith unto Peter, What, could ye not watch with me one hour? Watch and pray, that ye enter not into temptation: the spirit indeed is willing, but the flesh is weak. He went away again the second time, and prayed, saying, O my Father, if this cup may not pass away from me, except I drink it, thy will be done. And he came and found them asleep again: for their eyes were heavy. And he left them, and went away again, and prayed the third time, saying the same words. Then cometh he to his disciples, and saith unto them, Sleep on now, and take your rest: behold, the hour is at hand, and the Son of man is betrayed into the hands of sinners. Rise, let us be going: behold, he is at hand that doth betray me" (Matt. 26:36-46; cp. Mark 14:32-42; Luke 22:39-46).

John, and the Omission of Gethsemane

It is not without significance that John's Gospel has no reference to this aspect of the Garden episode, and, by this fact, we can gain an insight into the meaning of Gethsemane. In John, the time has come for the grain to die (John 12:23-33). But before He dies, He begins to reveal Himself personally and intimately to "His own" disciples (John 13-16). John 13 gives preparation for Christ to speak to His disciples by washing their feet, and by Judas leaving the others. In John 14, the Lord speaks in the Upper Room, after which they apparently sing a Psalm, and leave the room (14:31). As they travel that night through the streets of Jerusalem, the Lord speaks further to His disciples, as John 15 and 16 records. Then, just before they all cross over the

Kidron, the Lord prays (John 17). With the prayer being ended, the Lord and the disciples move over the brook (18:1), and go up into the olive grove on the west slope of the Mount of Olives.

We need to notice that John in his Gospel does not record many of the things found in the three synoptic Gospels of Matthew, Mark and Luke. Such things as the Last Supper, the prophecy of the denial of Peter, the prayer in the Garden of Gethsemane, Peter's use of the sword, to give an example, are omitted in John. All of these things are given only in the other Gospels.

But the very fact that John's Gospel omits certain events in our Lord's life is, in itself, the key to the significance and meaning of these events.

For instance, Matthew and Luke both refer in detail to the temptation of Christ. Matthew presents the temptation because Christ is the King of kings. The greatest opposing king—the prince of the world—comes to contest Christ's kingship. Matthew's concept is that the one who is greatest will come out victorious. We might as well settle, right at the beginning, which one is greatest. Thus Matthew does settle it before he presents this King to the nation of Israel. The Lord is tested by the greatest opposing king and kingdom, and is victorious, revealing once and for all He is sovereign.

Luke, on the other hand, presents the temptation of Christ because he is writing about the Son of man. If He is perfect and sinless man, the Second Adam, the Seed of the woman, He will have to be victorious over the enemy, and not succumb to him. The first man sinned, but the second man cannot sin if He is to be the Savior of the world. Luke's purpose in the temptation is much different from Matthew's, even though the events and words are similar. Christ is found, by Luke, to be victorious as perfect Man, and so may be our Savior to bruise the head of the Serpent.

Mark, however, only mentions that the temptation took place (Mark 1:12-13), and then goes right into the work of Christ. The reason is that Mark presents Christ as the servant, and you are only interested in what the servant can do. A servant's temptations are insignificant as long as he is victorious—that is all that matters—not what is involved. As long as he hasn't broken the law and is free to serve, this is all that is necessary to know. What He does—His performance—this is what counts; so Mark says, "Let us get right into His work."

John does not refer to the temptation of Christ at all. Why is this? Is it because John did not know about it? Not at all. Rather, John is not seeking to write for us a complete life of Christ. As he says when he concludes his Gospel, "And there are also many other things which Jesus did, the which, if they should be written every one, I suppose that even the world itself could not contain the books that should be written" (John 21:25). The reason John does not write about the temptation of Christ is because John presents the Lord as God. He is Deity incarnate. Even though He was perfect man, he never ceased to be God; and God cannot be tempted with evil (James 1:13). Therefore, to have a temptation in John would be foreign to his theme and message.

Let us consider one more episode before we consider Gethsemane. Matthew, Mark and Luke all refer to the transfiguration of Christ. John does not. The reason is that in John's Gospel, the Lord is always in glory as the Son of God, and John wants you to see that glory shining through, even in His incarnation. For this reason John does not mention his own name once in the Gospel so that Christ might receive all the glory. God doesn't transfigure Himself, for this would reveal He was something less than glory. A king, a servant, a man: yes. He may be glorified. But God: no!

Thus Matthew, Mark and Luke have a Gethsemane experience, but John does not. This, I say, opens the key to our understanding of Gethsemane. It is related, first to Christ's humanity and not His deity. It is related, secondly, to temptation over which the Lord is victorious. But these areas are outside the scope of the Gospel of John. John will record the High Priestly prayer (John 17), but not the Gethsemane prayer. Certainly there is a striking difference between the two. The one is related to His deity; the other to His humanity. The one sees His glory; the other, His humiliation in suffering and agony of an anticipated cross-death. The one stands on the other side of Calvary on resurrection ground; the other stands on this side of Calvary in full view of the Sacrifice who knew no sin being made sin for us, and bearing in His own body the fires of God's wrath, with the Father forsaking the Son.

With this background, let us walk with the Lord in the Garden.

The Lord and the Garden

This place was called "Gethsemane" which means, *the oil press.* Originally among the olive trees there must have been an oil press to press out the oil from the olive berries. The name remained even though the press may have no longer been there.

The name remained because, under the providence of God, it is going to have spiritual significance. Here in this Garden the Lord will labor in prayer and spiritually press out the oil from the olive which will become the balm for many a wounded lamb and sheep. Still today on Mount Olivet there remain eight ancient olive trees, unquestionably descendants of this original grove.

Our Lord had not spent a night in Jerusalem since He arrived in what is called the Triumphant Entry to keep the feast of the Passover, and to die as our Passover Lamb. Each night He had gone outside the city, but each day He was in the city teaching, as the Lamb to be sacrificed must be observed by the people to be without spot before it was killed. Luke tells us He went to the Mount of Olives "as he was wont" or "as was His habit." Oftentimes the disciples had resorted here to spend the night.

Jesus chose this Garden this night first so that Judas would know exactly where to come and find Him. John tells us (18:2) that "Judas also, which betrayed him, knew the place: for Jesus ofttimes resorted thither with his disciples."

But I feel there is even deeper significance than this. While the first Adam lost his right to live in a Garden, the Second Adam gained His right to resurrection in this Garden. Thus the writer of Hebrews tells us, "Who in the days of his flesh, when he had offered up prayers and supplications with strong crying and tears unto him that was able to save him from [i.e. 'out of'] death, and was heard in that he feared ['because of His piety' NASB] " (Heb. 5:7).

Adam was placed in a Garden, and he learned about disobedience and its consequences. Christ voluntarily went to a Garden, and He learned obedience through relating to the Father. Adam hid himself from God in the Garden; Christ agonized before the Lord God in this Garden.

Words Used that Convey the Heart Condition

The revelation of Christ's sufferings in Gethsemane is given to us in words. By examining these words, we can commence, in a little way, to realize something of the character of the sufferings the Lord experienced. Matthew 26:37 reads, "And he took with him Peter and the two sons of Zebedee, and began to be sorrowful." This word [*lupeo*] means "to make sorrowful; to affect with sadness, cause grief; to throw into sorrow." Matthew adds along with this "and very heavy." This verb [*ademoneo*] signifies "to be troubled, distressed." *The Amplified Bible* translates it, "deeply depressed."

In Matthew 26:38, the Lord begins to talk to His disciples about His mental and emotional anguish. "Then saith he unto them, My soul is exceeding sorrowful, even unto death." This word [*perilupos*] is hard to intensify any stronger. It translates, "very sad, deeply grieved; exceedingly sorrowful. By adding the phrase, "even unto death," something of the intensity of the Lord's condition is realized. It signifies that the sorrow and agony He was experiencing were so tremendous that He was at the point of emotionally collapsing under its weight.

Mark 14:33 uses a different expression. He says Christ "began to be sore amazed [*ekthambeo*], and to be very heavy [*ademoneo*]." This conveys "to be struck with amazement, or terror; to be thoroughly amazed, astounded." It is only used by Mark (9:15; 14:33; 16:5).

Luke adds two other concepts as found in Luke 22:44, "And being in agony he prayed more earnestly: and his sweat was as it were great drops of blood falling down to the ground." The words "agony, anguish" are both taken directly into the English from this Greek word used only here in the entire New Testament [*agonia*]. The cognate word in the Greek from which this is derived [*agon*] signifies "a struggle, trial, contest." It was used of the intense struggles of those who participated in the Greek games. The amazing thing is what the Scripture says concerning the Lord's struggle. Because of the intense anguish or agony, the Lord Jesus prayed the more earnestly. What a lesson for us all! The more we are in a struggle and cast down, the more intensely we should pray.

But Doctor Luke adds another fact: "His sweat was as it were great drops of blood falling down to the ground." This doctor would certainly be the one to bring out such a fact, as it would be of primary importance to him. It was a cool night being the spring of the year, A.D. 32, and Scripture substantiates this fact by Peter warming himself by the fire this night (Mark 14:54). But with such intense mental and spiritual strain on Christ, the blood was forced out through the pores, and it falls in great drops on the ground. Very few have ever experienced such agony as this—and no one this severe. Our Lord had a solitary experience never required of any other creature, and never repeated again.

These words were selected to convey to us something of the feelings and sufferings of Christ in the Garden. It was a suffering of soul, even as later He will leave the Garden and suffer in body. He is going through spiritual torment in Gethsemane, even as He will endure physical torment in the trials and crucifixion.

The Significance of Gethsemane

But even with this background, we are still only able to touch the fringes of the cause of the soul sufferings of our Lord. Yet there seem to be some indications as to what is involved in this experience through which He is passing. It appears that the Lord Jesus Christ is suffering in anticipation of bearing the sins of the world. He had previously said, "I have a baptism to be baptized with, and how am I straitened till it be accomplished" (Luke 12:50). He said moreover,

"Now is my soul troubled; and what shall I say? Father, save me from this hour: but for this cause came I unto this hour" (John 12:27).

We need to keep in mind the truth concerning the doctrine of the kenosis, namely, that the Lord Jesus, in becoming man, never ceased to be God. But He voluntarily surrendered the independent use of His divine attributes as God to the Father in order to become the true and faithful servant of the Lord. Thus many of the Lord's miracles were done by the power of the Holy Spirit as God, not by the Lord Jesus Christ's power as God. For instance, the unpardonable sin was the attributing of the miracles of Christ done by the Spirit's power to the power of Satan. What the leaders of Israel realized was that the Lord's miracles were performed through a spirit's power, and not through the Lord's own power. What they failed to realize was that this power was that of the Holy Spirit.

Moreover, the devil's temptation of Christ was actually, "Since you are the Son of God, command these stones to be made bread." But if He had done so, the Lord would have exercised His own deity apart from the will of the Father. The mockers, furthermore, said to Him, "Come down from the cross and we will believe." Had He come down, He could not have been man's Savior because it would have been an expression and use of His own deity, and not the operation of the Spirit of God working in the will of God. He would, then, not have been a perfect servant without sin, and so could not have been our Savior. Of a truth, if He saved Himself, He could not have saved others.

But not only was the Lord limited as to His expression of His deity through the incarnation, He was also in subjection to the Father in everything, including the Son's knowledge of what was future. As the Son of God, Christ knew everything—being omniscient. But as the Son of man, Christ knew only those things which the Father revealed to Him. Notice this fact in Scripture.

"But of that day and that hour knoweth no man, no, not the angels which are in heaven, neither the Son, but the Father" (Mark 13:32).

"I have many things to say and to judge of you: but he

that sent me is true; and I speak to the world those things which I have heard of him. They understood not that he spake to them of the Father. Then said Jesus unto them, When ye have lifted up the Son of man, then shall ye know that I am he [literally, 'that I am'], and that I do nothing of myself; but as the Father hath taught me, I speak these things" (John 8:26-28).

"For I have not spoken of myself; but the Father which sent me, he gave me a commandment, what I should say, and what I should speak. And I know that his commandment is life everlasting: whatsoever I speak therefore, even as the Father said unto me, so I speak" (John 12:49-50).

"For I have given unto them the words which thou gavest me . . . " (John 17:8).

So our Lord was in complete servitude to the Father. He exercised no attribute of deity except as the Father willed. This again does not say that He did not possess all the attributes, but He used none of them apart from the will of the Father. He had known why He came into the world from the beginning. It was to suffer and to die. The cross was ever before Him. But now as Christ stands before the cross in full view of its cup that He must drink and the baptism with which He must be baptized (Matt. 20:22), the Lord is experiencing the full anticipation of Calvary. The cup He must drink is that of being made sin—He, the Sinless One, who knew no sin. He comes within full consciousness of its awfulness and He is tormented in soul. Only true holiness can possibly feel the full effects of iniquity and sin. It is abominable to Him. He feels Himself as a culprit before God. He experiences something of the distress of the damned and the abandonment of God and man. He prays, but experiences no relief of soul. God is not answering Him, immediately. His disciples give Him no satisfaction. He seeks in desperation for some help from His disciples, but all in vain. He is going this road alone—all alone.

Not only did the Lord have a cup, He had a baptism. The cup is one thing; the baptism is another. He was to be identified with our sins—that is His baptism—but He must also drink the cup of God's wrath against sin without mercy in order that we might drink the cup of mercy without any wrath whatever (cp. Rom. 8:1). To bear sins is one thing; to bear the wrath of God for sins is another. But someone might well ask, how can the disciples—James and John—enter into this same cup and baptism which they said they were willing and able to take, and the Lord said they would partake (Matt. 20:23)? They can only enter into it the same as Paul desired to enter into the fellowship of Christ's suffering, which Paul speaks about in Philippians 3:10. James and John, and Paul, as well, did experience sufferings unjustly from man, and they were identified with death for the Lord's sake, but what they suffered was not efficacious in behalf of sinners as was the suffering and death of the Lord Jesus Christ.

In this experience in Gethsemane, Christ is experiencing what it is to be accursed. As the accursed one, Christ will have the Father to forsake Him. *Never* has the Son experienced this before, and it seems to be more than He can possibly stand. It seems His heart would break, and His grief is even to the point of death—a grief so intense that it produces a blood-letting through the pores of His skin. Physical suffering is bearable; soul suffering is bearable; but His Spirit suffering is nigh unbearable. Remember that the Lord Jesus was perfect body, soul and spirit in His humanity. In spirit there is a perfect God-consciousness, so that experiencing what it is to be made sin and to be accursed from God is something He feels to the point of infinity. Because of His suffering in spirit, Christ suffers in soul and in body. The reason is that man is one being, and these categories are interrelated.

Since there was no other way for man to be saved than for Christ to bear man's sin and punishment, Christ surrenders to the Father His will completely, gains the victory in prayer, and rises to go about the Father's will to Calvary, confident in the Lord. The very intensity of the Lord's suffering proves the completeness of His obedience. As Psalm 43:5 says, "Why art thou cast down, O my soul? and why art thou disquieted within me? hope in God: for I shall yet praise him, who is the health of my countenance, and my God." The writer of Hebrews admonished his readers who are going through testings to look "unto Jesus . . . who for the joy that was set before him endured the cross, despising the shame, and is set down at the right hand of God" (Heb. 12:2). When Christ comes to His disciples the third time, the agony and struggle is over. He no longer needs them. He has the victory of the Father's grace being sufficient. The Father has answered Him. He knows what His Father's will is, and goes about to do it. Not once from the Garden to the cross is the Lord tempted to despair. His spiritual torment is over—for now. His physical torment begins.

But with all that we have said, we seem not to have exhausted the entire truth of the Gethsemane experience. We have previously seen that the Garden is related to Christ's humanity, not His deity, and to temptation in His humanity over which the Lord is victorious. For these reasons it is not included in John's Gospel. Dr. Luke has stated following the temptation of Christ, "And when the devil had ended all the temptation, he departed from him for a season" (Luke 4:13). There is no other experience in the Gospels that corresponds to a temptation, if Gethsemane is not such an experience. I believe we have to say that it was just that, for several passages of Scripture seem to indicate this: "This is your hour and the power of darkness" (Luke 22:53). Darkness was ruling under the plan and program of God. "The prince of this world cometh . . ." (John 14:30).

On a previous occasion Satan had brought before Christ the glories of the kingdom of this world to tempt the Lord (Luke 4:5-6). Could it not be that God was permitting him to bring before the Lord the horrors and agonies of being a lost soul? Remember that the demons knew all about their future torment and suffering, and asked the Lord if He had come to torment them before their time. These horrors may have been so great that Christ in His humanity suffered unto death, or was tempted by Satan to take His own life and thus escape the agony He was going through. Remember, however, the doctrine of the impeccability of Christ. As the God-man it was impossible for Christ to sin, but the temptation was *real.* Christ did have the power to lay down His life (John 10:17-18). Had He laid it down in anything but a cross-death, however, our salvation would have never been experienced. Furthermore, the very fact that Christ enjoins His disciples to watch and pray lest they should enter into temptation seems to indicate that the temptation is there for Him, but He will be victorious because of His prayer life. He is tempted as man, and He is meeting this temptation as a man, not as God. Thus He can say, "The prince of this world cometh, and hath nothing in me" (John 14:30). An angel came to minister to Christ in the Garden because He was completely submissive to the will of the Father. But angels and a flaming sword kept Adam out of the Garden because he was disobedient to the will of his Maker.

Some have said that Christ was about to die a premature death in the Garden of Gethsemane, and this was the reason the angel was sent and even the reason for Christ's prayer burden itself. *This cannot be true.* First of all, death is because of sin, and Christ had no sin; therefore, death had no claim on Him. Furthermore, death was in His power, which is not spoken of as death, but the laying down of His life (John 10:17-18). Finally, those who say this, have never examined the Scripture carefully. The angel came to minister to Christ before His sweat was as it were great drops of blood (Luke 22:43-44). The angel strengthened Him so that He was able to agonize all the more earnestly in prayer and so gain the victory through prayer—not as God but as man.

The practical application of this is great. The Lord does not ask us to go through something that He has not gone through Himself. Furthermore, no man has ever suffered so intensely. Whatever trial we may be asked to go through, it will never match the intensity of Gethsemane. But the won-derfulness of this episode is that the Lord met this trial as a man relating to the Father. It is in this way that He demon-strated how any one of us can secure victory through prayer and reliance upon the Lord. The Lord Himself expressed it so simply in speaking to His disciples: "Watch and pray, that ye enter not into temptation: the spirit indeed is willing, but the flesh is weak" (Matt. 26:41; Mark 14:38). As His disciples, may we be more like our Master, and gain the victory through prayer.

Chapter 3

The Betrayal

It is somewhere about 2 or 2:30 A.M. when Christ returns to His disciples from the agony of Gethsemane. Between this hour and 6:30 in the morning, Christ will be arrested and experience six trials. Some of these trials will be formal, some of them informal. At 9 A.M. Christ will be on a little hill overlooking the city of Jerusalem. It will be a place called "Golgotha" where He is crucified. He will then hang on this cross for six hours, the last three hours being in total darkness. The total time from His arrest, to trial, to conviction, to sentence, to execution of that sentence will be at the most seven hours.

The Sanhedrin and Jesus Christ

There has never been in the history of mankind on earth a greater miscarriage of justice than what is about to take place. Everything that happens is illegal. From the arrest to the crucifixion, every principle of justice was violated, and the provision of both criminal and ecclesiastical law flouted. So much is this the case that the Jewish historian, Jost, plainly calls it murder, for he does not believe that there was an actual trial. Edersheim agrees with him, but I believe the facts show otherwise. There was a trial, if that is what you may call it, and *it was even done twice* in order to give it some semblance of legality. There is no other reason for trying the case twice by the Sanhedrin except they *considered it to be a legal trial.*

But the proceedings of the Sanhedrin that will lead to the death of the Lord Jesus Christ commenced following the restoration of Lazarus from the dead. At that time, John tells us, the following occurred: "Then gathered the chief priests and the Pharisees a council, and said, What do we? for this man doeth many miracles. If we let him thus alone, all men will believe on him: and the Romans shall come and take away both our place and nation. And one of them, named Caiaphas, being the high priest that same year, said unto them, Ye know nothing at all, nor consider that it is expedient for us, that one man should die for the people, and that the whole nation perish not. And this spake he not of himself: but being high priest that year, he prophesied that Jesus should die for that nation; and not for that nation only, but that also he should gather together in one the children of God that were scattered abroad. Then from that day forth they took counsel together for to put him to death" (John 11:47-53). The Sanhedrin decided the *fact* of His death at that time. The only undecided factors were the *time* and the *means.*

Then two days before the passover, the Sanhedrin met again. Matthew records their deliberation at this time in the following manner: "Then assembled together the chief priest, and the scribes, and the elders of the people, unto the palace of the high priest, who was called Caiaphas, and consulted that they might take Jesus by subtilty, and kill him. But they said, Not on the feast day, lest there be an uproar among the people" (Matt. 26:3-5). Here the Sanhedrin meet in secret session at the home of the high priest. But the Sanhedrin were to meet only at their place of meeting. Instead they were meeting in the courtyard of Caiaphas' house. Moreover, the Sanhedrin were to meet openly and not in private. There were to be no secret meetings of this highest ruling body in Israel. But this particular meeting had been called by the

High Priest that they might give official sanction to the death of Jesus Christ. Yet it was all illegal since they had judged the case before there was any accusation, trial and defense. They have taken counsel that they might put Him to death, but they want to do this quietly and to wait until after the Passover period is over and the great number of the masses that are in Jerusalem for the occasion have returned home. This will be done lest the people should not agree to His death and there be trouble in the city.

Then another event occurs. As the chief priests and scribes were seeking the means by which they might take Jesus and kill Him, an event occurred in their favor. "Then entered Satan into Judas surnamed Iscariot, being of the number of the twelve. And he went his way, and communed with the chief priests and captains, how he might betray him unto them. And they were glad, and covenanted to give him money. And he promised, and sought opportunity to betray him unto them in the absence of the multitude" (Luke 22:3-6).

The law had said, "Cursed be he that taketh reward to slay an innocent person" (Deut. 27:25), but this never phased Judas. Satan enters this man, and he covenants with the leaders of Israel to betray to them the Lord. This is Satanic possession, not demonic possession. It was experienced in the Garden of Eden when Satan took possession of the body of the serpent, and spoke through it. It now occurs again, but this time with a man. He, likewise, will be coming to a Garden, and it will be there in the Garden where his betrayal will take place.

Judas and Jesus Christ

Two days have now gone by. It is the night of the Paschal Supper, and John relates to us the events as they occurred in the Upper Room. The Lord says to His twelve disciples, "one of you shall betray me" (John 13:21). The disciples did not know who it was (v. 22). They were utterly bewildered. They continually looked around on one another. Matthew 26:22 reveals each disciple around the table one at a time was asking if he might be the one.

No one suspected Judas because, first, he was a clever hypocrite. He had not slipped up in any point. Secondly, he was treasurer. This was an elevated position of privilege. Jews were money minded, and material riches were considered a sign of approval. Thirdly, Jesus had not been cool toward Judas even though He knew he was the betrayer (cp. 6:70-71). If Christ had been distant with him, this would have given him away. In the fourth place, Judas was in the number one seat at the table. According to Edersheim, the left hand side at the table was the highest place. Every place at the table had more or less honor to it (cp. Luke 14:10; Matt. 20:21). John was lying on Jesus' breast. That was Christ's right hand (and the number two spot), as they were reclining on their left hands. Judas was on Christ's left hand (the position of highest honor), or immediately behind Christ. The final reason why no one suspected Judas as the betrayer was that the sop was given to Judas first. The master of the dinner gave the sop first to the *honored guest*. It was the custom to give the sop with an invitation for one to put their trust in the Messiah and the Messianic kingdom. This act was grace on the part of Jesus. The Lord treats Judas as the honored guest even though he has covenanted to betray Him.

But instead of receiving the Son, Judas receives Satan (John 13:27). So important were those events to Satan that he was not going to allow anything to go wrong by having Judas repent of what he had covenanted to do. We must remind ourselves that the same is true of Satanic possession as demon possession. The person himself is responsible for allowing or permitting this to take place. This occurred because Judas wanted it to occur.

But what is behind the movement of Judas to leave the feast and go to the Sanhedrin (13:27-30)? John tells us in his Gospel. Simon Peter had asked John to ask Christ who it was going to be who betrays Him (13:24). Evidently Peter was too far away to ask the Lord himself. John asked Christ this question for both Peter and also for himself, as he too wanted to know (13:25). Both John and Judas could hear the answer because of their positions (13:26a). The Lord said, "He it is, to whom I shall give a sop, when I have dipped it." Christ then prepares the sop (13:26b). In it was placed pieces of lamb, bitter herbs, being itself a piece of unleavened bread. These were wrapped up, dipped, and handed to Judas Iscariot. By this action, Judas now knows that Christ knows who it is that will betray Him. But he also knows that John knows, and he will soon tell Peter, and eventually everyone will know. Thus the gag is up; Judas knew he was discovered.

Matthew 26:25 reveals that Judas then asked Christ (probably in a whisper), "Rabbi, is it I?" (it is interesting that Judas never called Jesus, "Lord"). Christ replied, "Thou hast said," which is an idiom for, "Yes, it is." This forced Judas to act. He rushes out into the night (John 13:30) and tells the Sanhedrin he has been discovered. If they want him to betray Christ, it will have to be *at once* or never. This forces the Sanhedrin to act even though they had previously said, "Not on the feast day. . . ." The Lord is showing in this that He is master of ceremonies, and *He* is controlling everything that is occurring.

The Arrangement for the Capture

Through the entire time period of the Upper Room discourse, the walk and instruction through the streets of Jerusalem, the High Priestly prayer at the brook Kidron, and of the agony in the Garden, Judas was waiting while elaborate preparations were made to capture this One. Because it was the Passover, it was full moon. When everything was ready, there came a great company, being led by Judas, coming out of the city, crossing the Kidron and ascending into the Garden. John 18:3 reads, "Judas then, having received a band of men and officers from the chief priests and Pharisees, cometh thither with lanterns and torches and weapons." "A band" is actually "the speiran." It refers, in military language, to a cohort of Roman soldiers, which is a tenth part of a legion. Each legion at full strength was 6000 men plus auxiliaries, and was divided into 10 cohorts. A cohort of soldiers, then, would be around 600 men. These were the Romans who at this time were controlling Judea, along with Syria, and were administered by a Roman governor who resided in Cesarea, on the coast fifty miles away from Jerusalem, but had a palace in

Jerusalem. Pilate, at this particular time, was governor, and on this particular night was in Jerusalem. Along with him were a number of troops to preserve order on this occasion when so many additional people from all over Palestine had come to Jerusalem. These soldiers had already been used to put down an insurrection, for Mark 15:7 tells us "Barabbas . . . had committed murder in the insurrection." They were ready for anything. The high priest summons their assistance in capturing a dangerous rebel and conspirator. The fact is that this cohort of Roman soldiers was probably already under his control (Matt. 27:65), or this may have been the occasion that placed them under his control. Beside these Roman soldiers, there were the "officers from the chief priests and Pharisees" or "the temple guard." They were the sergeants of the temple, and had the actual task of arresting Jesus. The Roman cohort was there to give them assistance, if needed. Moreover, they made any resistance a crime against Rome. They all came with lanterns and torches and weapons. If He hides Himself, they need light to find Him. If He defends Himself, they need weapons to capture Him.

But why such a great company that approached close to 1000 men? First, this served as a mask to the Romans that they were capturing a dangerous conspirator and rebel. After all, they knew why they were taking Him, and it was to put Him to death. For this, they needed Roman cooperation since the Jews did not have the legal right to execute the death penalty (John 18:31). Secondly, they did not know whether He and His disciples would fight, but if they did, they had them outnumbered 100 to 1. But remembering also that the Sanhedrin had not wanted to apprehend Him on the feast day lest there be an uproar of the people, they needed enough forces to guard against such an uprising. They were forced to act this night because Judas had been found out. If they had to act, they were glad they could do their work under the cover of *darkness* (cp. John 3:20 spoken to a member of the Sanhedrin). Very definitely we may be assured that these soldiers were ordered to be as quiet as possible, for the one thing that they did not want was an awakened populace until they had completed their work.

But having said all this, we have probably not touched

one of the main reasons which would never have been even breathed by anyone that night, but of which all the Jews would have been aware. The Sanhedrin were well aware of the miracles of Christ. For instance, in John 3:2 Nicodemus had said, "we know . . . for no man can do these miracles that thou doest, except God be with him." The whole Sanhedrin knew of the miracles of Christ (cf. John 11:47). Furthermore, they knew of the events that transpired when soldiers were sent to capture Elijah in the Old Testament (II Kings 1:9-14). In this incident, twice fire came down from heaven and consumed the captain of fifty with his fifty men that had come to capture Elijah. Here this night was the power of darkness in operation, and there was unquestionably a secret fear of meeting opposition. Never before in the conflict of the ages between God and Satan had there ever been a time when Satan's works were not opposed by the Lord's forces, and the Lord's forces opposed by Satan's. Satan never expected that this would be any different. But here was a play in which the opposition was allowed to capture the ball and run for a touchdown without ever being opposed once. Nothing like this had ever occurred before.

The Man, Judas

Judas was in the lead because, first of all, he knew the place where Jesus could be found; and secondly, he was the one who had covenanted to betray Him with a kiss. The very fact Jesus Christ had to be betrayed with a kiss signifies that the Lord Jesus Christ in His humanity could not be distinguished from any other man, or even from His own disciples. There was no halo around His head. There was nothing about His appearance that made Him stand out from other men. Therefore, it was necessary for one to identify Him with a kiss.

Here were the disciples being awakened from a deep sleep. Here was the Lord Jesus standing in complete composure. Here was Judas coming ahead of the others with a covenanted task to perform. Though Scripture does not say, it is very likely that Satan still possessed him, for the point of all was to accomplish the actual betrayal.

The Lord has said, "And truly the Son of man goeth, as it was determined: but woe unto that man by whom he is betrayed!" (Luke 22:22). Judas had made a covenant with death, and with hell was he in agreement (Isa. 28:15). In this he is a picture of the nation itself, both then and in the tribulation. Christ had known from the very first who would betray Him, for in John 6:70 and 71, He had told His disciples, "Have not I chosen you twelve, and one of you is a devil? He spake of Judas Iscariot the son of Simon; for he it was that should betray him, being one of the twelve."

Besides the New Testament that speaks of Judas, the Old Testament gives a number of references also. In Psalm 41:9, it is said, "Yea, mine own familiar friend, in whom I trusted, which did eat of my bread, hath lifted up his heel against me." Then in Psalm 55, we read, "for it was not an enemy that reproached me; then I could have borne it: neither was it he that hated me that did magnify himself against me; then I would have hid myself from him: but it was thou, a man mine equal, my guide [companion], and mine acquaintance. We took sweet counsel together, and walked unto the house of God in company" (vv. 12-14; cp. Matt. 26:23). Verse 20 of Psalm 55 adds, "He hath put forth his hands against such as be at peace with him: he hath broken his covenant." Psalm 69 is a Messianic Psalm, and in it is recorded, "Let their habitation be desolate; and let none dwell in their tents." This is quoted in Acts 1:20 of Judas. In the near view of prophecy, it does refer to him; however, in the far view and the ultimate fulfillment, it refers to the nation of Judah and Jerusalem whom he represents. Psalm 109 gives the admonition, "Let his days be few, and let another take his office" (v. 8). This is also quoted in Acts 1:20 as referring to Judas. One other familiar reference is given in the prophecy of Zechariah, "And I said unto them, If we think good, give me my price; and if not, forbear. So they weighed for my price thirty pieces of silver. And the Lord said unto me, Cast it unto the potter: a goodly price that I was prised at of them. And I took the thirty pieces of silver, and cast them to the potter in the house of the Lord" (11:12-13).

What made Judas act as he did? Satan possessing his

body was only the end result of a long process. To summarize it in one word, it was "pride." It is the very same sin that caused Satan to fall in heaven. It seems that he had formed a grandiose picture of the kingdom, and visualized himself in an exalted position in it. When this did not materialize, and just the reverse was announced by the Savior—that is, that they would suffer and be persecuted and cast into prison, he seizes not only the money of the disciples, of which he was the treasurer, and hated that the costly ointment was not sold so he could have that money too (John 12:4-6), but adds to it 30 more pieces of silver. This, he felt, would compensate him in a small way for his disappointment for not being great in a glorious kingdom.

Remember, trials test men. Many an individual has turned against a church or a Spirit-directed movement to which he belonged when it did not materialize into that vision of grandeur that he had expected, or when he did not become a kingpin in it.

The Procession at the Garden

Here, then, are the events as they happened in sequence. Judas is with the entire company leading the way into the Garden when something unexpected happens. Jesus comes forward to meet them. John records it in the 18th chapter of his Gospel, "Judas then, having received a band of men and officers from the chief priests and Pharisees, cometh thither with lanterns and torches and weapons. Jesus therefore, knowing all things that should come upon him, went forth and said unto them, Whom seek ye? They answered him, Jesus of Nazareth. Jesus said unto them, I am he. And Judas also, which betrayed him, stood with them" (vv. 3-5). Judas had not expected this. They were to surprise Him, but He surprised them. He shows Himself again as the complete master of the situation.

But notice what happens. Jesus asked: "Whom seek ye?" They answered him: "Jesus of Nazareth." Jesus said unto them: "I am." The "he" is in italics and not in the original. The whole significance is found in Christ being the great "I am" which had spoken to Moses when he was called at the burning bush (cp. Exodus 3:14).

"As soon then as he had said unto them, I am, they went backward, and fell to the ground" (John 18:6). It is interesting to see what men want to do to this verse. One commented that the soldiers were falling over one another because Jesus surprised them. Some soldiers, if this be the case. But this is how ridiculous men become in trying to diminish the supernatural. When Christ said, "I am," these soldiers were struck to the ground with this *one word*, and they could not move. This merely shows the power of His word which He will exercise to the full when He comes the second time and smites the nations with the word of His mouth (Rev. 19:15). Had Christ desired—it being in the will of God—these soldiers would have remained on the ground until they rotted! This whole band lies prostrate at His feet by a single word from His lips.

Again He asked them, "Whom seek ye?" And they said, "Jesus of Nazareth." Christ replied the same but added, "if therefore ye seek me, let these go their way" (John 18:7-8). This gave permission for the Lord's disciples to move away, for this was His will for them. He has not requested their release, but commanded it. This was the Lord's signal to them to leave, but they didn't obey their commander-in-chief, and got into trouble.

The Kiss

It is only *now* that Judas comes forth to betray Christ with a kiss, this being his signal, and they were not taking anyone without the signal being given. Up to this time Judas has been pinned to the ground with the rest. As Judas approaches Christ to kiss Him, the Lord says: "Judas, betrayest thou the Son of man with a kiss?" (Luke 22:48). Judas went ahead anyway. "Master, master; and kissed him" (Mark 14:45). Again it needs to be repeated: Judas never called Jesus, "Lord." The word "kiss" [katathileo] signifies that intense warm kiss that a young man would give his bride-to-be. This same word is used of the woman who was a sinner, when she kissed the feet of the Savior.

The signal had been, "Whomsoever I shall kiss that same

is he; take him, and lead him away safely." Why *this* signal? The kiss was a sign of discipleship in the East. Students used this as an expression that they are followers of a teacher, and it is very likely that this custom prevailed among Christ and His disciples. Furthermore, when we become the Lord's disciples, we may be said to kiss Him. "Kiss the Son, lest he be angry, and ye perish from the way, when his wrath is kindled but a little. Blessed are all they that put their trust in him" (Psalm 2:12). Here is an act that is sacred, being profaned. This always has been Satan's tactic—to polute things "holy" and true. Here is hypocrisy to its fullest—to say one thing, to perform another. Judas confesses with his mouth, but his conduct belies him.

Christ then said to Judas, "Friend, wherefore art thou come?" (Matt. 26:50), which may be paraphrased, "Companion, why did you come and do this thing?" Here is the eternal farewell to the son of perdition. Think of what eternity will be with these words continually ringing in his ears.

Application

Why study Judas? If we feel that this doesn't apply to us, look out, we are quite deceived. Let none of us say, "I am thankful I am not like this man." There is a Judas living in every one of us in the person of the *old sin nature.* All that Judas was and did is what we have in germ in our breasts. "Let him that thinketh he standeth take heed lest he fall." God has no program of removing, nor of improving the old nature until we see the Lord face to face. It is destined for perdition, yet it still lives on within us seeking "opportunity" to betray Christ. Until this time, we are to "give diligence to make" our "calling and election sure." If we do these things we shall never stumble (II Pet. 1:10). We are to walk in the Spirit, and so we will not fulfill the lusts of the flesh (Gal. 5:16).

Chapter 4

The Arrest

After the kiss of Judas, everything occurs in rapid succession. With the kiss being accomplished, the one they were to capture has been identified, and so the temple guards move in to take their prey. As Christ is speaking for the last time to Judas, the disciples began to see the soldiers move in and apprehend Christ. Therefore they said to Him, "Lord, shall we smite with the sword?" (Luke 22:49). Before waiting for an answer, Simon Peter, having one of the two swords among the disciples (Luke 22:38), drew his sword "and smote the high priest's servant, and cut off his right ear. The servant's name was Malchus" (John 18:10). While the others were still talking, Peter was acting.

Peter and the Sword

Here was an historical fact that could be verified, thus John mentioned the servant's name, and Peter's name. In fact, John is the only Gospel writer who mentions Peter's name in connection with this incident. He mentions both of the men by name. Some have felt there is a specific reason why the Synoptics do not record who it was among the disciples that smote the servant of the High Priest. The Sanhedrin were still in power in Jerusalem, and Peter was living there as the Apostle to the circumcision. At the time of the writing of John's Gospel, Jerusalem is in ruin, and Peter has been martyred. But this does not seem to be the full answer, for at the time of the writing of the Synoptics, Peter could not then have been charged with this crime. No charge could be brought in Israel because the man was healed. For this reason, there must be something else involved.

Here are the facts that Scripture reveals about the situation. The Gospel of John brings out that John knew the High Priest (18:15), and that John was responsible for bringing Peter into the courtyard of the High Priest (18:16). Malchus may have been a personal servant of the High Priest, and, therefore, personally known by name by John. John further knew the kinsman of the servant of the high priest who recognized Peter and succeeded in causing him to deny Christ (18:26, 27). The very fact that one of the servants of the high priest was the one hurt by Peter's sword, shows us conclusively who was doing the actual arresting of the Lord Jesus. According to Luke 22:52-53, "Jesus said unto the chief priests and captains of the temple, and the elders, which were come to him, Be ye come out as against a thief, with swords and staves? When I was daily with you in the Temple, ye stretched forth no hands against me . . . " The chief priests and elders of the nation were there, and behind it all was the high priest whose servant came close enough to the center of things to get his ear cut off.

The very fact that John identifies the Lord's disciple as "*Simon* Peter," I feel is also significant. Whenever the name Simon is used, it seems to indicate the old man within Peter, as this was Peter's name before he met the Lord. Thus the *old man* of Peter was here in action.

By this action Peter had actually meant to kill this soldier, but Peter was better at casting nets than he was at wielding a sword. Christ had already told the disciples indirectly to go away (John 18:8). This was the Lord's will for them. Now Simon was about to get them all into trouble. When Peter drew his sword, there were nearly 1000 swords drawn and staves poised; and everyone was ready for expert use. The Garden of Gethsemane was, in that instant, prepared to become a battlefield.

Peter's sword was a *machaire,* a large knife, or a small ceremonial sword, in contrast to the large swords, *rhomphaia,* of the soldiers. Peter with his little ceremonial sword tucked away in his clothing, sets up and uses it as if it were one of the big Roman swords. The Roman soldiers had been trained to take their sword and with precision accuracy, split the helmet of their opponent at the exact, precise place of the weld so that one blow would not only divide the helmet, but the skull as well. Evidently Peter had seen it done, but fishermen make poor swordsmen. Being off target about 3 inches, he lopped off the man's right ear. Peter had not only involved himself in an act, but he had endangered the other 10 disciples as well as the Lord Himself (speaking on the human plane). How truthfully Paul wrote later, "None of us liveth to himself, and no man dieth to himself" (Rom. 14:7). Now in the very nature of Peter's action, we seem to have the key as to why this event was not spelled out until years later. Peter's action was an act of rebellion, not just against Israel, but against Rome itself due to the fact of the presence of Roman soldiers. Not until after Peter's death does any writer specify who it was that wielded a sword that night in the Garden.

Why was it that Peter did this? First, he hadn't prayed as Christ had suggested he should have done in the garden. Had he been in fellowship with the Lord, he would have known the perfect will of the Lord and would have done it. But from the human standpoint, Peter had bragged too much this very night. He had said, "Lord, though all forsake thee, yet will *I* not forsake thee" (Matt. 26:33-35). Thus Peter's *honor* was at stake. Oh how dangerous it is for the Lord's cause when our honor is at stake. Better that our honor and our name were dragged through the mud, and we had no reputation, than for us to keep our honor *at the expense of Christ's honor.* Peter, by his action, was giving the Lord's enemies justification for coming out with swords and staves as against a dangerous person. Oh, how great can be the damage of one careless act or word not in the will of God. It can undo the good of 10,000 words and a hundred acts done in the Spirit's power and in the Lord's will. This is always the fate of those who do not watch and pray. Simon, by this act, had almost removed the possibility of the Lord saying to Pilate, "If my kingdom were of this world, then would my servants fight . . . " (John 18:36).

The Crisis

Instantly Christ understands the danger of the situation, for the air has been electrified with tension. He steps in between His disciple who was about to have a premature death and the charging soldiers, and commanded, "Suffer ye thus far" (Luke 22:51); the Berkeley Version says, "Allow me this much." It is impossible from our vantage point to know exactly to whom this is addressed, for it could be addressed to (1) the soldiers Christ stopped, who were ready to cut Peter up; or (2) the soldiers that had apprehended Christ to permit Him to do this one thing of ministering to the bleeding head of this man; or (3) it could be Christ's words to His disciples that this is far enough. There are ways in which all three fit well into the context. It is not without possiblity that this spoke to everyone in this moment of crisis.

"And he touched his ear, and healed him" (Luke 22:51). Luke is the only writer that mentions this healing, though all four mention the event of the high priest's servant's ear being cut off by one of the disciples. It is the only incident recorded in the Gospels where Christ heals a fresh wound, and it is significant that the doctor records it. It is the only time that a miracle was performed on an enemy where there was no faith and no gratitude. This unveils the hardness of heart of His captors. It produced no effect upon this crowd. Had Christ not performed this miracle, there could have been a true charge brought against the Lord and His disciples.

The Purpose of this Miracle in Luke

But there seems to be more involved in this miracle than just what has been said. Since the miracle is only given in

Luke, Luke's Gospel alone should be considered to understand it (remembering that each Gospel writer was writing for a different purpose, and one event may be used by different men to teach different things).

First, Luke informs us Christ had specifically wanted the disciples to have swords (Luke 22:35-38).

Secondly, Luke alone records that all the disciples, including Peter, asked, "shall we smite with the sword?" Thus they were seeking His will as revealed in Luke's Gospel.

Thirdly, Luke records no prohibition to this. Christ never answered, "No. don't smite with the sword," and then one of the Lord's disciples did it anyway.

Fourthly, Luke, who certainly knew this was Peter who did this, does not record his name lest we would get our eyes on this particular disciple rather than *upon Christ* and what He is doing through this incident. It is the Lord in Luke's account (as is true in the other three Gospels) who is directing the entire series of events and is in complete control of the situation. His control included the disciples having swords, and it included one of the disciples using his sword so that Christ could perform His *last miracle* before His resurrection before this crowd that had come to apprehend Him.

Fifthly, Luke alone records Christ's words, "Suffer ye thus far," which may be taken as addressed to both Peter and the swordsmen of the opposition, "This is as far as you can go."

Sixthly, Luke alone records this miracle, as has been said.

Finally, Luke does not include in this Gospel any rebuke to the disciple that did this thing. The reason is because this would have been entirely out of keeping with the purpose of Luke's account. It records the action as necessary—this much being the Lord's will. After all, swords are to be used, not looked at; and it was necessary for the disciples to have swords that night.

How can we reconcile both of these avenues for truth? We can say that Luke presents this incident and subsequent miracle as a part of the Lord's program, while Matthew and John reveal that this was the permissive will of the Lord which He allowed and used, but not His directive will.

The Rebuke to His Disciple

Matthew records what happened next. "Then said Jesus unto him, Put up again thy sword into his place: for all they that take the sword shall perish with the sword. Thinkest thou that I cannot now pray to my Father, and he shall presently [immediately] give me more than twelve legions of angels? But how then shall the scriptures be fulfilled, that thus it must be" (Matt. 26:52-54). "Put up again thy sword into his place." Notice that the sword has a lawful place (cp. Rom. 13:1-6). Governmental authority and self-defense are one thing; rebellion is another.

Secondly, using the sword is inconsistent with spiritual truth. The battle is spiritual. If it is going to be won, it must be won on a spiritual basis (Eph. 6:10ff). The Lord is saying in effect, "If I asked the Father, I would have instantly 12 legions of angels. The Romans against us are only a cohort, or 1/10th part of a legion. Therefore, there would be one legion of spiritual forces, about 6000 angels, for each one of you disciples. Peter, if you fight the battle the Lord's way, you will always be able to say, 'They that be with us are more than they that be with them' (II Kings 6:16). But you must fight the spiritual battle on a spiritual basis if you want to win spiritually." Here was the Son of God who with a word could have had legions of angels minister to His every need, but He did not; and good angels cannot operate on their own. They are servants sent forth by the Lord to do His will at His command. All angels could do at this scene was "look on" as spectators (cp. I Tim. 3:16, "seen of angels"). Notice also that never once did Christ in His incarnation command angels Himself because of the kenosis. He had power to do so as God, but He relinquished His rights in order to be the perfect, submissive and obedient servant of Jehovah. Here in place of doing something evil to His enemies by praying the Father to send angels to destroy them, He bends down and does something good. He returns good for evil and so has become our example. That which gains the victory for the Lord's people is patience in the midst of trial and testing (I Cor.

4:12-13; II Cor. 10:4-5; James 1:2-4; etc.).

Thirdly, using the sword is inconsistent with *Scripture*. "I must be a willing sacrifice as is seen in a lamb being dumb before its shearers, and as is typified in the sacrifice of Isaac by Abraham on Mt. Moriah." Of a truth Peter needs to remember that Moses broke the type of the rock being smitten but once, and not be guilty himself of breaking the type. "Then said Jesus unto Peter, Put up thy sword into the sheath: the cup which my Father hath given me, shall I not drink it?" (John 18:11).

Fourthly, using the sword is inconsistent with *Gethsemane's answer* and *the Father's will.* "Peter, you have been talking too much and praying too little, and this is why your actions are getting you into trouble." This is only the beginning of Peter's mistakes and the Lord's rebuke to him.

The Rebuke to His Captors

Having corrected His disciple, He now reproves His captors. "In that same hour said Jesus to the multitudes, Are ye come out as against a thief with swords and staves for to take me? I sat daily with you teaching in the temple, and ye laid no hold on me. But all this was done, that the scriptures of the prophets might be fulfilled" (Matt. 26:55-56a). Mark 14:48-49 records the same thing. Luke 22:52-53 records, "Then Jesus said unto the chief priests and captains of the temple, and the elders, which were come to him, Be ye come out, as against a thief, with swords and staves? When I was daily with you in the temple, ye stretched forth no hands against me: but this is your hour, and the power of darkness."

The Lord addresses the rulers of Israel because they were responsible. They were doing their work under cover of darkness because their deeds were evil. "This is your hour." Whatever they want to do, they are going to be permitted to do unhindered. The holy angels will only be spectators and not participants protecting the Lord Jesus Christ as they always had done previously (Psalm 91:11-12). "And the power of darkness." Behind the actions of men will be the controlling influence of the whole underworld of fallen angels and demons. This is your hour—this is your inning, mine is coming later. Christ's hour is not a vindictiveness because of what has happened personally to Him, but as RIGHTEOUSNESS against iniquity, and JUSTICE against all injustice.

The Disciples Flee

With this, His disciples "all forsook him and fled" (Mark 14:50). The Lord had predicted this very thing: "All ye shall be offended because of me this night: for it is written, I will smite the shepherd, and the sheep of the flock shall be scattered abroad" (Matt. 26:31; cp. Mark 14:27).

Mark's Gospel alone goes on to record an incident that occurred concurrently with this that is interesting. "And there followed him a certain young man, having a linen cloth cast about his naked body; and the young men laid hold of him: and he left the linen cloth, and fled from them naked" (Mark 14:51-52). This has to be recorded for a reason. What is it?

Edersheim gives a very probable explanation. The Upper Room, where the Last Supper was held, was the home of John Mark's parents in Jerusalem. When Judas secured the forces who were to capture Christ when he betrayed Him, he evidently led them first to the Upper Room where Judas had last been with the Lord and His disciples. Finding them not there, Judas then took them to the Garden, figuring this was where Jesus would be, since He often went there with His disciples. However, with this armed band coming to the house of John Mark, there must have been considerable noise, and John Mark was awakened from his sleep. Like any young person he suspected something exciting was occurring, so he threw a linen cloth over his tunic or undergarment (which was the only garment worn by slaves, so it was not indecent), and he went along to see the excitement. As they get to the Garden, he lingered in the rear, perhaps going to follow as they lead Jesus away, never thinking that they might do anything to him. Somebody, however, spotted him, attempted to lay hold of him, and he lost his outer garment as he fled the scene.

Remember that it is this John Mark that is the writer of the Gospel of Mark. His including this historical incident in his Gospel would be marking his own personal indentification with this eventful night.

Jesus Bound

"Then the band," i.e. the Romans; "and the captain," i.e. the officer in charge of the Romans; "and the officers of the Jews," i.e. the temple guard; "took Jesus, and bound him" (John 18:12). Can you see it? The Son of God standing there bound before His captors. The Creator bound by creatures. The Sinless bound by the sinful. The only way this was possible was because this was *their hour and the power of darkness.* He was meek and gentle, as a lamb before its shearers is dumb—He will not resist. If the son of Manoah could break the strongest cords that bound him, how much more the Son of man who was given the Spirit without measure. What bound Him was love. What bound Him was the will of God. What bound Him was the Word of God that must be fulfilled. What bound Him was the accomplishment of the course set before Him.

The synoptic gospels show that the multitude laid hands upon the Lord before Peter struck the servant of the High Priest. In fact, this was the cause of Peter's action. Afterward, the Romans bound Him and led Him away. The arrest was actually performed by both the Romans and the Jews that all mankind might be guilty of this crime before God.

The Illegality Of The Arrest

The arrest was illegal because first, it was at night, and according to the law of the Sanhedrin, the taking of any steps in criminal proceedings after sunset was expressly prohibited. Secondly, it was accomplished on the charge of an accomplice or informer, and taking or giving a bribe was contrary to the Law of God (Ex. 23:8; Prov. 17:23). Thirdly, the court that was to try Jesus hired the betrayer, and some of the judges themselves participated in the arrest in their eagerness to see that nothing went wrong (Luke 22:52).

Chapter 5

The Trial
Before Annas

We are beginning a section of Scripture which staggers the imagination. In all the history of mankind on earth, there has never been the equal to the miscarriage of justice that is about to take place. It was a mockery at mercy, and this in spite of what the Law had said. In Deuteronomy 16, we read, "Judges and officers shalt thou make thee in all thy gates, which the Lord thy God giveth thee, throughout thy tribes: and they shall judge the people with just judgment. Thou shalt not wrest judgment; thou shalt not respect persons, neither take a gift: for a gift both blind the eyes of the wise, and pervert the words of the righteous. That which is altogether just shalt thou follow, that thou mayest live, and inherit the land which the Lord thy God giveth thee" (vv. 18-20). Notice that it says, "They shall judge the people with just judgments. That which is altogether just shalt thou follow."

The Local Sanhedrins

In order to carry out the letter of the Law, every locality where there were 120 men as heads of families, had what was called a Sanhedrin, consisting of 23 elders that would govern all matters. If the town were smaller, it was governed by three or seven members, or elders. This was the governing body of a synagogue community. One of them was designated the "chief ruler." The Sanhedrin served thus as a court.

In Jerusalem was the Great Sanhedrin, "The Council," consisting of 70 members plus the High Priest. This Council was the final Court of Appeal, and the highest ruling body of the nation of Israel, combining in themselves the executive, legislative and judicial branches of government.

The smaller Sanhedrins are referred to in passages like Matthew 5:22 which reads, "But I say unto you, That whosoever is angry with his brother without a cause shall be in danger of the judgment: and whosoever shall say to his brother, Raca, shall be in danger of the council . . . ." Then in Matthew 10:17, the Lord said, "But beware of men; for they will deliver you up to the councils, and they will scourge you in their synagogues . . ."(cp. Mark 13:9; etc.).

Their Code of Jurisprudence

Based on the Law, one of the finest codes of jurisprudence had been specifically laid out for the operation of each local Sanhedrin in criminal procedure. In legal terms, the Law demanded three things: publicity of the trial, entire liberty of defense allowed to the accused, and a guaranty against the dangers of testimony. Accordingly, one witness is no witness for there must be at least two who know the fact (Deut. 17:6; 19:15). The witness who testifies against a man, must affirm that he speaks the truth; the judges then proceed to take exact information of the matter. If it is found that the witness has sworn falsely, they compel him to undergo the punishment to which he would have exposed his neighbor (Deut. 19:16-19). The discussion between the accuser and the accused is conducted before the whole assembly of the people. In the case where a man is condemned to death, those witnesses whose evidence decided the sentence, inflict the first blows, in order to add the last degree of certainty to their evidence (Deut. 17:7). Thus Christ, speaking to men in their culture, exclaimed, "He that is without sin among you, let him first cast a stone" (John 8:7).

According to Joseph Salvador, quoted by Simon Greenleaf in his book, *The Testimony of the Evangelists*, a trial would proceed in the following manner.

"On the day of the trial, the executive officers of justice caused the accused person to make his appearance. At the feet of the Elders were placed men who, under the name of auditors, or candidates, followed regularly the sittings of the Council. The papers in the case were read; and the witnesses were called in succession. The president addressed this exhortation to each of them: 'It is not conjectures, or whatever public rumour has brought to thee, that we ask of thee; consider that a great responsibility rests upon thee: that we are not occupied by an affair, like a case of pecuniary interest, in which the injury may be repaired. If thou causest the condemnation of a person unjustly accused, his blood, and the blood of all the posterity of him, of whom thou wilt have deprived the earth, will fall upon thee; God will demand of thee an account, as he demanded of Cain an account of the blood of Abel. Speak.

"A woman could not be a witness, because she would not have the courage to give the first blow to the condemned person; nor could a child, that is irresponsible, nor a slave, nor a man of bad character, nor one whose infirmities prevent the full enjoyment of his physical and moral faculties. The simple confession of an individual against himself, or the declaration, however renowned, would not decide a condemnation. The Doctors say—'We hold it as fundamental, that no one shall prejudice himself. If a man accuses himself before a tribunal, we must not believe him, unless the fact is attested by two other witnesses; and it is proper to remark, that the punishment of death inflicted upon Achan, in the time of Joshua, was an exception, occasioned by the nature of the circumstances; for our law does not condemn upon the simple confession of the accused, nor upon the declaration of one prophet alone.'

"The witnesses were to attest to the identity of the party, and to depose to the month, day, hour, and circumstances of the crime. After an examination of the proofs, these judges who believed the party innocent stated their reasons; those who believed him guilty spoke afterwards, and with the greatest moderation. If one of the auditors, or candidates, was entrusted by the accused with his defense, or if he wished in his own name to present any elucidations in favour of innocence, he was admitted to the seat, from which he addressed the judges and the people. But this liberty was not granted to him, if his opinion was in favour of condemning. Lastly, when the accused person himself wished to speak, they gave the most profound attention. When the discussion was finished, one of the judges recapitulated the case; they removed all the spectators; two scribes took down the votes of the judges; one of them noted those which were in favour of the accused; and the other, those which condemned him. Eleven votes, out of twenty-three, were sufficient to acquit; but it required thirteen to convict. If any of the judges stated that they were not sufficiently informed, there were added two more Elders, and then two other in succession, till they formed a council of sixty-two, which was the number of the Grand Council. If a majority of votes acquitted, the accused was discharged instantly; if he was to be punished, the judges postponed pronouncing sentence till the third day; during the intermediate day they could not be occupied with anything but the cause, and they abstained from eating freely, and from wine, liquors, and everything which might render their minds less capable of reflection.

"On the morning of the third day they returned to the judgment seat. Each judge, who had not changed his opinion, said, *I continue of the same opinion and condemn;* any one, who at first condemned, might at this sitting acquit; but he who at once acquitted was not allowed to condemn. If a majority condemned, two magistrates immediately accompanied the condemned person to the place of punishment. The Elders did not descend from their seats; they placed at the entrance of the judgment hall an officer of justice with a small flag in his hand; a second officer, on horseback, followed the prisoner, and constantly kept looking back to the place of departure. During this interval, if any person came to announce to the elders any new evidence favourable to the prisoner, the first officer waved his flag, and the second one, as soon as he perceived it, brought back the prisoner. If the prisoner declared to the magistrates, that he recollected some reasons which had escaped him, they brought him before the judges no less than five times. If no incident occurred, the procession advanced slowly, preceded by a herald who, in a loud voice, addressed the people thus: 'This man [stating his name and surname] is led to punishment for such a crime; the witnesses who have sworn against him are such and such persons; if any one has evidence to give in his favour, let him come forth quickly.'

"At some distance from the place of punishment, they urged the prisoner to confess his crime, and they made him drink a stupefying beverage, in order to render the approach of death less terrible."

The Great Sanhedrin

With this code for the local Sanhedrins, the Great Sanhedrin in Jerusalem was in no way less lax in its administration of justice.

The appointment to the Great Sanhedrin was made by that tribunal itself. They would either promote to their ranks a member of one of the many lesser Sanhedrins of the various towns, or one from the foremost of the three rows of disciples or students who sat facing the Judges. Paul himself was a member of this last body—a disciple or student of Gamaliel (Acts 22:3). In fact, Paul tells us in Galatians that he had forged ahead of many his own age. "For you heard of my manner of life formerly in Judaism, that beyond measure I was persecuting the church of God and I was ravaging it, and I was advancing in Judaism above many of an equal age among my countrymen because I was more exceedingly zealous of the traditions of my ancestry" (Gal. 1:13-14, literal translation). The word translated "profited" or "advanced" is a word used of woodcutters of cutting their way through a forest, to make progress, to forge ahead. Paul made greater progress in Judaism beyond many of equal age. He was so outstanding that he had forged ahead of those who were his own age. He had been brought to a place of prominance which normally would have been reserved for a man of older age. Paul was certainly in line for becoming appointed a member of the Great Sanhedrin.

Membership consisted of the 24 chief priests, 24 elders, 22 scribes, and the High Priest, making a total body of 71 members.

Its grand function was the specialized interpretation and application of both written and oral law. Moreover, the Law itself gave to them this supreme authority (Deut. 17:8-13). Christ recognized this authority, for they sat in Moses's seat; and also He commanded that they be obeyed, but not to be imitated (Matt. 23:1-3ff). Thus the decisions of the Great Sanhedrin were binding upon all Jews everywhere. Just think of their position and responsibility.

Their Code of Jurisprudence

The axiom of this body was "The Sanhedrin is to save, not destroy life." The president of the Sanhedrin at the very outset of the trial was solemnly to admonish the witnesses concerning the preciousness of human life, and carefully and calmly to reflect whether they had not overlooked some circumstance which might favor the innocence of the accused.

For capital offenses the verdict of acquittal could be given on the same day, but the verdict of guilty had to be reserved for the following day. Therefore, such trials could not commence on the Sabbath or a feast day, nor on the day preceding them.

No criminal trial could be carried through the night, nor even in the afternoon.

The Judges who condemned a criminal had to fast all day.

The condemned was not executed the same day on which the sentence was passed.

The property of the accused was not confiscated, but passed over to his heirs.

Voting was from junior members to senior so that the lower members might not be influenced by the highest.

If the Sanhedrin voted unanimously for a verdict of

guilty, the accused was supposed to be set free since the necessary element of mercy was lacking.

The Sanhedrin's code of jurisprudence was the finest ever developed anywhere in the world.

A Man by the Name of Annas

With this background, we approach the darkest night in history. John 18:12 and 13 says, "Then the band and the captain and officers of the Jews took Jesus, and bound him, and led him away to Annas first; for he was father-in-law to Caiaphas, which was the high priest that same year." Who is this Annas? And what does he have to do with the whole situation?

He is one of the most notorious figures in Jewish history. He had the office of High Priest for only five or six years—twenty years before this time, and must have been now at least in his eighties. He had no fewer than five of his own sons fill the office after him, besides his son-in-law, Caiaphas, and one grandson. He had come originally from Alexandria in Egypt on the invitation of Herod the Great. He and his family became ambitious, arrogant and powerful. As their members multiplied, they promoted themselves into all the important offices.

Annas and his family had become intensely unpopular as far as the populace was concerned, but they were feared as greatly as they were disliked. The Temple-booths were known as Annas' Bazaars. He and his sons controlled everything that went on in the Temple, and, because of their greed, had developed a nice little system that worked to their personal benefit. According to the Law, when the people came before the Lord, they could not come empty-handed, but must give a free-will offering to the Lord. Of course, heathen money could not be given, but had to be changed into Temple coins. Thus there were the moneychangers who made this transaction. But they soon began to make an exorbitant profit from these transactions, not giving a just return in Temple currency.

The profit came also another way. It was possible for an Israelite to bring his own animal to sacrifice to the Lord—the best of his flock. But the priests were required to examine each animal to be sure no blemishes or other irregularities disqualified the animal (Deut. 17:1). Certain priests were set aside for this work, but the service was not free, and it just might be that they would find some blemish and pronounce the animal unfit for sacrifice. However, all this trouble could be avoided by going to the regular market within the Temple-enclosure, where sacrificial animals of each type could be purchased. These had already been duly inspected and passed and all fees paid before being offered for sale.

The entire setup was such that the market couldn't lose, or better, Annas couldn't lose, for he received his cut of all that was taken in.

Christ, and the Temple Operation

Because of this racket, Christ hated the whole operation. His work at the very first of His ministry, according to John 2, was to go into the Temple at the Passover season, and making a scourge of small cords, drive out of the Temple all those who sold oxen, sheep and doves, and the changers of money, overturning their tables (John 2:13-17).

Then again at the close of His ministry, once more at the Passover season, after riding on a donkey into the city of Jerusalem, He entered the Temple and "looked around about upon all things" (Mark 11:7-11). Then He went out of the Temple and the City. But the next day He cursed the fig tree (11:12-14), and came "to Jerusalem: and Jesus went into the temple, and began to cast out them that sold and bought in the temple, and overthrew the tables of the moneychangers, and the seats of them that sold doves; and would not suffer that any man should carry any vessel through the temple. And he taught, saying unto them, Is it not written, My house shall be called of all nations the house of prayer? but ye have made it a den of thieves" (11:15-17; cp. Matt. 21:12-14).

Annas Is Upset

Mark adds in the next verse, "And the scribes and chief priests heard it, and sought how they might destroy him: for they feared him . . ." (11:18). What were they fearing? They were fearing that the status quo would be upset, and the lucrative business would be toppled. The real problem was that Annas was upset. He was the political boss of Jerusalem. Everything had to be cleared through Annas.

This is why the next day after Christ overthrew the money changers, "there came to him the chief priests, and the scribes, and the elders, and say unto him, By what authority doest thou these things [That is, move into the Temple and overthrow the tables of the money-changers, and the seats of them that sold doves]? and who gave thee this authority to do these things?" (Mark 11:28). Annas was the boss of Jerusalem and he actually controlled the operation of the Sanhedrin, and the Sanhedrin controlled Israel; therefore, "Just who are You, and what is Your authority?" was their question.

Now we can understand why they led Jesus *first* to Annas. He was the one who had given the orders to have Him brought in this night. The Roman soldiers were now dismissed, for their work was done. They are not mentioned again. Annas wouldn't want them around, for he wants Pilate to know only what he wants to tell him. The proceedings before Annas were entirely informal. It allowed time, however, to gather the Great Sanhedrin together. With this background, we are now able to look in detail at the first trial of Christ. Let us now consider the entire account found in John 18.

John's Account

"Then the band and the captain and officers of the Jews took Jesus, and bound him, and led him away to Annas first; for he was father-in-law to Caiaphas, which was the high priest that same year. Now Caiaphas was he, which gave counsel to the Jews, that it was expedient that one man should die for the people.

"And Simon Peter followed Jesus, and so did another disciple: that disciple was known unto the high priest, and went in with Jesus into the palace of the high priest. But Peter stood at the door without. Then went out that other disciple, which was known unto the high priest, and spake unto her that kept the door, and brought in Peter. Then saith the damsel that kept the door unto Peter, Art not thou also one of this man's disciples? He saith, I am not. And the servants and officers stood there, who had made a fire of coals; for it was cold: and they warmed themselves: and Peter stood with them, and warmed himself.

"The high priest then asked Jesus of his disciples, and of his doctrine. Jesus answered him, I spake openly to the world; I ever taught in the synagogue, and in the temple, whither the Jews always resort; and in secret have I said nothing, Why askest thou me? Ask them which heard me, what I have said unto them: behold, they know what I said. And when he had thus spoken, one of the officers which stood by struck Jesus with the palm of his hand, saying, Answerest thou the high priest so? Jesus answered him, If I have spoken evil, bear witness of the evil: but if well, why smitest thou me? Now Annas had sent him bound unto Caiaphas the high priest" (John 18:12-24).

Christ is going to experience six trials. There will be three that may be called religious or ecclesiastical trials. There will be three that may be called political or civil trials. The total time for all the trials is less than five hours. Some have wanted to say that there were only two trials—one religious and one civil—with both trials having three different parts. This, however, doesn't answer to all the facts. As we shall see, each one was a trial in itself.

The Reasons for Knowing this is Annas

The trial before Annas was the first one, but it is the only religious trial that John gives in his Gospel. The reason John gives only this one is because the case was actually decided by Annas, and the other two religious trials were only carrying out what Annas had decided should be done.

At the first reading of John, one would not realize that the trial mentioned here was the one before Annas. This problem comes from John's use of the term "high priest" for both Annas and Caiaphas, and from a mistranslation of John 18:24. Let us consider both items.

As we observed, Annas was the first of a long line of high priests with five sons, one son-in-law and one grandson filling the office after him, all while he still lived. Now the Law made the office of high priests a lifetime position, but the Romans had forced Annas to give up the position—at least theoretically—for they felt it invested too much authority in one man for too long a time. This made the situation where there were, in fact, two high priests. Annas was still looked upon by Judaism as the true high priest as far as the Law was concerned. Caiaphas "was the high priest that same year" in which Jesus Christ was tried as far as the Romans were concerned.

The problem arises in John 18:15-23. Who is the high priest that John mentions, Annas or Caiaphas? From a very careful reading it is Annas, and the place is his home. The reasons are as follows. The events that take place in this private home are, first of all, making it possible for Peter to come inside. In the process, he gives a denial that he was one of Christ's disciples to the maid, or servant girl, who guarded the entrance to the courtyard (18:17). This never happened when Peter entered the courtyard of Caiaphas later on that morning. Furthermore, Peter warmed himself at both the house of Annas and Caiaphas (18:18, 25), but it was only at the latter fire that he denied Christ before the men. Here at this fire, Peter only stands; at the fire in the court of Caiaphas, Peter sat (cp. Psa. 1:1). Finally, there is no record of Caiaphas ever examining Christ in the manner stated here in John, nor of the servant smiting Christ with the palm of his hand with the resultant rebuke made by Christ for this act.

The whole problem is cleared up with a correct translation of John 18:24. Rather than read as the King James, "Annas had sent him bound unto Caiaphas the high priest," it should read, "Then Annas sent him bound to Caiaphas the high priest." *The New American Standard Bible* correctly translates the verse, "Annas therefore sent Him bound to Caiaphas the high priest." The issue at stake is the time of this action. The passage shows that after this private interview of Christ before Annas, the Lord was then taken bound to the home of Caiaphas. Thus all the events recorded before John 18:24 occur at the home of Annas. To state it another way, Christ was brought first to Annas (18:12), and He did not leave Annas' home until John 18:24. Therefore all in between occurs at the home of Annas. Now with this comprehension, we are able to look at the events of this trial with a deeper understanding of what is going on.

The Law required that trials be conducted before judges (Deut. 19:17; 21:5). There had to be more than one. For anyone to judge by himself, sitting alone, was strictly against the Mosaic law. Yet this is what we find here.

The Interrogation

"The high priest then asked Jesus of his disciples, and of his doctrine" (18:19). Annas begins to question Christ in order to form an accusation and bring a charge against Him. Annas is taking the place of what a Grand Jury does today. This, then, is a preliminary trial. Yet there is a basic difference between the work of a Grand Jury, and that of Annas. A Grand Jury seeks to determine guilt or innocence in a situation, and whether the state, for instance, should prosecute. With Annas, guilt was already determined, and all that he was seeking to determine was the best way to proceed with prosecution that would end with the death sentence.

There were two points that Annas specifically wanted to know about: (1) His disciples, and (2) His doctrine. Annas wanted to know "How many disciples do you have?" That is, "How widespread is your movement?" and, therefore, the dangers involved in doing away with Him. Furthermore, he wanted to know what Christ's teaching was in reference to the Law and the Prophets. He had felt that anything the Lord might have said either against the Law or the Prophets would form their best case against Him.

In place of interrogating Jesus respecting *positive acts* done, with their circumstances, and respecting *facts personal to Himself*, Annas interrogates Him respecting *general facts* respecting His disciples (who should have been called as witnesses had he desired information) and His doctrine, which has no bearing on the case as long as no external acts contrary to established law issued from it.

What Annas was trying to get Christ to do was to testify

against Himself. Christ recognizes this and doesn't reply, for neither Jews nor Romans required a man to testify against himself or stand as a witness against himself.

The Demand for Witnesses

The Lord's reply characterizes Him who is *truth*. He gives what we would say today is the lawful use of the Fifth Amendment.

"I spake openly in the world" (v. 20). The whole operation of the Lord and everything He did was done openly. Since He had nothing to hide, He had no reason for operating any other way.

"I ever taught in the synagogue and in the temple, whither the Jews always resort." This was the Lord's operation and no one had ever been able to prove He had taught anything contrary to the Old Testament Law or to established authority, even though men had many times been present to trick Him and trap Him in His speech.

"In secret have I said nothing." How different had been the actions of Christ in comparison to the man who was sitting before Him. Everything this man did was in secret.

"Why askest thou me?" (v. 21). Christ had a lawful right to ask this question because this was a preliminary trial in which He was asked to convict Himself.

"Ask them which heard me, what I have said unto them: behold, they know what I said." In any trial it is necessary to produce witnesses. Christ says, "Call your witnesses whether they be friend or foe, and let them testify, because they know exactly what I taught." The point is, why had they arrested Him if they did not know what He had said and done, and had witnesses?

His words have again been truth; but truth before error makes the error appear all the more wrong, and there is only one thing to do. Make the truth look as if it is the wrong.

Maltreatment

"And when he had thus spoke, one of the officers which stood by struck Jesus with the palm of his hand, saying,

Answerest thou the high priest so?" (v. 22). Here is the first maltreatment of the Lord Jesus Christ, and it gives the pattern and procedure for all that follows. The servant well knew that the High Priest was embarrassed by the direct and forceful truth that Christ had stated. This cruel blow was the only way that presented itself to the servant to rescue the High Priest from the corner that he had been backed into by the reply of Christ. All logic pointed to the fact that it was totally unjust, but as so often is the case, when the argument is weak, the actions and voice must be the loudest to make up for the other lack.

Whatever they want to do to Him, they are able to do. In the rebellion of Korah, who rebelled against Moses, the earth opened up and swallowed the rebels alive (Num. 16:28-34); but not here. Jeroboam, when he reached with his hand to apprehend the man of God, had his hand withered (I Kings 13:4), but not this Man. This was their hour.

Christ addresses the servant concerning the misdemeanor that he had committed: "If I have spoken evil, bear witness of the evil: but if well, why smitest thou me?" (v. 23). The man had no right to commit this act. He had only one right—bear witness, if he could, of evil that Christ had spoken. He still had that right to speak up and bear witness of any evil committed. Why didn't he exercise it? Because Christ had not spoken evil to Annas, but rather the truth.

Not only was Christ right, but, moreover, this was a *trial*. No judge is to allow violence in a trial. Yet the judge never censured this servant. Why? Because he approved of this act being done, and he became an accomplice to it, especially when this violence was committed under the pretense of avenging the alleged affront to his dignity.

Christ had previously said: "If they have persecuted me, they will also persecute you" (John 15:20). Paul experiences almost the same thing happening to him when he appeared later on in the Book of Acts before the Sanhedrin, and the High Priest, Ananias, was present. When Paul said, "Men and brethren, I have lived in all good conscience before God until this day" (Acts 23:1), "the high priest Ananias commanded them that stood by him to smite him on the mouth" (23:2). In the case of the Lord Jesus, it was the servant of the High

Priest that took the initiative for this action; but with Paul, the High Priest himself was directly responsible. Paul, likewise, testifies that this was against the Law of the Lord: "Then said Paul unto him, God shall smite thee, thou whited wall: for sittest thou to judge me after the law, and commandest me to be smitten contrary to the law?" (23:3).

Removal of the Prisoner

In the case of Annas, this is all he can take. He is being shown wrong before his own servants, and he has absolutely no defense. There is only one thing to do. Send this case on to Caiaphas and the Sanhedrin for trial. They will have to find witnesses to witness against Him, and this, we will see in the next trial, is the very first thing they seek to do.

But let us remind ourselves that the only reason you need witnesses is because you are conducting a trial. If this were murder—as Edersheim says—kill Him, and get it over with! But not so, if you are conducting a trial. They are going to give the Lord a trial—a trial where every point of their own code of jurisprudence is broken.

The first trial is over, and we may examine the case and ask ourselves, "How did Jesus fare?" He stands perfect in innocence Himself, and He has condemned His accuser.

"Then Annas sent him bound unto Caiaphas the high priest." It was customary to loose a prisoner when he was on trial, but to bind him once again when he was to be escorted to another place. Christ had been bound at the arrest, but was released as He stood before Annas. He was now bound again and led away.

F. W. Krummacher makes the statement: "Jesus bound! Can we trust our eyes? Omnipotence in fetters, the Creator bound by the creature; the Lord of the world, the captive of His mortal subjects! How much easier would it have been for Him to have burst those bonds than Manoah's son of old!" We must add: But this He did to fulfill all righteousness; or better, to fulfill all unrighteousness; for this was the hour of darkness, and it is still night as they lead Him through the streets of Jerusalem to the house of Caiaphas to be tried by the highest court in Israel.

Lessons for Living

What have we seen as we have looked at this trial? First of all, we have seen the awfulness of religion. Religion is just the opposite of Christianity. If Christianity would have become just another religion, Christians would not I have been persecuted. The world will always move over and allow another nitch in its religious pantheon. All the early church had to do was just acknowledge, "Lord Caesar," and they would have escaped martyrdom. Persecution comes today *only* when we refuse to be *one way among many*. This was the first compromise Pharoah offered Moses, and it will always be so. He wanted Moses and Aaron to go and sacrifice to their God in the land of Egypt (Ex. 8:25). So the world will always move over a little and make room for another religion—just don't leave the land. As long as you worship under the god-king of this world's system, room will be made for you. But whenever Christianity becomes just another religion in the land, it ceases to be Christianity. The Lord said to His own, "If the world hate you, ye know that it hated me before it hated you. If ye were of the world, the world would love his own: but because ye are not of the world, but I have chosen you out of the world, therefore the world hateth you. Remember the word that I said unto you, The servant is not greater than his lord. If they have persecuted me, they will also persecute you; if they have kept my saying, they will keep your's also" (John 15:18-20). Religion is that which caused all the problems for the Christians in the book of Acts. Religion would crucify the Lord Jesus Christ all over again, if He came today. Religion and Christianity are on opposite poles.

Secondly, we see the misuse of power or authority. All authority ultimately goes back to God. God-given authority can be used for good and against evil, or it can be turned around and used against good and for evil. There is nothing so wrong as misused authority that was given by God. The same is true today as in the time of the trials. The purpose of governmental law is to protect (1) life, (2) liberty, and (3) property. But that which is meant to protect can be turned to destroy (1) life, (2) liberty, and (3) property.

Thirdly, we see the finest program and procedures can be used to the worst of ends. This is true for any system. Something that is established for good can be used for evil. May God give all of us wisdom in these things.

Chapter 6

The Trial Before Caiaphas and the Sanhedrin

The first trial of Christ is over. Annas met with Christ in order to find some accusation with which to try Him. However, the Lord would not testify against Himself, but demanded witnesses. Annas sent the Lord bound to Caiaphas who was the High Priest that year, and who took over as the president of the Sanhedrin.

This second trial is given to us in detail in Matthew 26:57-66, and Mark 14:53-65. Luke mentions only Peter's denials and the maltreatment of Christ (Luke 22:54-65), and that is all. John mentions only the denials of Peter at this trial (John 18:24-27).

Both Matthew and Mark are writing to bring out the illegality of the trial: Matthew, to the Jews as an indictment to the nation of Israel; Mark, to the Romans who prided themselves in their code of judicial justice. But in Mark, Christ goes to Pilate after this trial, and He does no better before this Roman than He did before Caiaphas.

This trial before Caiaphas is *the main* religious trial. A mock repeat of the same events is held as soon as there is the light of day in order to try to conform to the Law. But that trial sees nothing new, and probably lasted no longer than five to ten minutes. We will follow this trial in Matthew's Gospel, and make comments from Mark when there is something additional that he gives.

The Assembly of the Sanhedrin

"And they that had laid hold on Jesus led him away to Caiaphas the high priest, where the scribes and the elders were assembled" (Matt. 26:57). By this time the entire Sanhedrin had had time to assemble themselves together and were waiting as Jesus was brought in. The case was so urgent that it could not await the daybreak. Everything had to be over when the populace awakened in the morning. It was still night, probably about 3:30 or 4:00 A.M.

Luke tells us specifically that He was brought "into the high priest's house" (22:54). This was where the Sanhedrin had assembled, but it was illegal for the Sanhedrin to meet anywhere but their own meeting hall, known as the Hall of Judgment, which was a part of the Temple complex. They will go to this Hall of Judgment at the first light of day in order to give a repeat performance of the trial that is about to take place.

Mark tells us, "And they led Jesus away to the high priest: and with him were assembled all the chief priests and elders and scribes" (14:53). Thus the entire Sanhedrin was present, which is important. This thing was not railroaded through by just a few.

"But Peter followed him afar off unto the high priest's palace, and went in, and sat with the servants, to see the end" (Matt. 26:58). Peter follows the procession from a distance as they move from the home of Annas to the home of Caiaphas. He is going along with the servants, and feels he will not be noticed this way.

In the Oriental house of this magnitude there would be the large room on one side of an open court or patio. In the case of Annas, Jesus was only taken into the court (John 18:15 R.V.). In the case of the trial before Caiaphas and the Sanhedrin, Christ is tried in the large room, while Peter is out in the court where the fire was burning (Matt. 26:69 R.V.). The inside room would have been lighted so everyone in the court could see beyond the large pillars into the area and watch the entire proceedings.

"Now the chief priests, and elders, and all the council, sought false witness against Jesus, to put him to death" (v. 59). The word "council" is "Sanhedrin." Think of it. Here was the greatest assembly in the world! These men sat in Moses' seat with *divine authority* over the entire nation of Israel. Not only did these men possess governmental authority given to mankind after the flood (Gen. 9), but theocratic authority given by God from Mount Sinai.

These were the interpretors of the Law of Moses, and it was their task to administer justice. It was their task to guard the nation against heresy and false prophets even as the Law itself said (Deut. 13:1-11. For open enticement, see 13:1-5; for secret enticement, see 13:6-11). It is in this category that the Sanhedrin feel they are justified in assembling and trying this case. Though He has done miracles, these miracles are attributed to being performed by the power of Satan. Their verdict is that He is turning the people to "another God" in claiming to be the Son of God Himself. *This is the issue!*

Dr. Edersheim, in *Life and Times of Jesus* (I, 309), states, "The Sanhedrin did not and could not originate charges. It only investigated those brought before it." Yet the entire procedure of this court, in its relationship to the Lord, reveals that it originated the charges as well as proceeded to try the case. The Court thus became both the prosecution and the judge.

They Seek False Witness

Now you notice that the Scripture states that they "sought false witness against Jesus to put him to death." They were seeking false witnesses when as yet they have not stated His crime. Any trial is to begin with a clear statement of the crime alleged and with the production of witnesses already secured to support the charge and to testify against the person.

In this case there is no charge, and they have to seek for witnesses, or as Matthew says, "false witness." Why do they have to seek? Because unsought, nothing presented itself. But

Annas has said, "Get witnesses and get rid of Him!" They are seeking to be obedient.

Think of the judges trying a case *seeking witnesses*. This is not the work of the judges, who are to be impartial and administer justice. But here the judges had already reached the verdict before they tried the case. The verdict was guilty, and the sentence was "death." All they needed now were the witnesses to substantiate this decision.

"But found none: yea, though many false witnesses came, yet found they none" (v. 60a). Before we stand to condemn them, let us be careful we are not guilty of the same act in another area. I have seen many people with the verdict rendered already—with their minds already made up—seeking for passages of Scripture to support their preconceived position. The act is the same; the difference is only in the area involved and in the magnitude of the case.

There were many who wanted to testify against Christ, each one for his own reasons. Someone expressed it well when he said, "A man's life is known by his enemies." He that has no enemies has sought to be a manpleaser—he has done no lasting good; he has failed honestly to deal with gut issues in men's lives.

"He has no enemy, you say;
My friend your boast is poor,
He who hath mingled in the fray
Of duty that the brave endure
Must have made foes. If he has none
Small is the work that he has done
He has hit no traitor on the hip;
Has cast no cup from perjured lip
Has never turned the wrong to right;
Has been a coward in the fight."
                    —Anastasius Griin (Free Translation)

But each witness destroyed the witness of someone else. Thus Mark tells us, "For many bare false witness against him but their witness agreed not together" (14:56). The Law required two witnesses to agree. One witness was no witness.

At last two witnesses gave a semblance of agreement to something they heard Him say. This was enough. They were rushed into the meeting room to testify. "At the last came two false witnesses, and said, This fellow said, I am able to destroy the temple of God, and to build it in three days" (Matt. 26:60b-61).

Mark goes into fuller detail as to what they testified: "And there arose certain, and bare false witness against him, saying, We heard him say, I will destroy this temple that is made with hands, and within three days I will build another without hands" (14:57-58). To this Mark adds, "But neither so did their witness agree together" (14:59). That is, the two witnesses did not testify that He said the same thing. Thus Matthew gives the one version of what they thought Christ said, while Mark gives the other.

Matthew's witness said He had the power both to destroy the Temple of God and to build it up in three days. If they are going to use this against Him, they have to prove that He doesn't have this power.

Mark's witness testified that Christ said, "I will destroy this handmade temple and I will build another (of the same kind) not handmade in three days time." In order to use this against Him they have to prove that He will not do this.

So very often what we think a person said, and what he actually said, are two different things. Here is a case in point. The fact is that Christ said neither. His exact words are recorded in John 2:19, "You destroy this sanctuary [inner sanctuary, i.e., Holy of Holies—the dwelling place of God] and in three days I will raise it up." Christ here referred to *His body*, as John testifies. This was the sign of His authority for casting out the moneychangers from the temple. "You men destroy My body, and in three days I will raise it up."

With the witnesses not agreeing as to His statement, they were destroying themselves and were becoming no witness at all. Furthermore, even if they had agreed, no legal accusation could have been formed against Christ by their testimony. The case is falling apart. But this will never do, for the case has already been decided. Something must be done, and done in a hurry.

The Action Of Caiaphas

"And the high priest arose, and said unto him, Answerest thou nothing? what is it which these witness against thee?" (v. 62). This is the first time that Caiaphas has addressed Christ in the Scripture.

There is something as far as criminal code is concerned that is very important in reference to this man. John brings this to our attention in John 18:14, "Now Caiaphas was he, which gave counsel to the Jews, that it was expedient that one man should die for the people." This refers to a previous statement given in John's Gospel in 11:47-53. This is the decision the Sanhedrin had made. The Council met after the resurrection of Lazarus from the dead. They knew they had to do something, but what? "If we do nothing, the gullible people will be taken in by Him, and this will cause the Romans to come and take away our authority and nation from us." Caiaphas, at this time, addresses the Sanhedrin, clearly not acting as president, but only as "one of them." Many authorities state that it was illegal for the High Priest to be president of the Sanhedrin as occurs in this trial of Christ. B. W. Westcott paraphrases his statement to them this way, "Ye, who dwell on these scruples and these fears, do not even know the simplest rule of statesmanship, that one must be sacrificed to many." Then John adds a footnote in verses 51 and 52 that whereas Caiaphas made the statement in one way, God would use it as truth in another. Verse 53 shows us the counsel of Caiaphas was accepted, and their action was decided. Their indecision was now only in reference to time and means.

But the point of criminal prosecution and justice is that no judge qualifies to render justice in a case which he himself has already formed a preconceived decision as to the outcome. Here we have the Judge, who has previously given his verdict of what must be done in the case, now taking over in the trial of the case in his own home—all of which was contrary to their own code, let alone to every code of criminal prosecution.

It is in this situation, with the witnesses breaking down, that the High Priest arises from his seat and says to Christ, "Answerest thou nothing?"

Why should He? If He has done wrong, produce the witnesses, but this they could not do. Had not Christ previously challenged His adversaries, "Which of you convinceth me of sin?'' (John 8:46). Here was the Lamb of God without spot or blemish.

Why should He answer anything? Were not these witnesses destroying themselves and testifying of nothing that could possibly bring an indictment against Him?

"*What* is it which these witness against thee?'' You answer that Caiaphas? They witnessed nothing against Christ, but only witnessed to the vile, corrupt, depraved heart of their sin nature.

The Silence of Christ

"But Jesus held his peace" (v. 63a). He was absolutely silent. It was not His place to testify against Himself; it was their place to bear witness if He had done any wrong.

The trial before Annas had gone from bad to worse, and the same thing was occurring here before Caiaphas and the Sanhedrin. The witnesses had failed. The two that were used did not agree among themselves. The High Priest tried to have Christ speak, but this failed. His silence was golden as He stood in absolute innocence. There was only one final way that the High Priest knew in order to achieve the decision that they had already reached.

Placed Under Oath

"And the high priest answered and said unto him, I adjure thee by the living God, that thou tell us whether thou be the Christ, the Son of God" (v. 63b). Stalker says, "He put Him on oath to tell what He claimed to be; for among Jews the oath was pronounced by the judge, not by the prisoner.'' This is the climax of the life of Christ on earth. The person sworn answered without repeating the form itself with a simple "Yes" or "No." If he deviated from the truth, he could know that the living God who had been invoked as a witness to the statement would punish him.

Before we consider Christ's answer, let us consider two things. The High Priest knew, first of all, that to claim to be the Messiah would be to claim to be the Son of God, and thus deity. This was clear to him as a student of the Old Testament Scriptures. Thus, whoever would be the Messiah, would be the Son of God, which in the mouth of an Israelite was deity incarnate (cp. John 5:18; 10:33). Secondly, the High Priest knew precisely what Jesus Christ claimed to be. They all knew that He claimed to be the Messiah. They knew of the works He had performed, including His last main miracle of raising Lazarus from the dead.

If He answers "No," they will forget the trial and drop the case. He has discredited Himself—His word will stand.

If He answers "Yes," He will not be making any new statement nor new claim, but they will charge Him with blasphemy and execute Him as they have planned. In either case they feel they will win, and Christ will lose.

The reply of Christ is in two parts. Matthew records the first part, and Mark the other. He replies, "Thou hast said" (Matt. 26:64). This is an idiom for "Yes, that is right. You said it as you asked Me the question." But Mark states that the Lord then went on to make it as emphatic as possible by adding His own divine affirmation. He added, "I am" (Mark 14:62). Keep in mind what this phrase meant to an Israelite, and also what had occurred when He said "I am" in the Garden. He is claiming not only to be the Christ, but deity itself.

He then added, "Nevertheless I say unto you, Hereafter shall ye see the Son of man sitting on the right hand of power, and coming in the clouds of heaven" (Matt. 26:64). The answer the Lord gave means suffering and death for Him, but it means "life" for us. The Lord cannot but speak the truth. Let the scoffers have their hour; His hour will come when they shall see He was right and they were wrong.

Again let us remind ourselves that the High Priest and all the members of the Sanhedrin were completely cognizant of what the Old Testament Scriptures taught, and that when the Messiah came He would be the Son of God, and He would be exalted to the highest seat of authority. Psalm 110:1 says, "The Lord said unto my Lord, Sit thou at my right hand; until I make thine enemies thy footstool." (Christ had already quoted this in Matt. 22:44.) Daniel 7:13 states, "I saw in the night visions, and, behold, one like the Son of man came with the clouds of heaven . . . ."

Christ makes the same claim He has made from the very beginning, which was made even by His forerunner—John the Baptist. He is the Christ. To be the Christ He must fulfill all the Scriptures prophesied about the Messiah. *This He claims* He will do. They may take away His earthly life, because the Father wills and He lays it down, but they can never touch His eternal life, nor His stated destiny. He shall sit, and He shall come again.

It was this same group, this same Sanhedrin, that later sat and tried Stephen (Acts 6:8-15). Stephen gave his address before this body (Acts 7:1-53), but was never allowed to complete it before they became so enraged that they were willing to kill Stephen to stamp out the light. "But he, being full of the Holy Spirit, looked up stedfastly into heaven, and saw the glory of God, and Jesus standing on the right hand of God, and said, Behold, I see the heavens opened, and the Son of man standing on the right hand of God" (Acts 7:55-56). The witness had been borne. They saw the fulfillment of what Christ had predicted in the face of Stephen, and then snuffed out his life.

With Jesus bearing testimony for the very last time of whom He was, He places His accusers and judges on trial. They must now prove that what He has said is not true. But they have already decided this, first when they committed the unpardonable sin, and later in secret meeting. They had already considered the evidence and rendered the verdict. They have judged the case in private session and given the sentence of death. The procedure that has been followed is only their means of carrying out that sentence.

Now they sit as His judges; but then He will sit as their Judge—and He has the greater judgment both in extent and duration. It is not a matter that they do not believe; they will not believe. It is a willful rejection.

Caiaphas Rent His Clothes

"Then the high priest rent his clothes" (v. 65a). The rending of the garments is designed to be a sign of intense sorrow or anguish, in this case because the High Priest heard blasphemy. By tearing his garments, he was saying to the other judges, "I mourn because my ears have had to listen to the greatest possible blasphemy they could hear."

But you who sit in Moses' seat and judge according to the Law, do you hear the Law? Leviticus 21:10 reads: "And he that is the high priest among his brethren, upon whose head the anointing oil was poured, and that is consecrated to put on the garments, shall not uncover his head, nor rend his clothes." Here is the High Priest condemning One who was guiltless before the Law, for no witnesses could be produced to prove otherwise, and no witnesses were allowed to prove His Messiahship; yet here he is breaking the Law himself in his eagerness to condemn Christ to death.

Who ever heard of the chief justice acting in such a manner? All protocol is set aside to achieve the desired decision. Yet this act was to be employed by God as symbolic of the rending of the Aaronic priesthood in order to establish a new priest and priesthood after the order of Melchisedec (Heb. 7:11-12).

The Plea for a Decision

At this time the High Priest addresses the other members of the Sanhedrin. "He hath spoken blasphemy; what further need have we of witnesses; behold, now ye have heard his blasphemy. What think ye?" (vv. 65b-66a). The High Priest renders his decision: "He hath spoken blasphemy." But the decision among the members of the Sanhedrin was to begin with the junior member and work toward the senior, one by one, so that the lower members might not be influenced by the highest.

Not only does the High Priest render his verdict first, but he renders the decision that there is no further need of witnesses, and this in spite of the fact that the law demanded them.

But Caiaphas and members of the Sanhedrin: You have had the Man to testify against Himself, and accepted that testimony as convicting evidence contrary to your own code, but you have not proved Him to be wrong. You must first prove His claim to be false before you render your decision. Furthermore, does this claim that Jesus is the Christ remain without testimony? Why have you not allowed witnesses on His behalf to substantiate His claim?

Matthew tells us why. You committed the unpardonable sin when the signs of His Messiahship were first presented to the nation, and now there was no sign, but the sign of the prophet Jonah (Matt. 12:39; 16:4). That sign is the death, burial and resurrection of Jesus Christ, and the Gospel going to the Gentiles. The resurrection of Jesus Christ is the sign to Israel that His claim of Messiahship was correct (cp. Rom. 1:4; Acts 2:32-36). This is why so many priests came to believe later (Acts 6:7).

The High Priest continues, "Behold now ye have heard his blasphemy." You will remember that a man's words before the Sanhedrin could not be used against him apart from other witnesses. Here again they break their code.

"What think ye?"—Render your decision. The whole Sanhedrin rendered the predetermined verdict: "He is guilty of death." Thus they voted simultaneously in contradiction to their own law.

The trial itself is over, or shall we say better, "The mockery of justice" is finished.

The verdict has been rendered.

The charge for which He was condemned: "Blasphemy."

The verdict: "Guilty."

The sentence: "Death."

The Afterglow

We have just seen religion at work with words; now we will behold its deeds. There is nothing as bad as religion. Religion always has and always will be the greatest enemy of truth and righteousness until the Lord destroys religion in the tribulation. It was religion that put Jesus Christ on the cross. It has been religion that has slain the martyrs of Jesus (Rev. 17:6). Politically, Satan controls the kingdoms of this world as the Prince of this world's system. Religiously, Satan controls the world as the prince and power of the air. The whole world lies in the power of the wicked one (I John 5:19), therefore, on these two counts.

What is taking place is something that startles the imagination. These men have just sentenced a man to die—that was their verdict. Any court that has the power of life and death ought to be a place of solemnity and dignity. The judges are responsible before the very law and authority given them to try a case, to protect the criminal against all injustice and maltreatment when he is found guilty.

These outrages would have been inexcusable even toward a man irrevocably condemned to punishment, but were all the more criminal toward Jesus, who had never been proven guilty of anything.

The very fact that these things were done in Caiaphas' house too, makes him culpable just as a citizen, let alone as presiding officer of the Sanhedrin. But these displays of feelings which occurred were just the aftermath of Caiaphas' own rage which he himself displayed upon the bench. Behind it all is more than the wickedness of the human heart. What is displayed against Christ is an infernal wickedness of the forces of the underworld. This is their hour.

Here is the record of the proceedings. "Then did they spit in his face" (Matt. 26:67). This fulfills Isaiah 50:6, "I gave my back to the smiters, and my cheeks to them that plucked off the hair: I hid not my face from shame and spitting." For someone to spit in another person's face was to show the greatest contempt possible for that one (cp. Job 30:10. For instance, when Miriam complained that Moses, her brother, was taking too much authority to himself and that God speaks through others also, God taught her quickly when she became leprous, white as snow, in Numbers 12. When Moses intercedes for her, the Lord's reply was, "If her father had but spit in her face, should she not be ashamed seven days?" (12:14). Thus we see in Scripture something of the shame and disgrace connected with a person spitting in your face.

Besides this, they "buffeted him" (Matt. 26:67). This word is "to strike with the fist," from the Greek word "the knuckles." Paul used the same word in I Corinthians 9:27 of "keeping under" his body by giving blows with the fists.

When they got tired of doing this, someone suggested they play a little game. So they covered His face (Mark 14:65) and someone then "smote him with the palms of their hands, saying, Prophesy unto us, thou Christ, who is he that struck thee?" (Matt. 26:67-68). Here is the first mockery. He claimed to be Messiah. If He were Messiah, He could give the name of the person who struck Him even though He was blindfolded. These servants ridicule the Lord's claim at being the Messiah and Prophet who was to come. The Roman soldiers later ridicule His claim at being a King. When He answered nothing, they laughed and jested and mocked. He had given His word, "An evil and adulterous generation seeketh after a sign; and there shall no sign be given to it, but the sign of the prophet Jonah," and this must stand.

"He was oppressed, and he was afflicted, yet he opened not His mouth: he is brought as a lamb to the slaughter, and as a sheep before her shearers is dumb, so he opened not his mouth" (Isa. 53:7). One word would have destroyed them all, yet He opened not His mouth. One word, and He would have been vindicated, but this was not the Father's will nor way. The Son was to be vindicated by His resurrection from the dead (Rom. 1:4), not by demonstrating His Messiahship to an evil mob. The Father's will for Him now was to be "dumb" though He be the Lord of all.

Chapter 7

The Denial

The denials of Peter are inseparable from the trials of Christ. It is a part of the whole story, for it occurs simultaneously with the trials and was not a separate picture. In order for us to treat it properly, it is necessary for us to look, however, at the denials of Peter as a unit by itself.

The Accounts in the Four Gospels

All four Gospels speak first of Peter's self-confidence when he stated he would not deny the Lord, but Christ predicted that he would. Each Gospel gives truth not covered by the others and needs to be considered. "Peter answered and said unto him, Though all men shall be offended because of thee, yet will I never be offended. Jesus said unto him, Verily I say unto thee, That this night, before the cock crow, thou shalt deny me thrice. Peter said unto him, Though I should die with thee, yet will I not deny thee. Likewise also said all the disciples" (Matt. 26:33-35).

"But Peter said unto him, Although all shall be offended, yet will not I. And Jesus saith unto him, Verily I say unto thee, That this day, even in this night, before the cock crow twice, thou shalt deny me thrice. But he spake the more vehemently, If I should die with thee, I will not deny thee in any wise. Likewise also said they all" (Mark 14:29-31).

"And the Lord said, Simon, Simon, behold, Satan hath desired to have you, that he may sift you as wheat: but I have prayed for thee, that thy faith fail not; and when thou art converted, strengthen thy brethren. And he said unto him, Lord, I am ready to go with thee, both into prison, and to death. And he said, I tell thee, Peter, the cock shall not crow this day, before that thou shalt thrice deny that thou knowest me" (Luke 22:31-34).

"Peter said unto him, Lord why cannot I follow thee now? I will lay down my life for thy sake. Jesus answered him, Wilt thou lay down thy life for my sake? Verily, verily, I say unto thee, The cock shall not crow, till thou hast denied me thrice" (John 13:37-38).

Christ's Predictions of Peter's Denials

All Bible study begins with first determining what Scripture says about an event or a subject, and then and only then, to interpret and apply the truth of Scripture. There is, first of all, the piecing together of facts so as to discover what happened, and then there is understanding the significance of those facts.

The first part is tedious and time consuming, but it alone produces the true significance and a correct interpretation and the application that may follow. Never forget that everything Scripture gives has significance, and it is up to the Bible student to discover the reason and purpose behind what is recorded. The denials of Peter are no exception.

When we analyze the passages involved, we discover an amazing fact. The Lord did not give just one prediction concerning the denials of Peter, but two separate and distinct predictions. Mark's Gospel gives the one; while Matthew, Luke and John record the second.

The Lord first made the statement that Peter would deny Him "this day," i.e. within the 24-hour period (Mark 14:30a). He then narrowed it to "even this night," and narrowed that further to "before the cock crowed twice" that Peter would three times deny the Lord (Mark 14:30b).

It seems that when Peter persisted in saying that regardless of what the other disciples would do, he was ready to go with the Lord "both into prison and to death" (Luke 22:33), the Lord added, "I tell thee, Peter, the cock shall not crow this day, before that thou shalt thrice deny that thou knowest me" (v. 34).

What is going to happen, then, is a multiplicity of denials of the Lord by Peter. Luke records also Christ's words to Peter that this is because Satan wants Peter and desires to sift him as wheat. Yet Christ prayed for Peter and for his restoration.

Looking at each Gospel individually, we find that each one is content to record but three denials that Peter made. Mark alone records three before the cock crowed twice (Mark 14:66-72); the other three Gospels state three denials before the cock crowed at all (Matt. 26:69-75; Luke 22:54-61; John 18:17,25-27). In fact, this is the emphasis of the Lord's prediction in all three of these Gospels that *the cock would not crow* until Peter had denied the Lord three times (Matt. 26:34; Luke 22:34; John 13:38).

What we find, then, is that each Gospel is content to record just three denials out of the many that took place. It took only three to fulfill the prediction of Christ, and to record more than this would be only adding insult to an already pathetic situation. What appears to have happened is this: Peter was so sure of himself and so vehement about it, that the Lord just had him stumble all over the place by multiplying his denials.

Peter's Denials

In order to construct the chronological sequence of events, we need to consider all four Gospels. In doing so, here is what we find.

The Trial before Annas

John alone records that Peter denied Christ when He appeared before Annas. When our Lord was led first to

Annas, Peter followed at a safe distance behind the procession; but as Christ was taken into Annas' home, he was left outside in the street with the gate closed (John 18:15-16). Evidently both Peter and John started following the procession together, after fleeing the scene in the Garden. John may have then moved quickly ahead so as to join in with the end of the procession as they entered the home of Annas. But getting inside, John realized Peter had not. So John, knowing Peter was on the outside, and knowing personally the maid who kept the door, went out, found Peter, and came back in with him.

James Stalker reminds us: "A Western house looks into the street, but an Oriental into its own interior, having no opening to the front except a great arched gateway, shut with a heavy door or gate. When this door is opened, it discloses a broad passage; penetrating the front building and leading into a square, paved courtyard, open to the sky, round which the house is built, and into which its rooms, both upstairs and downstairs, look. . . . On the side of the passage, inside the outer gate, there is a room or lodge for the porter or portress, who opens and shuts the gate; and in the gate there is a little wicket by which individuals can be let in or out."

John felt he was doing Peter a favor by bringing him into the house, but while John might enter without being tempted to deny his Lord, Peter could not. What a graphic illustration of the doctrinal truth Paul presents in Romans 14 and 15 and in I Corinthians 8-10 concerning the weaker brother. If we do something that causes our brother to sin, we have sinned against our brother. We may not fall, but if he falls, we have sinned against him.

John, because he was known to the high priest and therefore to his servants, would have been able to move around with perfect ease, but not Peter. He was in a strange place and was probably fearful of being recognized as one of Jesus' disciples.

Whether John was present at Peter's first denial is not known; however, he is the only one who mentions it. It may have been that John hurried away, not wanting to miss anything that was going on, and Peter was left behind. I personally feel John was there. At any rate, the very maid who let Peter and John in, questions Peter, "Art not thou also one of this man's disciples?" He saith, "I am not" (John 18:17). In the Greek language, whenever a question was asked, the expected answer was given. In this case, the expected answer is "No." "You are not *also* one of this man's disciples, are you?" This maid knew John was a disciple of Christ for he was known unto the High Priest, and, therefore, to his servants. She is asking Peter if he were also a disciple although she does not herself believe that he is. Peter goes along with her expectation and denies that he is Christ's disciple. He emphatically says, "I am not."

I imagine if you would have asked Peter right after this, "Why did you say that?" he would have answered, "I don't know." It was something he said without thinking about it or premeditating it at all. Subconsciously Peter is fearful.

No other denial took place in Annas' court. Peter only "stands" with the servants and officers at this fire.

The Trial before Caiaphas and the Sanhedrin

All the rest of the denials of Peter take place before Caiaphas and the Sanhedrin in the second trial. Neither Peter, nor any of the other apostles, ever attended the third trial, which took place after the light of the morning rays. When this second trial was concluded, Peter's denials were over, and he went out and wept bitterly.

While the order of events cannot be absolutely determined, there seems to be a logical sequence within each Gospel as chronologically presented.

The second denial occurs, then, before the servants and officers as Peter is "standing" and warming himself by the fire. This was soon after the Lord Jesus was sent bound unto Caiaphas. "And Simon Peter stood and warmed himself. They said therefore unto him, Art not thou also one of his disciples? He denied it, and said, I am not" (John 18:25).

The third denial occurs by the same fire as Peter sought to lose his identity with the others by sitting among them. Peter's denial is to one of the maids of the high priest who spotted him as he sat in the light of the fire. "And when they had kindled a fire in the midst of the hall [court], and were set down together, Peter sat down among them. But a certain maid beheld him as he sat by the fire, and earnestly looked upon him, and said, This man was also with him. And he denied him, saying, Woman, I know him not" (Luke 22:55-57; cp. Matt. 26:69-70; Mark 14:66-68).

In Mark's Gospel we discover that Peter decided that he had better change his position after this denial, so he got up and went out into the forecourt or entrance way from the street to the court proper. Some of the later manuscripts of Mark's Gospel add, "and the cock crowed," but this is not contained in the earlier manuscripts, nor does it harmonize with the rest of Scripture as to the time and place for the crowing of the cock.

But Peter needed more than a change of position; he needed a change of heart. Therefore he experiences denial number four. "And a maid saw him again, and began to say to them that stood by, This is one of them. And he denied it again" (Mark 14:69-70a). This is not another maid, but "the maid," i.e., the same one who identified him by the fire.

But soon, in the same location, there came along another maid to cause him to deny the Lord the fifth time, and this time with an oath, i.e., he called God to record that he never knew the man. "And when he was gone out into the porch, another maid saw him, and said unto them that were there, This fellow was also with Jesus of Nazareth. And again he denied with an oath, I do not know the man" (Matt. 26:71-72).

In the next three denials, the locations are nowhere stated. The sixth denial is found in Luke 22:58, "And after a little while another saw him, and said, Thou art also of them. And he said, Man, I am not." This denial is to a male servant (unless his exclamation, "Man," does not identify the sex of the servant). In which case this incident could be identical to the above given by Matthew. Against this, however, is the Greek word "another" which signifies another of a different kind. Moreoever, the expressions "Woman" (Luke 22:57) and "Man" (22:58) seem quite contrastive. It must be said also that this male servant was different from the male servant next recorded by Luke which appears to be the same as the last one recorded by John. All things considered, then, this denial stands alone as separate and distinct.

The seventh denial, John lists. "One of the servants of

the high priest, being his kinsman whose ear Peter cut off, saith, Did not I see thee in the garden with him? Peter then denied again; and immediately the cock crew" (John 18:26-27). Luke 22:59-60 must be the same incident, which says: "And . . . another confidently affirmed saying, of a truth this fellow also was with him: for he is a Galilean. And Peter said, Man, I know not what thou sayest. And immediately, while he yet spake, the cock crew."

So the cock has crowed—the first time—right as Peter was speaking, but evidently it never registered on his consciousness.

Therefore, probably almost immediately following, occurred the last and final denial. "They that stood by said again to Peter, Surely thou art one of them: for thou art a Galilean, and thy speech agreeth thereto. But he began to curse and to swear, saying, I know not this man of whom ye speak. And the second time the cock crew. And Peter called to mind the word that Jesus said unto him, Before the cock crow twice, thou shalt deny me thrice. And when he thought thereon, he wept" (Mark 14:70-72; cp. Matt. 26:73-75). This final time, you will notice, Peter began both to curse and to swear. The cursing would be using the language of the unbeliever (but not taking the name of God in vain as in today's cursing), and the swearing would be the act of again calling God to witness to the statement he made, "I know not this man of whom ye speak."

This last denial followed the third denial recorded by John, and the third recorded by Luke. There the cock crew the first time right as Peter was speaking. Here the cock crew the second time right after Peter had spoken.

This takes into account all the denials. We find that there were not three of them, but eight. Seven of these take place during this second trial. Seven take place before the cock crowed once; all eight before the cock crowed a second time.

Summary of the Eight Denials of Peter

Place	Persons Involved	Significant Events
1. Door	Servant girl	Trial before Annas

(Place)	(Persons Involved)	(Significant Events)
2. Fire (standing)	Men	Trial before Caiaphas
3. Fire (sitting)	Servant girl of High Priest	
4. Forecourt	The same servant girl as above	
5. Forecourt	Another servant girl	Peter gives oath
6. Unknown	Male servant	
7. Unknown	Servant of the High Priest, and kinsman to the servant whose ear Peter cut off	

The first crow of the cock

8. Unknown	Before all	Peter curses and swears

The second crow of the cock

Four events now happen in rapid succession, following the last denial. First, the cock crew the second time, and Peter heard it this time with conscious significance. For the first time it registered what he had done. Secondly, the Lord turned and looked upon Peter (Luke 22:61a). Then Peter remembered what Christ had predicted (Luke 22:61b; Matt. 26:75; Mark 14:72). Evidently while these events were in progress, Peter never called to mind what Christ had said. Finally, Peter went out of the grounds of the High Priest's house and wept bitterly (Matt. 26:75).

Footprints of Backsliding

Having looked at Scripture concerning the facts of Peter's denials, let us now go back and look at the significance behind these facts. What was behind Peter's fall? This is practical because if we can discover what was behind his fall, we can begin to see areas that correspond to things behind our fall.

Peter did not fall because Christ prophesied that he would. Rather, it is the reverse. Christ prophesied he would because Peter was going to fall. The cause of Peter's fall was not Christ's prediction, but *Peter's life.* It is always true. As someone well expressed it, "No one suddenly becomes base." Peter's fall was not a blow out, but a slow leak; and such is the case for every man and woman that appears suddenly to deny his or her Lord and does that which is wrong morally and spiritually. There have been certain steps taken "in the flesh" before this. The steps may be somewhat secret or concealed, but they *always* exist. They may be found in every child of God who has ever "fallen into sin." It wasn't a fall at all. It was a deliberate walk in the flesh.

Notice Peter's footprints as he takes this downward path.

1. Self-confidence

"But Peter said unto him, although all shall be offended, yet will not I" (Mark 14:29). This was Peter's confidence in Peter, or better, confidence in Simon. Later on Peter would write that we are "kept by the power of God" (I Pet. 1:5), even though in manifold temptations and trials (1:6-7). It was no longer the flesh that kept Peter. Peter, then, would say with Paul, "For I know that in me (that is in my flesh,) dwelleth no good thing" (Rom. 7:18).

2. Unreprovable

"And Jesus saith unto him, Verily I say unto thee, That this day, even in this night, before the cock crow twice, thou shalt deny me thrice. But he spake the more vehemently, If I should die with thee, I will not deny thee in any wise" (Mark 14:30-31). Peter knew it all. The *Word of God* could not reach him to reprove and correct him (cp. II Tim. 3:16-17). Whenever the Word cannot reach us before we fall, there is nothing left but a fall. Here is one who would not listen to God speaking to him.

3. Prayerlessness

"And he cometh, and findeth them sleeping, and saith unto Peter, Simon, sleepest thou? couldest not thou watch one hour?" (Mark 14:37). *Simon, are you of all people sleeping?* Christ here gives further warning to Peter which again goes unheeded, "Watch ye and pray, lest ye enter into temptation. The spirit truly is ready, but the flesh is weak" (14:38). Without prayer, and the victory gained through prayer, the flesh will overpower the spirit of a man. He may will to do good, but have no power to perform it.

Christ's words go unheeded (Mark 14:40), and they have no answer because there is none. The person out of fellowship is so at ease and unaware of his spiritual state that he has no trouble sleeping (cp. Jonah 1:5).

I feel there is a lesson here also that needs to be

emphasized greatly. Whenever I will not pray with another, I am the one who is wrong. Whenever there is a problem to be faced by the Lord's people, and one will pray and another will not, the one who will pray is always right, and the one who refuses to pray is always wrong. The flesh never wants to pray, and the one controlled by the flesh will not pray, for that very act (and continuous state) of prayer would reprove him and his wrong position. God's man loves to pray, and the one in fellowship with the Lord loves the time of fellowship with Him. If we are not in fellowship, His presence is the last thing we want, and we will soon be following Him afar off.

It will be noticed that these footsteps of Peter are a series of chain reactions. Each one leads to the next, and to the next. Having taken the first step, and refusing to be converted or reproved, one merely continues on the downward course.

4. Impulsive action

"Then Simon Peter having a sword drew it, and smote the high priest's servant, and cut off his right ear. The servant's name was Malchus. Then said Jesus unto Peter, Put up thy sword into the sheath: the cup which my Father hath given me, shall I not drink it?" (John 18:10-11; cp. Mark 14:47). Peter was acting without thinking of the consequences of his action, as we have already seen. He was acting to maintain his honor, because he had previously boasted of what he would do. What happened to Christ's honor was immaterial. In the Garden when Peter should have been active, he was passive and asleep; now when he should have been passive, he is active. Oh, how characteristic this is of the "flesh"!

5. Unfaithfulness

"And they all forsook him, and fled" (Mark 14:50). Now this should have been enough to cause Peter (and all of the others) to realize their spiritual condition. It was this prediction in Mark 14:27, "And Jesus saith unto them, All ye shall be offended because of me this night: for it is written, I will smite the shepherd, and the sheep shall be scattered," that caused Peter to say, "Although all shall be offended, yet will not I" (14:29). It had now been fulfilled, but Peter did not weep bitterly at this time. He has not hit bottom, but is

rapidly moving down.
6. Following Christ afar off
"And Peter followed him afar off . . . " (Mark 14:54a).
Intimate fellowship with the Lord has now been broken. This
will only lead to further sinning. Peter once had said he was
ready to go to prison and death, but now he is walking afar
off. We already discussed how John was able to get Peter into
the home of Annas, but right at the very entrance, Peter
denies his Lord. And this condition only leads to another
problem.
7. Wrong company
Peter stands with the officers and servants and warms
himself by the fire. This was the situation first in the
courtyard of Annas, and nothing happened (John 18:18), so
he did it likewise in the courtyard of Caiaphas (John 18:25).
But there something does happen. They ask him, "Art not
thou also one of his disciples?" He denied it, and said, "I am
not" (John 18:25). Peter has emphatically said, "No," and he
figures this will suffice; so the next time we see him, he has
sat down at the fire, and in the light of the fire one of the
maids of the high priest spots Peter. She intently looks him
over and then speaks up, "Thou also wast with the Nazarene,
even Jesus." But he denied, saying, "I neither know, nor
understand what thou sayest" (Mk. 14:68). "Woman, I know
him not" (Luke 22:57). Oh Peter, have you forgotten,
"Blessed is the man that walketh not in the counsel of the
ungodly, nor standeth in the way of sinners, nor sitteth in the
seat of the scornful" (Psa. 1:1)?
At this, Peter felt he had better change location. So he
went into the precourt or forecourt which is the archway
leading from the gate to the court.
8. Fearful
Peter is now controlled by fear, and in this state the
whole nature of the flesh will manifest itself—given enough
time. The very same maid who spotted him in the light of the
fire sees him again in the forecourt and begins to say to them
that stood by, "This is one of them." But he denied it (Mark
14:69-70a).
Another maid saw him and said unto them that were
there, "This man also was with Jesus the Nazarene." Being

controlled by fear, Peter felt now the need to make his denial even more emphatic than he had done before, so he denied with an oath, calling God to witness, "I know not the man" (Matt. 26:72).

Thus we have another step taken by Peter.

9.   Oath—Calling God to witness his lie

Then after a little while, a male servant saw him, and said, "Thou also art one of them." But Peter said, "Man, I am not" (Luke 22:58).

Then the servant of the High Priest who was a kinsman to the man whose ear Peter cut off, said to Peter, "Did not I see thee in the garden with him?" Peter denied it. But the man confidently affirmed, "Of a truth this man was also with him: for he is a Galilean." To this Peter said, "Man, I know not what thou sayest."

While Peter was in the process of speaking, the cock crowed. Then again, they that stood by said to Peter, "Of a truth thou art one of them; for thy speech betrayeth thee that thou art a Galilean." This causes Peter to panic, and so to take his final step on his downward course. He began to curse and to swear and said, "I know not this man of whom ye speak."

10.   Cursing: Peter's language as a fisherman before he met the Savior.

Peter says in effect, "Does my speech betray that I am His disciple? Well then, listen closely to my speech. Does this sound like someone who is His follower? Would anyone who was His follower use language like this?" Peter knew that they knew no one belonging to Jesus would use such language as Peter was using. What a testimony Peter was unconsciously giving of Christ and of His disciples, but oh how wrong that such a testimony of Christ's purity and of His power to transform men should have been borne in this negative way from the Lord's own disciple. Still today the world does not expect cleanness of speech and conduct from its own, but it does expect and demand it—and rightly so—of one of the Lord's disciples.

Can the disciple of Jesus revert back to the old life and conduct? Yes he can, and Peter is an example of this. But he can never do so *as a life*. Formerly, before he met Jesus, this was the way he lived. He can now only do this *as an act*, after which he will be convicted by the Holy Spirit within. Should he persist in sinning and hardening his heart to the Holy Spirit's reproving, he is on dangerous ground simply because he is God's child and will not be condemned along with this world. He cannot continue to live this way, for God will take him off the scene (Acts 5; I Cor. 5; 11; James 5; I John 5).

The Backward Glance of Christ

The cock now crows the second time. Peter hears it, and there comes to his mind all the words that Christ spoke to him, when he refused to listen and believe. The day was just beginning to break; the trial and beatings before Caiaphas and the Sanhedrin were over; Christ was being led out. At the very instant Peter was swearing and cursing, Christ was close enough to His disciple to pick up every word. With the crowing of the cock, "the Lord turned, and looked upon Peter" (Luke 22:61).

Eye met eye, and while no words were spoken, yet a volume of words were communicated. What a look it must have been. It had to bring conviction, and yet be filled with compassion, else Peter would have been brought to despair. It was both a sword to cut, and a balm to heal. It was used as the climactic turning point in Peter's life. It brought Peter back to reality and spiritual truth. For the next fifty days, Peter will be moving upward until on the Day of Pentecost, filled with the Holy Spirit, he delivers to these same people the message of their taking and crucifying the Lord of Glory, but God raising Him from the dead and exalting Him to His own right hand as both Lord and Christ.

How far have we sinned against our Lord? It makes no difference how far we have gone; there is always *forgiveness* if we will but turn and seek it. The Apostle John's admonition to us is, "If we confess our sins, he is faithful and just to forgive us our sins, and to cleanse us from all unrighteousness" (I John 1:9). The Lord is always faithful to His child. Satan would love to bring the child of God to the place of despair so that he plunges himself over the precipice that Judas used to end his life. If Satan can succeed in having the child of God do this, he can gain the victory and defeat the Lord's plan in that life. If Satan can make him a mental wreck over his sin, it will be for Satan, a good second best.

What do we need? We need to look into the face of the One we have denied, just as Peter did. When Peter looked at Him, he saw One who loved him with an infinite love even in his sin. The Lord loved Peter even though Peter had denied Him. He was on the way to the cross to die for him—greater love hath no man than this.

The very fact that Christ loved Peter was what broke Peter's heart. As James Stalker has penned it, "He saw now what kind of Master he had denied; and it broke his heart. It is this that always breaks the heart. It is not our sins that make us weep; it is when we see what kind of Saviour we have sinned against."

The remembrance of his fall and restoration never left Peter for one moment the remainder of his life. It colors everything in Peter's First Epistle.

I have heard some say that they never like to see a man cry. I would to God we had men today who could cry. Many of the men God has used have been men that wept before Him:

Job	— Job 16:11	
David	— Psalm 102:9; II Sam. 15:30	
Jeremiah	— Jer. 9:1; 13:17; Lam. 1:16	
Nehemiah	— Neh. 1:4	
Christ	— Luke 19:41	
John	— Rev. 5:4	
Paul	— Phil. 3:18; Acts 20:37	

"Blessed are ye that weep now: for ye shall laugh" (Luke 6:21). "Be afflicted, and mourn, and weep" (James 4:9). "Weep with them that weep" (Rom. 12:15). Here is weeping, not because of any personal sin, but because of a heart of compassion. Many times Scripture portrays weeping as the sign of the true repentance of the heart and conviction of sin. "They that sow in tears shall reap in joy. He that goeth forth and weepeth, bearing precious seed, shall doubtless come again with rejoicing, bringing his sheaves with him" (Psa. 126:5-6).

Let us never forget, earth has no sorrow that Jesus cannot heal.

Chapter 8

The Trial Before the Sanhedrin

It is shocking to find how few who write about the trials of the Lord even deal with this trial. Edersheim passes over it with just a few sentences. Many others do not even mention it at all, or combine it with the previous trial before Caiaphas. It is true that two of the Gospel writers pass over it with just a summary word but even this is a very significant word. Dr. Luke alone brings out the details as to what took place. But in passing over events, let us remind ourselves that Luke and John pass over completely the trial before Caiaphas with the exception of referring to Peter's denials, yet no one would dare deny its importance. Some books devoted to being verse by verse exposition of the Gospels even omit this trial.

Here is what Scripture says occurred. "When the morning was come, all the chief priests and elders of the people took counsel against Jesus to put him to death: And when they had bound him, they led him away, and delivered him to Pontius Pilate the governor" (Matt. 27:1-2). "And straightway in the morning the chief priests held consulation with the elders and scribes and the whole council, and bound Jesus, and carried him away, and delivered him to Pilate" (Mark 15:1).

What Matthew and Mark give in a summary statement, Luke gives in fuller detail (Luke 22:66-71). Remember that none of the apostles were at this trial. Luke, who thoroughly investigated these things, probably received his information from Joseph of Arimathaea, or from Nicodemus—both of whom were members of the Sanhedrin. Let us consider point by point what is taking place.

"And as soon as it was day . . . " (v. 66). All three Gospels mention this fact. The day has dawned. Thus this trial can in no way be confused with those trials before Annas and Caiaphas during the night. This is an entirely new trial. In fact, this is, supposedly, the legal ecclesiastical or religious trial. All that had transpired during the night was illegal, and every member of the Sanhedrin knew it. If it had not been, there is no reason for them to meet again after it became light; but the very fact that they all meet again after dawn to ratify and legalize the illegal action that they took in the early morning stands as condemnation to them all. The very fact, furthermore, that the entire Sanhedrin meets and does so in their Judgment Hall shows that they do intend for this to be a legal trial and handled according to their code of jurisprudence. They are officially trying the case.

It will be before this body that Peter and John will be questioned (Acts 4:5-22). Then again a second time they appear before this same body (Acts 5:27-42). Stephen also had his day to witness to them (Acts 6:8—7:60). Later on Paul is brought before this tribunal (Acts 22:30—23:10).

The Distinctives of this Trial

Many things are different in reference to this trial when compared to the trial that had occurred in the darkness before Caiaphas and the Sanhedrin.

The place is different.

Previously it was at the home of Caiaphas. Now it is at their council hall.

The time is different.

It was dark then—before the crowing of the cock. It is light now; morning has come. The morning light came and the cock crowed at the very end of the previous trial.

The officer in charge is different.

The High Priest, Caiaphas, was officiating when the trial was conducted in his home. Now nothing is mentioned of Caiaphas, and the implication is that he is in no way acting as president of the Sanhedrin, which action at the previous trial was completely contrary to the rules of the Sanhedrin.

The procedure is different.

Before Caiaphas, the first thing they sought to do was to secure witnesses. Now there is no mention of witnesses whatever as this did not work out satisfactorily. They seek to convict Christ alone on His own testimony which was the end result of the trial before Caiaphas. After Christ makes the statement in this trial that they desire, they say that there is no need for witnesses. Thus they seek to get around both the Law, and their own code by this act.

The action in the trial is different.

Caiaphas rent his clothes previously; no such action occurred at this trial.

Christ's answer is different.

Previously, when He was asked under oath by the High Priest if He were the Christ, the Son of God, His answer was "Yes, I am." Then, He spoke of sitting at the right hand of power and coming with the clouds of heaven. Now, they do not put Him under oath. "If you are the Christ," they said, "tell us so." "If I tell you," replied Jesus, "you will not believe me; and, if I question you, you will not answer. But from this hour 'The Son of Man will be seated on the right hand of God Almighty.' " "Are you, then, the Son of God," they all asked. "It is true," answered Jesus, "I am." (Luke 22:67-70 *Twentieth Century New Testament*).

The method of voting is different.

At the conclusion of this trial, they did not take a voice vote as had previously been done, but now they merely stand and indicated by this action their decision.

The action following the trial is different.

Here they lead Jesus out immediately to take Him to Pilate. There is no violence in this court as there was after the previous trial.

The people present at the trial are different.

There is no indication of anyone present at this session

of the Sanhedrin other than its members, while the servants of the High Priest, officers and at least two disciples, Peter and John, were present at the home of Caiaphas. All the denials of Peter had taken place at the previous trials, and no such events occurred at this trial, for Peter is not even present at this trial.

The Events of this Trial

Before we leave the truth that it is now morning, we need to remind ourselves that this morning was the anniversary of that day when Israel moved out of the land of Egypt to the Red Sea, having partaken of the Passover lamb the night before and applied its blood to their dwelling. What a day of deliverance for Israel it was, and it was to be commemorated each year. While Israel had deliverance, there was no deliverance for the Lord. He was paying the price for deliverance and redemption of others—*His own blood* (1 Pet. 1:18-19).

"As soon as it was day, the elders of the people and the chief priests and the scribes came together" (Luke 22:66). The minute that the Sanhedrin could legally assemble, they did so because they wanted to hurry this up before the populous could get wind of what was happening. It is probably close to 5 A.M. Normally the Sanhedrin did not assemble until after the morning sacrifice at 9 A.M., but they cannot wait that long this day. This is not a normal day. The morning and the evening sacrifice this day will be the person of the Lord Jesus Christ Himself.

"And led him into their council," i.e., into their council chamber of meeting hall. "Saying, Art thou the Christ? tell us" (v. 67a). Literally, their first question was, "If (as you say is true) you are the Messiah, tell us once and for all."

"And He answered them: If I should tell you, you will in no wise believe" (v. 67b). This is a double negative with the aorist subjunctive which gives the strongest possible negation. Christ's point is that they are not about to be convinced by anything He says. He had told them in the darkness of the morning hour, and *look what they did to Him*. Will they do any differently now? Christ says they will not.

"And if I should ask you, you will in no wise answer" (v. 68). That is, *You members of the Sanhedrin will not enter into a fair discussion with Me. If I interrogate you as to what the Messiah will be and do when He comes, and whether these are fulfilled in Me, you will in no wise give Me an honest answer. You are resolved not to listen to truth, but to condemn Me to death.* Previously Christ had asked them questions, but they would not answer, simply because they came each time to a wrong conclusion. When they didn't want to accept the conclusion, they refused to answer the question (cp. Matt. 21:24-27; 22:41-46). Thus *the issue* is brought to the front and exposed to the light: the issue is *they will not believe.* The problem is *willful blindness* and *willful rejection.*

Having stated this, Christ then replied, "And from henceforth the Son of man shall be seated at the right hand of the power of God" (v. 69). When asked whether He was the Messiah, He replies that He is the Son of man and the Throne-sitter. This is the last time Christ refers to Himself as the *Son of man.* Again the reference is to Daniel 7:13-14. We find that the Lord Jesus Christ applied this designation to Himself 86 times in the Gospels. The expression characterizes the One through whom God is working and giving a revelation to others. It does not indicate what the prophet is in himself, but what he is to God. He is a Son of man: (1) chosen by God; (2) endued with the Spirit; and (3) sent by God with a message. Jesus Christ is the Son of Man. He is the representative of man—the head of regenerate humanity. The Sanhedrin, knowing the Old Testament prophecies, knew that the Throne-sitter would be the Son of God (cp. Ps. 110:1). They therefore interrogate Him further.

"And they all said: Are you then the Son of God?" (v. 70a). This is the issue upon which they have decided to condemn Him.

"And He declared to them: You say that I am!" (v. 70b). Here is a Greek idiom for "Yes, I am." Christ combines three epithets and claims them all: Messiah, Son of Man, and Son of God. The last involved both deity and humanity and was the one the Sanhedrin refused to accept. Not one of them will ever be able to say, "He never told us who He was."

"And they said, What further need have we of witnesses? for we ourselves have heard from His own mouth" (v.
71). They have not called witnesses. They say now they do
not need them. They have all witnessed what He said. This
makes about 70 witnesses who have heard His "blasphemy."
On account of His own testimony, they condemn Jesus to
death. They had previously reached the verdict that for Jesus
to claim to be the Son of God was wrong and necessitated
that He die. It is exactly as Christ said. They are not in truth
trying the case. They are not interested in evidence or
discussion or witnesses. They will make no reply to reason or
logic. They have completely and totally rejected light since
the day they committed the unpardonable sin, so there is
nothing left to them but darkness. They met, not to try the
case, but "to put him to death" (Matt. 27:1). The Sanhedrin
in court session has officially ratified the action taken during
the darkness of the morning. There was physical light now,
but still spiritual darkness. They had made an attempt to
legalize their illegal actions. But, as A. T. Robertson says,
"No ratification of a wrong can make it right."

The End of One Action—The Beginning of Another

The work of the Sanhedrin is officially over, but they
cannot rest for they must now deliver the Lord over to Pilate,
and will stop short of nothing but His death. Jesus is now
bound (Mark 15:1), and taken to Pilate. The whole assembly,
rather than remain in their Judgment Hall, arises and leads
Jesus to Pilate. This is contrary to their own code of conduct
in a criminal case, but they are forced into it in order to
secure from Pilate the verdict of death, which they want.
They cannot turn back now; their work is not yet over. They
will not rest until they stand beneath His cross with folded
arms and mock.

Previously Christ has predicted "he must go unto
Jerusalem, and suffer many things of the elders and chief
priests and scribes . . . "(Matt. 16:21). And again, "Behold,
we go to Jerusalem; and the Son of man shall be betrayed
unto the chief priests and unto the scribes, and they shall

condemn him to death, and shall deliver him to the Gentiles . . . " (Matt. 20:18-19). Thus far, every word has been established. The Jews have had their part in His condemnation; now the Gentiles will have their part so that the whole world will stand guilty before God that the Lord might have mercy on all and to all to offer them salvation by grace alone.

The Latest Twist

Each generation must often contend with the same problems which were dealt with by the previous generation. However, sometimes these attacks take new turns or twists. Such is the case of Israel's Supreme Court Justice, Haim Cohn, who claims to be an expert in the history of Jewish legal traditions. It is his contention that not only did the Jews have no part in the trial of Christ, but that the Sanhedrin was actually trying to save Jesus from death. Here is how he arrives at such a proposition, in a recent issue of the *Israel Law Review.*

He holds, in light of the known facts about legal customs and traditions of Jesus' time, that it is just improbable that there would have been a trial commence after sundown—especially on the eve of the Passover, when most members of the Sanhedrin would have been busy with ritual preparations for the feast. Moreover, if they had met, under existing Jewish law, any condemnation would have required the sworn testimony of at least two trustworthy witnesses. In all these points he is absolutely right. Yet he does not stop here, but goes on.

Cohn insists that Jesus was tried and condemned for the political crime of insurrection—a charge that could be handled by no one other than the Roman Procurator, Pilate. He feels this is verified by the fact that when Pilate asked Jesus if he were King of the Jews, he answered, "You have said so"—in effect, Cohn says, a *nolo contendere* admission of guilt.

"Why," Cohn asks, "did the Jewish authorities summon Jesus?" He believes they were trying to save Jesus; and that by saving a prophetic teacher, beloved by the masses of

Jerusalem, their own waning popular prestige would have been enhanced. As Cohn reconstructs the events, the Sanhedrin first examined witnesses, not to condemn Christ, but to find men who would convincingly testify in His favor before the Romans. When it could not find any, this highest court in the land attempted to persuade Jesus to plead not guilty before the Romans; He refused. Thus the buffeting recorded that Jesus received from the Sanhedrin members was not punishment for blasphemy, but simply the product of bitter frustration. According to Cohn, "Jesus had refused to cooperate and to bow to their authority, and there was nothing that could be done to prevent the trial from taking its course." Thus Cohn holds that the Sanhedrin was seeking to work for Jesus and against the hated Pilate.

I have presented the evidence, and will let you be the judge if this is what Scripture presents.

Chapter 9

Judas Iscariot — The End of the Betrayer

The Holy Spirit gives us one final glimpse into the life of Judas Iscariot before He continues with the trials of Christ. There are a number of reasons why the Spirit desires us to have this final portrait, as we shall see as we uncover what He has recorded.

Two passages deal with Judas' death: Matthew 27:3-10 and Acts 1:16-19. These two accounts are not contradictory, but complementary. Matthew is speaking in general terms in regard to the suicide of Judas, while Dr. Luke in the book of Acts is recording the specific statement of Peter with its details "known unto all the dwellers of Jerusalem."

The Action of Judas

Let us look first at Matthew's account. "Then Judas, which had betrayed him . . . brought again the thirty pieces of silver to the chief priests and elders" (Matt. 27:3). There is no reason to seek to place this incident as occurring other than where it is placed in Matthew's account. Morning has come. The Sanhedrin have completed their trial of Jesus and condemned Him. They now lead Him to Pontius Pilate, the governor. As they are taking Him, Judas comes to the chief priests and elders. After this event (which Matthew carried to its completion for the sake of clarity), Jesus stood before the governor to be tried by him.

Observe carefully this fact: when Judas met the members of the Sanhedrin, they were traveling with Jesus to take Him to Pilate. Jesus Christ was in their midst. Did Judas repent to the Lord and plead for mercy and forgiveness? Not at all! Scripture says, "he repented himself." What does this mean?

In order to answer this question, we must understand that Scripture uses two verbs for "repent." The word translated here "repented" (*metamelomai*) is used only six times in Scripture. This word is in contrast with a much more frequently used verb and noun (*metanoeo* and *metanoia*) used 34 and 24 times respectively in the New Testament. The last two words involved in Scripture the idea of a *change of mind* and, consequently, of action and life. It is the only word used when we are commanded to *repent* in the book of Acts or Revelation. The other word translated also "repent," used here of Judas and five other times, has more of a connection with emotion, and thus "remorse" and "regret." Let us look at *each* of the six occurrences of this word in Scripture in order to understand exactly what Judas is doing.

The Six Occurrences of Metamelomai

Matthew 21:29, "He answered and said, I will not: but afterward he repented [he regretted it], and went." This is the parable of the two sons where one said he would go into the field, but didn't while the other son said he could not go, but then regretted he had said this, and went.

Matthew 21:32, "For John came unto you in the way of righteousness, and ye believed him not: but the publicans and the harlots believed him: and ye, when ye had seen it, repented not afterward, that ye might believe him." That is, the Sanhedrin had no regret for not believing in John's message, even though the publicans and harlots did believe him. The reason they did not regret it was|that if they had believed John, they would have had to accept the One of whom John spoke—Jesus Christ—and this was to them unthinkable. Thus they never regretted not believing John. (This shows the meaning of the repentance mentioned in verse 29 and why it is brought into the context).

Matthew 27:3, "Then Judas . . . when he [Judas] saw that he [Christ] was condemned, repented himself, and brought again the thirty pieces of silver to the chief priests and elders." This was a remorse and regret of what he had done. The full impact of his action now lay upon him. He realized he had done wrong, as he will testify to the Sanhedrin, and that Jesus was innocent (27:4). But this remorse for the action he had taken, and his regret that he had performed it, is not repentance at all in the true Scriptural sense. It is not repentance unto salvation. We shall see this clearer as we come back to this scene and notice specifically what Judas did.

Hebrews 7:21, "(For those priests were made without an oath; but this with an oath by him that said unto him, The Lord sware and will not repent, Thou art a priest for ever after the order of Melchisedec:)." Here "repent" is not the idea of a change of mind, but a change of feeling, of remorse, of regret. This will never come to pass. The Lord gave this prediction in Psalm 110:1, and He will never regret this prediction because the Lord Jesus Christ will be all that the Father has anticipated, etc.

In II Corinthians 7:8-10, the verb is used twice, and stands in context in contrast to the other word for "repentance" which signifies a change of mind. It reads, "For though I made you sorry with a letter, I do not repent [regret it], though I did repent [regret it at first] . . . . Now I rejoice, not that ye were made sorry, but that ye sorrowed to repentance [i.e., to a true repentance or change of mind. It wasn't just an emotional response only, but also a change of action and life]: for ye were made sorry after a godly manner, that ye might receive damage by us in nothing. For godly sorrow worketh repentance [i.e., a true repentance or change of mind] to salvation not to be repented of [i.e., not to be regretted. True repentance will never cause regrets or remorse of heart or action]: but the sorrow of the world worketh death." Judas is an example of this. His sorrow was more than he could bear, and it worked death.

What Judas Did

These are the six occurrences of this word. Now, what do we find? Judas regretted he had betrayed Jesus when he saw Him condemned by the Sanhedrin and taken bound to Pilate for execution. This whole thing had not worked out as he had thought. Perhaps he had calculated that Jesus would not have allowed Himself to be captured and condemned. If this or something similar was his thinking, he is still without excuse, for over and over again Christ said what was going to happen in minute detail. Judas' problem was he was *an unbeliever.* But he is still an unbeliever. He never falls before the Lord and asks forgiveness for his deed. Why? Because he is an unbeliever, and he died an unbeliever, as Acts 1:25 says, "that he might go to his own place." Had Judas fallen before the Lord, he would have been forgiven. It was Ambrose, who said, "If only Judas had said, 'I have sinned,' to Jesus, instead of to the priests, he could have been saved."

The issue for Judas was salvation. This was his one need. Now notice what took place concerning Judas:

(1) He had a feeling of guilt (conscience). Remember the words that Christ had spoken to him in the garden? They seem to be eating into his soul.

(2) He had a great emotional response. He was sorry for his sins, and would have given anything if he had not done this one act.

(3) He gave up his sins and made restitution. He brought back the silver to the priests; and when they refused to take the money back, he forced it upon them, for he wanted no reminder of this deed.

(4) He confessed both his sin and Christ's innocence. Now someone will say, you cannot ask a man to do much more than this!

(5) He would have done penance, had someone told him what to do to try to relieve his guilty conscience. But even if he had done all these things, and penance too, he still would have been lost. The reason is that none of this is salvation. The Lord Jesus Christ is salvation.

The Difference Between Remorse and Salvation

It is possible for a man to feel the full depth and consequences of his sins, and be grieved for them so as to be under a strong conviction of guilt with a great emotional response and distress of mind and deep remorse—all of this—and yet never experience true repentance and salvation.

The reason is that there is a wide gulf between remorse and repentance. True repentance leads to the light; remorse leads from it. Many a person has had remorse because of his sins, but never repented of them. True repentance leads the sinner to the Savior. That which is false and wrong leads the sinner away from his only means of salvation, and it seeks to destroy his life so that he cannot come to the Savior. The end of following Satan is death, but before death, comes remorse. Everyone who follows Satan ends up his life with the testimony, "I played the fool." Yet this confession in no way saves him at all.

Beloved, if you should be reading these words, and you have been remorseful because your life has been controlled by Satan and you have done things that you ought not, do not allow him to seal your doom in the Lake of Fire. Flee to the Lord Jesus Christ. Many others have fled for refuge before you and no one has ever been turned down (Heb. 6:18). All that will come unto Him He will in no wise cast out. The Lord Jesus is your only Savior.

Was Judas too Great a Sinner to be Saved?

Someone may say that Judas was too big a sinner to be saved by the Lord. We need to pause here and meditate for a moment, for the poet Dante and all medieval writers considered Judas to be in the lowest part of the pit, where the worst of all sinners are. There is no question that this act of Judas was a great sin. None other than Christ Himself said so (Luke 22:22). In fact, He said, "It had been good for that man if he had not been born" (Matt. 26:24). But what Judas Iscariot did in reference to the Lord Jesus Christ in betraying Him and causing the Lord to suffer, Paul did as an unbeliever to the body of Christ—the church. This is why the Lord said to him, "Saul, Saul, why persecutest thou me?" (Acts 9:4). Because of Paul's actions against Christians, he identifies himself as the chief of sinners. Listen to his words as recorded in I Timothy 1:12-16.

"And I thank Christ Jesus our Lord who hath enabled me, for that he counted me faithful, putting me into the ministry; who was before a blasphemer, and a persecutor, and injurious: but I obtained mercy, because I did it ignorantly in unbelief. And the grace of our Lord was exceeding abundant with faith and love which is in Christ Jesus. This is a faithful saying, and worthy of all acceptation, that Christ Jesus came into the world to save sinners; of whom I am chief. Howbeit for this cause I obtained mercy, that in me first Jesus Christ might shew forth all longsuffering, for a pattern to them which should hereafter believe on him to life everlasting."

Notice the words "mercy," "grace," "all longsuffering." Paul realized a very important truth. If he had not obtained this grace and mercy, and had he gone to hell as an unbeliever, he would have had the greatest punishment of anyone born of woman. When he calls himself the chief of sinners, he is not being dramatic, but infinitely truthful. No one had done more against the truth and the Lord than Paul had done, and punishment in hell will be determined on the basis of one's works against the truth (cp. II Tim. 4:14; Rev. 20:12). Judas was not the chief of sinners; Paul the apostle was. And one of the reasons Paul loved the Lord so very much was that the Lord had forgiven him such a great amount (cp. Luke 7:47).

Could Judas have been saved, then? Yes, because Paul was saved, and Paul was a greater sinner than Judas. But why had the Lord worked to lead Paul to salvation and not Judas? There is an indication given to us in I Timothy 1:13, "I obtained mercy, because I did it ignorantly in unbelief." Judas was not in ignorance, though he was in unbelief. Judas had light, and rejected light because his deeds were evil. He refused to come to the light lest his deeds would be manifested that they were wrong. He hardened his heart and rejected light. The love of money is the root of every kind of evil (I Tim. 6:10), and Judas was a thief. His love for money finally caused him to sell the Lord Jesus for 30 pieces of silver. Paul, on the other hand, was not so controlled. Paul was in ignorance, not in willful sin. Touching the righteousness which is in the law, he was blameless (Phil. 3:6). Paul never sinned willfully, that is, with full knowledge that he was rejecting truth and light (Acts 23:1; 26:19).

Why Judas was not Saved

Why are we going into this? Because it brings out one of the basic truths concerning salvation. From the human standpoint, men are unsaved because they refuse to come to the light, because they reject the light and, by an act of their volition, harden their hearts against it. Consequently, every man is saved or lost because of himself, not God. God has provided salvation for everyone. He is not willing that any be lost. No one will ever stand before the Lord and say, "But I could not have been saved because you didn't choose me." Not at all. Judas will never be able to say this either. Judas is lost because Judas chose to be lost and refused to come to the Savior. It is choice that determines our eternal destiny. It is "sin" that hardens the heart. This is a law that operates in both the unbeliever and the believer as well. Thus the exhortation to all of us is "But exhort one another daily, while it is called Today; lest any of you be hardened through the deceitfulness of sin" (Heb. 3:13). The Holy Spirit is the only One who can soften the heart and bring the sinner to the Savior. He leads no other place than to Christ (John 16:8-11). If we are being driven any other place, look out—it is the devil.

Application of the Truth

But there is one more practical point that needs to be emphasized today. Satan is a master at causing us to have an emotional response to truth when we hear a soul-searching message. This is "to repent"—as Scripture uses the term six times—with emotion and "regret" that we haven't lived for the Lord as we should, ad infinitum. If this is all we have—and usually it is—it accomplishes nothing. True repentance goes beyond the emotions to the mind which thus activates the will. Until the will is activated, there is no true repentance.

Let us take two examples: one, the message preached to the unsaved, and the other, our own response to revelation as saved. In Acts 2:38 we read, "Then Peter said unto them, Repent, and be baptized every one of you in the name of Jesus Christ on the basis of the remission of sins . . . ." Verse 37 shows that the people hearing Peter had an emotional response. Peter tells them to go on and repent, i.e., change your mind about Jesus Christ that He did not blaspheme when He claimed to be the Son of God. "And be baptized." Seal your faith in action by being identified through water baptism with the believers in the Lord Jesus Christ. It would have caused them to be excommunicated from the synagogue, but God would take care of them and their needs.

What do we mean when we say to a sinner, "repent," or "repent of your sins?" The last phrase is anything but Scriptural. If we mean by "repent," be sorry for your sins, this is completely wrong. Judas was extremely sorry for his sin. Being sorry for sins does a person no good whatever. If we mean by "repent," "Change your mind about Jesus Christ. He died for your sins and rose again from the dead," then we are right. It is best never to even use the word "repent" in dealing with an unsaved person because his concept of the word is "to be sorry for his sin," but this is not the Scripture's concept.

In each of the seven churches of Revelation 2 and 3, the Lord Jesus is giving a message to the believers in these separate churches. In every church He uses the word "repent" which signifies a change of mind about what the essentials are, and then having done that, to "act" accordingly. The Lord's word to all of us is to "repent and do. . . ." Our task is to apply the Word to our lives and be doers of it and not hearers only, having merely an emotional response.

The Testimony of Judas Iscariot

"Then Judas, which had betrayed him, when he [Judas] saw that he [Christ] was condemned, repented [had an emotional reaction in himself of remorse, regret], and brought again the thirty pieces of silver to the chief priests and elders" (v. 3). Many Bible scholars feel that when Judas covenanted with the chief priests and elders to betray Christ, it involved not only his arrest, but also Judas testifying against Christ as a witness. Judas, however, was nowhere to be found during the trials before the Sanhedrin. Thus, the Sanhedrin was forced to try to secure others to witness against Jesus. Judas' conscience would not permit him to testify against Christ, for he knew He was innocent.

Now the Sanhedrin's chief witness steps forward, not to testify against Christ, but, because of a stricken conscience, testifies for Him. He testifies of Christ's innocence first by action and then by word.

First, he brought again the thirty pieces of silver. This silver, which was so dearly coveted, brought Judas no pleasure when it was in his possession. "Treasures of wickedness profit nothing" (Prov. 10:2). "Every good gift and every perfect gift is from above, and cometh down from the Father of lights" (James 1:17). "A man can receive nothing, except it has been given him from heaven" (John 3:27).

Oh, the times we saw something that we thought would be the one thing that would make us happy, only to gain it and have it bite like an adder. Sin's pleasures are but for a season, if they are enjoyed at all. The wages of the sin nature is death, but before death is that bitter agony of sorrow, remorse and shame (cp. Rom. 6:21). They that sow to the flesh always reap, in the end, corruption.

Amnon felt he just had to have Tamar. Nothing would satisfy his heart but her. He said, "I love Tamar." Amnon sowed the flesh and reaped corruption. "Then Amnon hated her exceedingly; so that the hatred wherewith he hated her was greater than the love wherewith he loved her" (II Sam. 13:15). The end was death for Amnon. Look out for the lusts of the flesh, the lusts of the eyes, and the pride of life. These things never satisfy the unbeliever, let alone the believer. "He that loveth silver shall not be satisfied with silver; nor he that loveth abundance with increase" (Eccl. 5:10).

"The folks who spend their days

> In buying cars and clothes and rings
> Don't seem to know that empty lives
> Are just as empty filled with things."

Secondly, he testified to the members of the Sanhedrin, "I have sinned in that I have betrayed the innocent blood" (Matt. 27:4a). Now just stop and think what is involved in this testimony. Here is the Sanhedrin's chief witness testifying to them, but he is testifying of what? He is testifying for Christ's innocence. I remind you again: This is the highest court in Israel whose code of jurisprudence was the finest ever developed of any nation. They have the responsibility of administering justice; and after a criminal trial, when a man was condemned to death, they were to remain in their seats in case any witness might appear to speak in the criminal's defense. Then they would call back the prisoner, and hear the evidence of the witness.

Is this what is happening here? Not at all. The entire Sanhedrin is moving as a body to go to Pilate in order to secure from him the verdict of death. Will they go back and retry the case, hearing the new witness that has come before them? Not at all. They reply to Judas, "What is that to us? see thou to that" (27:4b).

What do they mean, "What is that to us?" Why, it is everything to them! It is their responsibility, and it cannot be side-stepped. In fact, this is the very reason that Matthew brings in this incident of the Sanhedrin with Judas. He is writing to the Jews, and, in his account, he is bringing a legal indictment against the Sanhedrin which would be valid in any court for their impeachment. The testimony of Judas, being the very one who in the first betrayed Him, should have been more valuable to the Sanhedrin than any other man. It stands today as a monument to the Lord's innocence.

"What is that to us? see thou to that," not only has a bearing concerning Jesus, but also against Judas himself. If Judas had sinned by betraying innocent blood, it is the responsibility of the Sanhedrin to retry the case in order to condemn Judas and let Jesus go free. The law says: "Cursed be he that taketh reward to slay an innocent person" (Deut. 27:25). If Judas was guilty of this, it was the Sanhedrin's responsibility to show it. If Judas had witnessed against

Christ by his betrayal of Him, as he had, he deserved to bear the punishment that was to be given to Christ according to the law (Deut. 19:16-19), and it was the Sanhedrin's responsibility so to punish him. Why didn't the Sanhedrin reopen the trial? Because the very evidence that would condemn Judas would also condemn themselves.

But here is their answer to Judas. When Judas came to them and he could be used by them in their scheme to apprehend Jesus, they were his bosom friends. Now that he has done what they want, they have no more use for him, but cast him aside. He finds himself despised by those whose tool he was. This has been repeated over and over again in time. The world loves for what it can get, and after they have obtained what they were seeking, they have no more use for the victim of their desires.

The Sanhedrin have no grace for this man that has come to them, in desperation. The guilty can never comfort the guilty. So the world can give no help to the sinner. The Lord Jesus Christ is the only One who can give grace to the sinner regardless of his sin, and it is never too late to come to Him. Judas failed to come to the only One that could help him. One penitent thief did come in the last hour before he died to show us this mercy seat is open to all, yet there was only one saved in this manner lest any man might presume on the grace of God and so wait until the last hour. Now is the day of salvation. If you reject light and do not come to the Lord Jesus now, you may not have the opportunity later. Oh come while you may.

Thirty Pieces of Silver

Evidently the Sanhedrin were just in the process of leaving the Temple; and with Jesus being bound, Judas knew immediately the decision they had reached. Since they refused the money, he forces it upon them, "And he cast down the pieces of silver in the temple, and departed, and went and hanged himself" (Matt. 27:5). The price of treason is thrown into the Temple. The expression Matthew uses for Temple is *naos*, which is always used in the New Testament of the Sanctuary itself where only the priests could enter, and not of the outer courts (cp. John 2:19-21).

Judas does not leave this money just any place, but the one place in all the world where the priests must decide what to do with it. They have refused to hear the witness; they will now try the case in absentia. Judas has forced them to it through the providence of God. In all probability, Judas may not even have realized why his impulse was to cast this money into the Sanctuary. Had he left it at his home, it would have become the possession of his heirs. Had he left it on the street, it would have become the property of the one who found it. Had he put it into the treasury in the Temple, the Sanhedrin would undoubtedly have left it there, saying it was his to do with as he desired. But, having left it in the Sanctuary, it becomes an issue for the chief priests to meet and decide what to do with it. Let us follow the money as Matthew traces it, and then come back to the suicide of Judas.

"And the chief priest took the silver pieces, and said, It is not lawful for to put them into the treasury, because it is the price of blood" (Matt. 27:6). Whether they met in session immediately or a little later in the day is not the issue. In all probability it was later in the day, after their encounter with Pilate had been entirely successful, for without this, what happened to the money meant little. Matthew, however, traces the money through to completion, and then he resumes the trial.

"It is the price of blood"—Notice this! They, the chief priests, witness the truth concerning this money, and thus concerning the whole trial. It was the price of a life. A man died, not because he was guilty, but because of thirty pieces of silver—the price of a slave. Here was the legacy of a crime, and the chief priests knew it. Their consciences would not allow them to put it into the treasury, nor to keep it for themselves. But this money could just as honestly have gone back into the treasury as it came out. Yet those who unscrupulously take it out cannot decently put it back in.

These chief priests have just committed the greatest travesty of justice that the world will ever see, without one qualm of conscience. Now, on this little thing their consciences are religiously scrupulous. What irony! Of a truth,

Christ spoke of them, "Woe unto you, scribes and Pharisees, hypocrites! For ye pay tithe of mint and anise and cummin, and have omitted the weightier matters of the law, judgment, mercy, and faith: these ought ye to have done, and not to leave the other undone" (Matt. 23:23). Many are very scrupulous in small things and commit the greatest felonies before the Lord in gossiping and sins of the tongue—which things really count.

But do you understand what the chief priests are testifying here? They are meeting in council of their own group: 24 chief priests. What they are doing is far more than deciding on 30 pieces of silver. It is an issue that is at stake. This money is blood money, and the chief priests testify to this fact. But when they so testify to this, they are testifying to the Lord's innocence. They are saying clearly His life was bought, not justly condemned. He was innocent, but He died anyway. This money caused His death, and thus it is "blood money."

Purchase of the Potter's Field

"And they took counsel, and bought with them the potter's field, to bury strangers in " (Matt. 27:7). Someone among them had an idea. Why not use this unclean money for unclean people in an unclean place? The old potter's field is no longer of any value for making pottery, as the land has been completely worked over. It is of such a nature that nothing will grow on it either. It is available today on the market, and could be purchased for this very sum of money. We could use it to bury the heathen that die in the city of Jerusalem and thus solve the problem of what to do with them. Motion seconded and passed. Meeting adjourned. The purchase was made.

Whether they were cognizant of it or not we cannot say, but it is very likely that they realized also that this land had the curse of God upon it, placed there through Jeremiah. They will use this unclean money to buy an unclean place in which to bury unclean people. "Strangers" refers to those outside of the nation. Many times money gained in an unjust way has sought to be cleansed by using it for charitable purposes. The field was formerly called, "The potter's field." The Sanhedrin desired it to be called "A field to bury strangers in" (v. 7). The people called it correctly, "The field of blood" (Aceldama, Haqal Doma), even at the time Matthew wrote his Gospel (v. 8).

This thing was not done in a corner. The people knew that blood money was used to buy this land, and they so nicknamed it accordingly. More than this, the name persisted in spite of all attempts to wash it away. At the time of the writing of the Gospel of Matthew, about 30 years after the events took place, the name for the graveyard was still "The field of blood." Here, Matthew says, is the historical reason why. It is not a name that would normally be attached to a graveyard, even a heathen one. Thus, the people also testify to the Lord's innocence, for they knew it was purchased with blood money. Yet, the only way this money could have been blood money was for the Lord to have been innocent.

Here was erected a perpetual monument, not to Judas, but to the Sanhedrin and to the infamous deed that they had committed. They have tried the case *in absentia* and have found the Lord innocent. "They" are the ones who act the decision of their own council, as Matthew says in the following verses, and so seal their decision in deed. By this very act, they stand self-condemned. It is a very important principle of Scripture that the Lord often allows a man to pronounce his own sentence (Luke 19:22; Job 9:20; Psa. 64:8).

Fulfillment of Prophecy

"Then was fulfilled that which was spoken by Jeremy the prophet, saying, And they took the thirty pieces of silver, the price of him that was valued, whom they of the children of Israel did value; and gave them for the potter's field, as the Lord appointed me" (Matt. 27:9-10). Matthew's quotation is full of meaning at this point, and yet it presents some problems. The quotation is said to be from Jeremiah, and yet the idea comes from Zechariah. Here, then, is a problem. Various solutions have been offered.

(1) Some feel that Jeremiah originally gave the prediction,

but that it was not written down. It was transmitted orally until Zechariah recorded it. This would be similar to our Lord's statement in Acts 20:35, recorded by Paul.

(2) Some think that Matthew originally wrote the words, "the prophet," without giving any name, and that some early scribe placed the name Jeremiah by mistake. In favor of this view, the Syriac version, which is one of the oldest, reads simply, "the prophet." The Persian version also omits it.

(3) Some held that Matthew originally wrote the words, "Zechariah the prophet," and that an ignorant transcriber very early changed the word into Jeremiah. In favor of this position is the fact that in manuscripts, names were often written in a shortened form in which only the initial letter would be different (IRIOU and ZRIOU). By the change from Z into I the mistake might easily have been made.

(4) Some contend that originally the former prophets began with Joshua in the Hebrew Scriptures, and the later prophets began with Jeremiah rather than the present-day arrangement which finds Isaiah first. Since each division in the Old Testament canon was known by the first book in the section (e.g., Psalms refers often times to the entire third division, cp. Luke 24:44), Jeremiah would then stand in place of the prophetic prophets which would include Zechariah.

The solution offered by Augustine is no solution at all. He said, "Matthew forgot what he was doing and made a blunder. He quoted from memory, and inaccurately. He meant Zechariah and not Jeremiah." If writers of the New Testament can make blunders, then we can never know what is truth and what is not. We have no word of truth.

My own position is this. Matthew wrote Jeremiah and he meant Jeremiah, but he also quotes from Zechariah the essence of his prediction. Matthew is not confused; he knows what belongs to Jeremiah and what belongs to Zechariah, having quoted Zechariah less than one chapter before (Matt. 26:31). In Matthew's thinking, Jeremiah's prophecy is the more important of the two, while Zechariah's is the specific prediction.

The entire 19th chapter of Jeremiah is devoted to this area of ground known as the Potter's Field. It was called "The valley of the son of Hinnom," since he owned the ground. It had been called Tophet (in the King James), better Topheth which is the Hebrew word signifying the place of burning. It is first mentioned in II Kings 23:10 at the reforms of Josiah. Topheth was where the idol Moloch had been set up and where the Israelites were sacrificing their infant sons and daughters, placing them in the brass arms of this god that had been heated to destroy whatever was placed there. Jeremiah gives a prophecy against it, first in Jeremiah 7:31-32. He then enlarges upon this in Jeremiah 19. This place will no longer be called Tophet nor the valley of the son of Hinnom, and it wasn't. It will be called, "The valley of slaughter; for they shall bury in Tophet, till there be no place" (7:32; 19:6, 11). Now in the enlargement of the prophecy, Jerusalem receives the curses of the land of Tophet (Jer. 19:12-15).

This is what is behind the thinking of Matthew. "God so ordered it that the elders of Israel purchased the field of which the curse of Jeremiah rested, thus making it the property of the Jewish State. By so doing, they transferred that curse to themselves and the people." The curse of Tophet becomes the curse of the city of Jerusalem. God will make this city as Tophet, till there be no place to bury.

The chief priests of the nation, as heads of State, have purchased the land of Tophet and with it its curses to themselves and the people of Israel by this act. It will be fulfilled to the letter in A.D. 70 under the seige and destruction of Titus. The city will be laid "even with the ground, and thy children within thee" (Luke 19:44). God will not be mocked. They have set their own judgment by this act.

Zechariah's prophecy gives us added detail. In Zechariah, chapter 11, we find the true Shepherd coming and ministering to the nation. But the Lord tells the Shepherd that it is "the flock of slaughter" He is ministering to (11:4, 6, 7). In verse 12, the Shepherd asks the nation to price His ministry. How faithful and how wonderful do you consider my ministry to have been? What is your estimate of the value of my ministry as the Shepherd? "So they weighed for my price thirty pieces of silver" (Zech. 11:12).

Is there anything significant about this? Most certainly there is. In Exodus 21:32, this is the price of a slave gored by an ox. This is their utter repudiation and contempt for the ministry of the Lord's Shepherd. But with it the nation, in truth, becomes the flock of slaughter. To prove this, the very money with which they valued the Shepherd was cast to the potter. According to Zechariah, this transaction was carried out in the house of the Lord (Zech. 11:13). This is an amazing prediction. The nation valued the Lord, and then bought the potter's field with this same money that they used to value His ministry. Jeremiah gives the curse; Zechariah shows the price; Matthew records it was transacted just as predicted.

The Death of Judas Iscariot

Having traced through the money and the purchase of the land with it, we need to go back and take a final look at the death of Judas. Matthew records only that Judas went out and hanged himself. "And he cast down the pieces of silver in the temple, and departed, and went and hanged himself" (Matt. 27:5). Dr. Luke in the book of Acts enlarges upon the details of the death of Judas. "Now this man purchased a field with the reward of iniquity; and falling headlong, he burst asunder in the midst, and all his bowels gushed out. And it was known unto all the dwellers at Jerusalem; insomuch as that field is called in their proper tongue Aceldama, that is to say, The field of blood" (Acts 1:18-19).

Only two men in all of Scripture commit suicide by hanging: Ahithophel in the Old Testament, and Judas in the New. Scripture had pronounced anyone hanging on a tree as cursed (Deut. 21:23). Ahithophel was the counsellor and friend of David. He betrayed his master and went with Absalom in his rebellion against David, only to have his own words rejected. This led to his ignominious end (II Sam. 17:23). In all of this Ahithophel is a portrait of Judas.

Suicide

Suicide is treated by Scripture as being one of the most contemptible acts of which mankind is capable. In it all reason is cast to the wind. The law of self-preservation becomes deadened. Unbelief takes over as the person's master. The individual reasons it is better to leave than to stay and cope with life, failing to realize that it will be worse in death than in life, for after death is the judgment. In such an act the person seeks in effect to strike back at God. It is a way of saying to God that He has not been good, righteous and loving; that it is impossible for the person to cope with the circumstances of life; and that there is no source of strength or place of help. Such an act, then, denies the goodness of God to all men. It denies the providence of God that He is seeking our repentance and turning to Him through the events that happen unto us. It denies the love of God, and God loves *me*, and the Lord Jesus Christ gave Himself for me (Gal. 2:20). Socrates said that God has placed us here, as at some military post and, until He recalls us, it is our business to hold it. In this he is in line with the revealed truth of Scripture.

Peter tells us, "Now this man purchased a field with the reward of iniquity." How is this possible when Matthew tells us that it was not Judas at all that bought the land, but the chief priests? The point of law is this: The money was still considered to be Judas', and to have been applied by him in the purchase of that potter's field. It is very frequent in the Word to represent a man doing that which he is merely the cause or occasion for another to act. Acts 2:23 is an example. Speaking to the men of Israel, Peter says, "Him, being delivered by the determinate counsel and foreknowledge of God, ye have taken and by wicked hands have crucified and slain." The men of Israel had crucified Him through their leaders and through the Roman soldiers, yet the act was theirs. So with the property. The chief priests would have made the act of valuing, selling, and purchasing all Judas'; but they themselves were equally guilty for all that transpired.

Looking at what happened to Judas, we find him dying a double death. Judas hung himself on a tree, but either the rope he used broke, or the branch of the tree, so that having suspended himself over a cliff, he falls, not feet first, but he is thrown head first, perhaps caused by a slight incline in the slope. In this manner, he hits at the bottom of the cliff, and a sharp rock pierces his intestines so that he dies an aggrevated death. Only too late did Judas learn that the Lord Jesus Christ, whom he failed ever to call "Lord," holds the world and all things therein together. Those who have visited Palestine tell us that there is a precipice over the valley of Hinnom where trees still grow quite near the edge. A rocky pavement exists also at the bottom of the ledges. Dr. Luke records the vivid account of his death from the lips of Peter which was known unto all the dwellers at Jerusalem. He tells us further that at that time, some 43 days after the events took place, the people had called the place the field of blood (Acts 1:19). Thus we find that the name, "The field of blood," has a dual significance. In Acts, it is so called because it was the place where Judas died a horrible death. In Matthew, the name is used thirty years later as an indictment against the Sanhedrin because blood money was used to buy this field. Both accounts are right, but are approaching the events from a different point of view.

"Judas by transgression fell" from the ministry and apostleship to which he was appointed. He fell because of unbelief in the Lord Jesus Christ, and he went "to his own place." He refused mercy so there was only judgment left. He spurned coming to the only One who could extend mercy to him, so now he will receive justice for all eternity.

Friend, though "all have sinned, and come short of the glory of God," we may be "justified freely ['without a cause,' John 15:25] by his grace through the redemption that is in Christ Jesus, whom God hath set forth to be a propitiation through faith in his blood" (Rom. 3:23-24). The word propitiation may be translated "mercy seat." There is one place where God may show His mercy and manifest His grace to the vilest sinner. It is at the cross where the blood becomes the basis of God showing mercy to the sinner. If you come—mercy. If you spurn the invitation—justice. You make the decision, but eternity is in it!

Chapter 10

The First Trial Before Pilate

We now come to the civil trials, which are three in number. Christ will be first tried before Pilate, and pronounced innocent. He will then be sent to Herod who makes a mockery of the whole thing, signifying the Lord's innocence. Finally, He comes back to Pilate, who tries the case for a final time, ultimately rendering a decision.

The Time Involved

The time of day "was early" (John 18:28), which is an expression that signifies the fourth watch of the night. The sun had not risen as yet over the horizon. The Sanhedrin had met in their hall for their condemnation of Jesus just as soon as it began to be daybreak. Matthew and Mark mention only that it was morning, and Luke, "as soon as it was day" (Luke 22:66). This trial of the Sanhedrin could not have lasted over five minutes at the most. Since it becomes light an hour before sunrise, the Sanhedrin may have been before Pilate by 5 or 5:15 A.M. Jesus Christ's first trial before Pilate could easily have been limited to five minutes, after which time He was sent off to Herod. There before Herod, Christ answered nothing. He was mocked and sent back to Pilate. All this could have taken place within a half hour, making it 5:45 A.M. The second time before Pilate demands more time, but by 6:15 A.M. Pilate could have said to those gathered before him, "Behold your King," which John says was *"about the sixth hour"* (John 19:14). John in all his Gospel, living among the Gentiles, reckons time according to the Roman method, which begins the new day at midnight, rather than the Jewish method of naming the hours from sunrise. (Westcott adequately shows from ancient writings that the Romans reckoned their civil days from midnight, and that all of John's times in his Gospel are Roman times since there was no longer a Jewish nation when John writes, and he is writing among the Gentiles in the Roman Empire. See B. F. Westcott, *The Gospel According to St. John*, p. 282). Thus, all the events of the trials may be harmonized together as far as time is concerned, with the fact that Christ was crucified at 9 A.M. in the morning which was the third hour as reckoned by the Jews (Mark 15:25).

Why Christ Was Taken to Pilate

Why was it that the Sanhedrin took Jesus to Pilate? Why did they not execute Him themselves even as they stoned Stephen to death (Acts 7:57-60), and as they would have killed Paul had he not been rescued by the Romans (Acts 22:22; 23:10)? The stoning of Stephen was mob action, and it was illegal. So was their action against Paul, and this is why the Romans stepped in to rescue him. Judea was a conquered country, and, while the Romans sought to work with the existing governments of their conquered states, the right of the sword remained in their sole control. The Jews could try a man according to their own law, but they could not legally put a man to death. This they acknowledge before Pilate when they are seeking from him the death penalty for Christ (John 18:31).

John records that this was, in actuality, fulfilling our Lord's own prediction that He was not going to be the victim of mob rule, but was to be delivered by his own nation to the Gentiles (Matt. 20:18-19), and receive, not stoning, but death by crucifixion (John 18:32). Krummacher observes, "For the second time they hand over their brother Joseph to the uncircumcised and to strangers. By this transfer, they typified, at the same time, their own fate. The world's salvation intended for them in the first instance, was by them most ungratefully given up to the Gentiles; while they themselves were thenceforward left to languish in darkness and the shadow of death." But we might add that just as Joseph ultimately became the savior of Israel, so will the greater than Joseph be the same to His people in the future.

Pilate was Procurator of Palestine, and was thus the representative of Caesar in Judea. To him was delegated authority from the Roman Governor of Syria for the condemning to death of any person. The right of the sword was Rome's not Israel's; and they knew this. Even though the Jews had tried a man, he was retried all over again in a Roman court by Roman law before the death sentence could be passed against him. The procedure to this point had been private, or nearly so, but it was the very essence of proceedings of Roman law that they were public. While the private proceedings worked to the detriment of truth and righteousness, the public proceedings will also work to the same end. It is not the method that is wrong or right in either case; it is the heart of man that is defiled.

Pilate

Before looking at the trial itself before Pilate, we need to take a look at this man who is the Procurator at this time. Palestine was a district under the authority of the Roman Governor of Syria. Pilate was Procurator from A.D. 26 to 36. He had been appointed by the Roman Emperor and made his residence in Caesarea—a Roman name meaning "Caesar's town"—which was a Roman or Gentile city, a small imitation of Rome with its theatres, baths, games, etc. On special Jewish feast days he would go up to Jerusalem with a large band of soldiers in order to keep order. While in Jerusalem he would make his residence in what had formerly been the royal place built by Herod the Great. It was situated on the hill southwest of the one on which the Temple stood. It is said to have been a magnificent building, rivaling the Temple itself in appearance, and large enough to be capable of containing a small army. It consisted of the main building with two wings on either side. In between the two wings and in front of the main building was a broad pavement. It was on this pavement in the open air where the trial before Pilate occurs.

Pilate had been born in Sevile, Spain. He hated the Jews, and was detested equally by them. The former Procurators had ordered the removal of the image of the Emperor from the standards of the Roman soldiers before marching them into Jerusalem, in order to avoid the appearance of the worship of the Caesars, and so offend the Jews. Pontius Pilate did no such thing. He forces this hated emblem on them, even though later he retracted. Also during his time as Procurator, he had robbed the Temple treasury and used the money to build an aquaduct to bring water into the city of Jerusalem. A number of revolts had arisen in Palestine against his regime. Each time there was a revolt, he would kill a number of Jews, and so use this tactic to suppress further revolts.

One such revolt is spoken about, in the current headlines in Luke 13:1-3, where we read, "There were present at that season some that told him of the Galileans, whose blood Pilate had mingled with their sacrifices. And Jesus answering said unto them, Suppose ye that these Galileans were sinners above all the Galileans, because they suffered such things? I tell you, Nay: but, except ye repent, ye shall all likewise perish." Josephus does not even mention this particular incident, which indicates something of it being a rather commonplace occurrence. Most Bible scholars feel this is a reference to "the followers of Judas of Galilee, who . . . taught that Jews should not pay tribute to the Romans, and of whom we learn, from Acts 5:37, that he drew after him a multitude of followers, who, on his being slain, were all dispersed. About this time that party would be at its height, and if Pilate caused this detachment of them to be waylaid and put to death, as they were offering their sacrifices at one of the festivals, that would be 'mingling their blood with their sacrifices' " (David Brown, *A Commentary*

Critical, Experimental and Practical on the Old and New Testaments, V, 279).

Even among Roman leaders, Pilate was known for his inhuman cruelty. The discharge of his office in Judea had been brought to the attention of the Roman Emperor himself. It seems that at this precise time he was investigating Pilate's running of his office. There had been so many revolts that he felt Pilate cannot be a good administrator. The Emperor Caligula does banish Pilate from his job subsequent to this time. Caligula himself was known for his inhumanity, but even he could not stand for Pilate's inhumanity. He banished Pilate to Gaul. It was while in Gaul that Pilate committed suicide. Thus you can see what kind of a man Pilate was.

With this background in mind of the Sanhedrin's hatred for Pilate and for Rome itself, think of the irony of their statement that they will make. While their hatred for Rome was great; their hatred for Jesus Christ was greater. They will, in the course of the trial, take the part of Rome and Rome's interest until finally they exclaim, "We have no king but Caesar" (John 19:15).

The passages that bear upon this trial are Matthew 27:11-14; Mark 15:1-5; Luke 23:1-6; John 18:28-38; and I Timothy 6:13. Using John's Gospel at this point, which is the most detailed, let us move through the events as they occurred.

The Jews and Their Scruples

"Then led they Jesus from Caiaphas unto the hall of judgment: and it was early; and they themselves went not into the judgment hall, lest they should be defiled; but that they might eat the passover" (John 18:28). Pilate was sitting in the Judgment Hall when they arrived with Jesus. The reason he was seated here is that someone had come ahead and notified him that the Sanhedrin were coming. He was prepared for their arrival.

But when they came, the Jews would not enter into the Judgment Hall "lest they should be defiled." This was to them a very important principle. Once again we see how

meticulous they were to seek to keep the minute details of
the Law but "omitted the weightier matters of the law,
judgment, mercy, and faith" (Matt. 23:23). They "strain at a
gnat and swallow a camel." Christ went in, and He was not
defiled; they stayed out and were defiled with His blood
upon their hands.

John says they would not enter in "lest they should be
defiled; but that they might eat the passover." Here is given
to us both the negative and positive reason for their action.
Not entering in to the Judgment Hall was not the Jew's
problem; bringing their Messiah to Rome, seeking His death,
was the problem. Israel had kept the action of separation
from things that defile, but not the meaning of it intended by
God. She was going through the ritual without the reality.
She had the ceremony without its significance. But, beloved,
this is our danger too. Israel had made the Law into a religion
where acts or things defiled and other acts made you holy.
This was totally wrong. Holiness is a matter of the *heart*, and
defilement is a matter of the *heart*. "Who shall ascend into
the hill of the Lord? or who shall stand in his holy place? He
that hath clean hands, and a pure heart" (Ps. 24:3-4). The
Lord's disciples were criticized for eating with unwashed
hands, i.e., hands that had not been ceremonially washed
according to the traditions of the elders after that person had
walked in the market place and may have come into contact
with something common or unclean (Matt. 15:2). Our Lord's
answer was that defilement was not an external thing, but a
heart condition (Matt. 15:17-20). Let us never forget it.
Israel here was defiled because their hearts defiled them.
Christ was pure, righteous and undefiled because His heart
was right (Heb. 7:26). "Keep thy heart with all diligence; for
out of it are the issues of life" (Prov. 4:23). The issues of life
are heart issues, not church traditions or personal standards.

Pilate Yields to the Jews

"Pilate then went out unto them, and said, What
accusation bring ye against this man?" (John 18:29). Because
the leaders would not come to Pilate he was forced to yield
to their scruples lest his failure to do so result in

uncontrollable mob action and tumult for which he would be called into question. Even though Pilate yields to their whims, the subsequent language reveals there is no love for these people in his heart. Here is the Judge rising from his judicial bench and going out to the mob to try the case.

What does Pilate know about Jesus even before he steps out to speak to the crowd? Matthew will tell us later on that Pilate "knew that for envy they had delivered" Jesus to him (Matt. 27:18). His wife also will send word to him later that morning saying, "Have thou nothing to do with that just man: for I have suffered many things this day in a dream because of him" (Matt. 27:19). Pilate certainly knew something of what was going on in the area, and in all probability he and his wife had even spoken about Jesus Christ. Pilate displays, through the entire proceedings, a real interest in Jesus and a genuine respect, so that he must have had some previous knowledge of Him and knew that the Sanhedrin had for envy delivered Jesus over to him. Pilate's wife had, moreover, dreamed this vivid nightmare. Since Pilate had risen early this morning, he was not around when his wife, Procula (as tradition calls her) arose. She was so terror stricken by her experience that she felt compelled to send word to her husband.

Pilate's Call for the Accusation

"What accusation bring ye against this man?" For Pilate to try the case, there must first be an accusation presented to him. Mark it well. Pilate is not asking them for the verdict they have reached in their trial with a view to merely carrying out the sentence they have passed. He begins from the beginning to try the case himself according to Roman law.

This puts the Sanhedrin in an embarrassing position. You will remember that their charge against Him, for which they had tried Jesus, was blasphemy. He was found guilty by them, and the penalty was death. But blasphemy was not a capital crime according to Roman law. Consequently, the leaders never mention the true charge, for they knew if they did, the case would have been thrown out of court (see Acts 18:14-16 for an example).

But there is another reason why they do not dare
mention blasphemy as their true cause for condemning
Christ. Blasphemy in the Jewish sense was a man claiming to
be God, but for a man to claim to be god was true to a
Roman. The Roman Caesar was god, and all were to worship
him. "You mean you Jews do not accept Caesar as god?"
Pilate would have asked them, and then *they* would have
been on trial, not Jesus.

Their first approach is to side-step the issue. They put
up a smoke-screen seeking to evade the question and hoping
this will suffice. "They answered and said unto him, If he
were not a malefactor, we would not have delivered him up
unto thee" (John 18:30). By this haughtiness of speech they
hope to cover up the weakness of their case. They are asking
Pilate to forego any trial and merely pass sentence since they
only bring malefactors to him, i.e., the worst of criminals,
and if He were not one, they would not have bothered Pilate
with Him.

"Then said Pilate unto them, Take ye him, and judge
him according to your law" (v. 31). Pilate is not about to
yield. Rome was known the world around at this time for its
legal justice and for its court system. This was the Roman's
pride even as the philosophies were the pride of the Greeks.
Roman law demanded that criminal proceedings could be
entered into only on definite accusations. Pilate is being
investigated by the Roman Emperor at this very time, so he is
forced to be very careful. He demands legal charges—a civil
and not a religious accusation—against this prisoner. If the
Sanhedrin does not wish to comply with Roman law, then
they will have to try the case themselves according to their
own law.

The Sanhedrin is losing the situation fast, and they
know it. Their indirect approach has backfired on them. In
desperation they yell out the bitter and painful fact that they
are subject to Rome. "The Jews therefore said unto him, It is
not lawful for us to put any man to death." Their stoning of
Stephen, not too far distant, was an unlawful action on the
part of the Sanhedrin. The power of life and death among
conquered people of Rome resided in the authority of Rome
alone. While lesser powers might be given to the governments

of conquered nations, Rome never relinquished the right of the sword.

John adds one of his characteristic footnotes that what is happening is merely the fulfillment of what Christ predicted. "That the saying of Jesus might be fulfilled, which he spake, signifying what death he should die" (18:32). Had the Sanhedrin taken things into their own hands, as they did with Stephen, Jesus Christ would have been stoned, and not have died by crucifixion (John 3:14; 8:28; 12:32-33).

Since the Sanhedrin has sought the death penalty from Pilate, they are forced to yield and submit their articles of accusation. John does not record them, because Dr. Luke already has given these to us, and John is content to record events not covered by the other Gospels.

The Accusation of the Sanhedrin

"And they began to accuse him, saying, We found this fellow perverting the nation, and forbidding to give tribute to Caesar, saying that he himself is Christ a King" (Luke 23:2). Think of this. They have tried the Lord Jesus Christ and convicted Him on one charge, and now they present an entirely new charge before Rome. Many have thought this charge was a three-fold one; others, two-fold. I personally feel it was all one charge, and is so understood as such and treated by Pilate. It reads literally, "This One we found perverting the nation, even [namely] forbidding to give tribute to Caesar saying He Himself is Christ King." The way they claimed Jesus was perverting the nation was forbidding to give tribute to Caesar, saying He was Himself Messiah-King.

Notice that the Sanhedrin here takes the position of Rome, and stands up for Rome's interests. They accuse Jesus Christ of treason, not against His nation, but against Rome. When the nation of Israel went after idols, the Lord sent them to Babylon, the center of idolatry, where Jeremiah said, "They are mad upon their idols" (Jer. 50:38). It was there that the nation got its fill and was cured of idolatry. Now the nation is going after Rome, and is mad after Rome, so that they will cry out: "We have no king but Caesar" (John

19:15). The Lord will yet bring judgment upon them, for their false Messiah will make a covenant with the head of the revived Roman Empire, which will be a covenant with death and sheol (Isa. 28:15). Israel will learn, but only through great trial. God will give them up to their own heart. They want Caesar to be their king, and they will have it so until they acknowledge their offense and cry out, "Blessed is He that cometh in the name of the Lord."

How truthful is this accusation? Was it true that Jesus was perverting the nation? The answer depends upon how you look at the situation, and this is the point. It was a half truth, but was made to Pilate with the intent to deceive him in taking it the wrong way. According to the Sanhedrin, Jesus Christ was perverting the nation, not against Rome, but against themselves. This was the true issue, and this is why the Sanhedrin felt forced to act to get rid of Jesus Christ (John 11:48, "If we let him thus alone, all men will believe on him . . ."). But the leaders used this as if Christ was perverting the nation against Rome. This was not so. In reality, they were the ones who had perverted the nation and the Law through their traditions. They were the ones getting rich through religion. They were the ones also who were seeking a Messiah who would overthrow the Roman yoke. They rejected Jesus as their Messiah because He was not such a Messiah as they wanted (John 10:22ff).

Their proof offered that Jesus was perverting the nation is an absolute falsehood. Christ never forbid to give tribute to Caesar. The Sanhedrin had sent certain ones to catch Him in this very thing, but He refused to be caught (Matt. 22:15-22). When shown a Roman coin He had said, "Render therefore unto Caesar the things which are Caesar's; and unto God the things that are God's." This charge was a deliberate lie. Yet we know from history that the chief priests and the crowd there were the ones who were trying every scheme there was to get around paying taxes to Rome. A person on the spot will always accuse someone else of the very thing of which he himself is guilty. The thought is that if I am guilty of this, he must be also. The Sanhedrin are on the spot, and so, having told a lie, they must cover it with some semblance of truth. Christ had said that He Himself is

Christ-King. In this they were right. He had claimed to be their Messiah, and had authenticated those claims with signs. The Sanhedrin had rejected His claims and signs saying His power was satanic power, not Holy power. They know His claim, and now seek to use it for their advantage. They speak the truth, but they say it in a way to deceive. They know Pilate would understand this in a political sense and so try the case.

Pilate's Interrogation of Jesus Christ

The charge has been made. Pilate must now act. He has the accusation, and he knows that if he dismisses this charge without investigation, he will sure enough be in "hot water" with those higher up in the Roman government which could pronounce him guilty of malfeasance in office. He now leaves the crowd and goes into the Praetorium to talk to Jesus (John 18:33). Remember that it was the very essence of proceedings under Roman law that they were conducted in public. But the Jews themselves would not enter into the Praetorium, thus making this talk between Pilate and Jesus private. At this point all four Gospels record certain aspects of the proceedings (Matt. 27:11-14; Mark 15:2; Luke 23:3; John 18:33-38a). Right at this point John's Gospel is the most complete, so we will follow the trial in John.

"Then Pilate entered into the judgment hall again, and called Jesus" (John 18:33a). As Pilate went back into the Praetorium and sat upon the judgment seat, he had the prisoner brought before him. The Lord had not been outside listening to what had transpired, but was inside the Praetorium while Pilate had secured from the Sanhedrin their accusations against Jesus.

Here Pilate comes face to face with Jesus Christ, and, whether he realizes it or not, he, and through him the Roman Empire, are on trial. The true Judge is Jesus Christ, and the prisoner on trial is Pilate. The very secrets of his heart are going to be exposed. The very same thing is true of Paul and Agrippa in Acts 26. No man comes near the light without having the light expose what he, in truth, really is.

"And said unto him, Art thou the King of the Jews?"

(18:33b). Because of the situation and the circumstances as they have developed, Pilate is endeavoring to make the prisoner incriminate Himself contrary to Roman law. He asks a question which is a true question, for Pilate really wants to know, and it stands in contrast to verse 37 where the question is asked and the expected answer, is "Yes." There the question in the English should be translated, "Thou are a King then?" with the expected answer, "Yes." Here the English is correct: "Art Thou the King of the Jews?"

This title "King of the Jews" will remain before Pilate, and he will place it over the cross to the gall of the Sanhedrin. In this he will not change. The term "Jew" is the way the heathen had of designating all twelve tribes of Israel, and it was so used from the time of Esther (cp. Acts 2:36; 21:20-21; 26:7). Christ is King not of just the one tribe of Judah, but of the entire nation and through them, of the whole world.

"Jesus answered him, Sayest thou this thing of thyself, or did others tell it thee of me?" (John 18:34). The Lord answers first with a question, *Why are you asking this of me? Is it because it has been reported to you by your soldiers that either I or my disciples have acted in insurrection against Rome, or are you asking this because others of the same as I am—Jews—have told this of me?* Christ questions whether Pilate is asking this as Commander of soldiers that have told him about the incident of insurrection in the Garden that very morning, or is he asking this as Governor because the Jews have told him that this was His claim. The reason the question was asked is that it makes a great difference in the Lord's reply.

This questioning of Pilate nettles him, since he does not realize its significance. He thus has not been told about the incident in the garden when Peter used his sword.

"Pilate answered, Am I a Jew? Thine own nation and the chief priests delivered thee unto me: what hast thou done?" (18:35). Pilate knew nothing except what the Jewish leaders had just told him. Moreover, he was not a Jew himself so as to know the significance of being the Christ, nor to judge whether this One standing before him was or was not the Christ-King. *You are accused by the Jews: therefore what have You done?* This is what Pilate wanted to know. Christ then proceeds.

"Jesus answered, My kingdom is not of this world: if my kingdom were of this world, then would my servants fight, that I should not be delivered to the Jews: but now is my kingdom not from hence" (18:36). Every word is carefully selected by the Lord of Truth. The question cannot be answered yes or no, but takes explanation. Christ three times says, "My kingdom." He has a kingdom. It is not of this world. It is not a temporal kingdom that is a political threat to Caesar nor usurps any power given to Caesar. If this had been the case, then My servants, Christ says (literally "officers"; same word used in verse 3, 12, 18 and 22) would fight that I should not have been delivered to the Jews and by them to the Romans. The very fact that I am a prisoner shows I am not politically motivated. "Now my kingdom is not from hence."

Oh how significant is this word "now." There will come the day when He will be against Rome and against Rome's Caesar, whom He "shall consume with the spirit of his mouth, and shall destroy with the brightness of his coming" (II Thess. 2:8). But that is another day and another hour. Not now is His kingdom of force and power against Rome.

"Pilate therefore said unto him, Art thou a king then?" (18:37a). This is logical in light of the fact that three times Christ spoke of His kingdom. "You are a King then?"

"Jesus answered, Thou sayest that I am a king. To this end was I born, and for this cause came I into the world, that I should bear witness unto the truth. Every one that is of the truth heareth my voice" (18:37b). The other three Gospels merely record "Thou sayest"—an idiom for "Yes, I am." John gives the enlarged, the complete, the emphatic answer. A king is born a king, and I was so born. And not only born, but I came into the world. I was in existence before my appearance in flesh. I came to bear witness unto the truth. My kingdom is not a Jewish kingdom, it is a universal kingdom. It is for all men everywhere. Every one that is of the truth heareth My voice.

The Lord is seeking the soul of this man and is approaching him on his own ground. Would he be truthful? If he would, he would, thereby, manifest that he belonged to the Lord's kingdom. Or would he play politics? Politics it had been for Pilate, and politics it was to be. Here was the difference between Rome and Christ. The kingdom of Rome was governed by expedience. The kingdom of Christ was governed by truth. The one was temporal and passing; the other, eternal and abiding. The one governed the bodies of men who were its citizens; the other, the hearts and souls of its citizens. The one was physical, the other spiritual. Just as Rome had extended its influence out beyond its borders; so Christ's kingdom was more than Jewish. He came unto His own, but His own received Him not. Therefore, as many as received Him, whether they be Jews or Gentiles, whether they be paupers or kings, to them He gave authority to become the sons of God (John 1:11-12).

Now the Judge has spoken. Would the prisoner, Pilate, play politics and do that which was expedient, or would he abide by the truth regardless of the outcome? Pilate is on trial. Christ had come to bear witness of the truth. The truth already existed, but Christ only bore witness of it. As such, He is Prophet as well as King.

To this invitation by Christ to Pilate for him to be His disciple of truth, "Pilate said unto Him" synically, "What is truth?" (18:38a). Even though he asked the question, he wasn't honestly seeking its answer. With the asking of the question, he leaves the Praetorium and goes out once again to the Jews. His whole background is that truth is relative, not absolute. Pilate, while not a master of the philosophies, was certainly familiar with them. He realized that one system contradicted another, and while the search for truth was at this time the ambition of thousands, yet it was the attainment of none to his knowledge. As a politician, he had always done the expedient thing at any given time. To him at one time one thing might be the right thing, and at another time, another course of action. Again, things were relative, not absolute.

"What is truth" was his question, but he never waited to be instructed by the One who was Truth, but went out to act on his own. Here the Eternal Truth will be batted around, and, finally, Pilate will succumb to the pressures of a moment.

Christ has spoken to Pilate, but will now be silent. During the remaining trials *Christ will utter but one more word.* Why? Is it because He has changed? Not at all. He is the same yesterday, today and forever; He changes not. But Pilate has rejected truth, and he will be given no more truth until he acts on what he knows. The only revelation is that of sin and judgment to follow. Thus the Lord deals with all in the same way, being the unchangeable and eternal God. He who spurns truth will receive no more truth to trample under foot, and it makes no difference whether he is an unbeliever or a believer. Spiritual things are spiritually discerned, not naturally discerned. "No man knoweth the Father, save the Son, and he to whomsoever the Son will reveal him" (Matt. 11:27). Unless you are in right relation to the Son you will never know the Father, nor will you ever know the Son. "Now we have received, not the spirit of the world, but the spirit which is of God; that we might know the things that are freely given to us of God . . . . But the natural man receiveth not the things of the Spirit of God: for they are foolishness unto him: neither can he know them, because they are spiritually discerned" (I Cor. 2:12, 14).

As Pilate leaves the Praetorium this time, he has the One who was handed over to him escorted out of the Praetorium with him, all prepared to release Him. We know this from the subsequent things that happen.

The Verdict

"And when he had said this, he went out again unto the Jews, and said unto them, I find in him no fault at all" (John 18:38b). Dr. Luke records the same words: "Then said Pilate to the chief priests and to the people, I find no fault in this man" (Luke 23:4).

The trial is officially over.

The charge was treason against Rome.

The verdict of acquittal was given.

The legal order to discharge the defendent was all that remained. But it never came. For the Sanhedrin had not come for the verdict of acquittal. They had come for His

death, not His release; and they were prepared to pay any
price to accomplish it.

A New Barrage of Accusations

"And they were the more fierce . . ." (Luke 23:5). The
announcement of His innocence sent them to more urgent
pressure upon Pilate, and he was no match for them.

Josephus records for us in his *Antiquities of the Jews*
(XVIII, 3, 1) what happened when Pilate tried to force
Caesar's image upon the people of Jerusalem that were on the
standards of the soldiers. Pilate was the first to bring those
images into Jerusalem, and he did it secretly at night. When
the Sanhedrin knew it, they went to Caesarea in multitudes
and interceded with Pilate for five days. On the sixth day
Pilate had his fill and ordered his soldiers to have their
weapons concealed and he would appear on his judgment-seat
with the army concealed ready for action. When the Jews
petitioned him once again, he gave the signal and his soldiers
surrounded the Jews, and Pilate threatened them with
immediate death unless they would leave off disturbing him,
and go home. At this they threw themselves to the ground
and laid their necks bare, saying they would take their deaths
very willingly rather than have their laws transgressed and
their city defiled. When Pilate saw their fanatical devotion to
keep their laws inviolable, he gave the order to bring the
images back from Jerusalem to Caesarea.

It was to those same people Pilate had condescended to
leave the Praetorium and go out to them because of their
religious scruples. He was no match for the dedication they
had to their cause when it was fixed and immovable. In this
case, it was the death of Jesus Christ.

Here came a barrage of fresh accusations, with the
Sanhedrin being more vocal than before. At this point we
must integrate the accounts of Matthew and Mark together in
order to acquire the complete picture.

"And the chief priests accused him of many things"
(Mark 15:3). "And when he was accused of the chief priests
and elders, he answered nothing. Then said Pilate unto him,
Hearest thou not how many things they witness against

thee?" (Matt. 27:12-13). "And Pilate asked him again, saying, Answerest thou nothing? behold how many things they witness against thee. But Jesus yet answered nothing? so that Pilate marvelled" (Mark 15:4-5). Or as Matthew states, "And he gave him no answer, not even to one word; insomuch that the governor marvelled greatly" (Matt. 27:14 R.V.).

He would not give any more truth to Pilate. He would not speak in His own defense. His resurrection from among the dead would be His vindication. Now He was as the Lamb led to the slaughter. "He was oppressed, and he was afflicted, yet he opened not his mouth: he is brought as a lamb to the slaughter, and as a sheep before her shearers is dumb, so he opened not his mouth" (Isa. 53:7).

Everyone was excited and disturbed in the entire gathering, but Jesus Christ. This was their hour to do what they wished, and He was completely surrendered to the will of the Father. He had complete calmness, and why not? His heart alone was right of all that were there. Pilate marvelled, and well he might, for others would have sought witnesses and sought to vindicate themselves. But "Jesus appealed to no one, either in heaven or on earth."

The Way Out of a Dilemma

In the new group of charges, someone was heard saying, "He stirreth up the people, teaching throughout all Jewry, beginning from Galilee to this place" (Luke 23:5). Galilee had been a hot bed of insurrection against Rome, and the mention of it was the purpose of inciting guilt by association of place. But the charge now was sedition—"the excitement of discontent against the government." With the mention of Galilee, Pilate feels there may be a way out of the dilemma in which he finds himself. "When Pilate heard of Galilee, he asked whether the man were a Galilean. And as soon as he knew that he belonged unto Herod's jurisdiction, he sent him to Herod, who himself also was at Jerusalem at that time" (Luke 23:6-7).

It was not an unusual procedure in Roman law to transfer a prisoner from the territory where he had been arrested to his place of origin to be tried. Herod was then governor of Galilee, while Pilate was of Judea. As a Galilean, Christ came under Herod's jurisdiction. Christ, in place of being released after the verdict of acquittal, is bound now once again, and is conducted to Herod's residence to be tried by him.

Chapter 11

The Trial
Before Herod

Only Dr. Luke records the trial that took place before Herod (Luke 23:6-12). This trial would add nothing to the theme of Matthew, Mark or John, but it does add greatly to the theme of Luke. The Man Jesus Christ went through this experience, and He came out vindicated of any wrong whatever even though it was in Galilee under Herod Antipas' domain where the Lord had spent most of His time and performed most of His miracles. Pilate will take the fact of His innocence by Herod as an argument for Christ's release (Luke 23:15). Moreover, Dr. Luke also refers to this trial in Acts 4:27.

In order to understand the full significance of the events that transpire as the Lord Jesus appears before Herod, we must understand something of the background behind this man's life.

The Herods of Scripture

There was a family of Herods, and it is essential to keep the various Herods distinct in order to understand the events that occurred. Thus the name "Herod" was not a personal name, but the family or surname (for the Herods in Scripture see the accompanying chart), page 147.

In each generation there is one major Herod who involved himself in the Scripture account. Herod the Great was the Herod who sought to kill the Lord Jesus by putting to death all the babies up to two years of age around Bethlehem. Herod Antipas was the one responsible for killing John the Baptist, and it was before this Herod that Jesus Christ appears now to be tried. Herod Agrippa I killed James the brother of John, with the sword in the days of the early church, and this pleased the Jews so very much that he was planning to kill Peter also after Passover, but Peter was miraculously delivered out of prison by angelic ministry. Herod Agrippa's son, Herod Agrippa II was the king before whom Paul stood and testified, and it was this man who said: "Almost thou persuadest me to be a Christian" (Acts 26:28). Herod Antipas is the major Herod of Scripture, but his life cannot be fully understood apart from the whole family.

The family history starts with Antipater, the father of Herod the Great. He was an Edomite, a descendant of Esau, who was appointed ruler of Judea by Julius Caesar. He ruled as Procurator of Judea from 47-43 B.C.

His son became known as Herod the Great, born in 62 B.C. and died in 4 B.C. In all, Herod the Great had nine wives. His career began in 47 B.C. when his father, Antipater, gave him the territory of Galilee. By winning the favor of Antony, he and his brother were appointed tetrarchs of Judea by the Roman Senate. Then in 37 B.C., by the aid of Antony, he was made King of Judea. He conquered Jerusalem in that year, and slew Antigonus, the last of the Maccabean king-priests. Thus at this time an Idumean dynasty replaces the Asmonean that had been governing Palestine. Under Emperor Augustus, nearly all of Palestine was added to his territory.

Wanting to promote his position more favorably with the Jews, Herod the Great desired to rebuild the temple of Zerubbabel that had stood for nearly 500 years. According to Josephus it commenced in the eighteenth year of Herod's reign, or 20-19 B.C. The Jews permitted the workmen only to tear down one section at a time and then to reconstruct it.

CHART OF THE HERODS INVOLVED IN THE NEW TESTAMENT

Antipater
(Procurator of Judea 47-43 B.C.) (Descendant of Esau)

Herod the Great
(King of Judea 37-4 B.C.) Matt. 2:1-19; Luke 1:5

Sons of Marianne I
(The Asmonaean) Murdered by Herod 6 B.C.

Aristobulus
Murdered by Herod 6 B.C.

Alexander
Murdered by Herod 6 B.C.

Herod Agrippa I
(King of Judea A.D. 37-44) Acts 12:1-24

Herod Agrippa II
(Tetrarch of Chalcis and northern territory A.D. 48-70) Acts 25:13-26:32

Drusilla
Married Felix Procurator of Judea A.D. 59-61 Acts 24:24

Bernice
Acts 25:13

Son of Marianne II
(Daughter of Simeon, the High Priest)

Herod Philip I

Herodias

Her first marriage was to Herod Philip I Matt. 14:3; Mark 6:17

Her second marriage was to Herod Antipas.

John the Baptist denounced this marriage and lost his head. Mark 6:18-28

Salome
Daughter of Herodias by Herod Philip Matt. 14:6-11

She danced before Herod Antipas and at her mother's request asked for the head of John the Baptist.

Sons of Malthace
(Samaritan)

Herod Antipas
(Tetrarch of Galilee and Perea, 4 B.C.-A.D. 39) Matt. 14:1-12; Mark 6:14-29; Luke 3:1, 19-20; 9:7; 13:31-33; 23:7-12

Archelaus
(Ethnarch of Samaria and Judea, 4 B.C.-A.D. 6) Matt. 2:22

Son of Cleopatra
(of Jerusalem)

Herod Philip II
(Tetrarch of Iturea & Tranchonitis 4 B.C.-A.D. 34) Luke 3:1

The construction, done by the priests, commenced with the sanctuary itself which was completed in a year and a half, but the entire temple complex, with its many buildings, was not completed until A.D. 64, just six years before it was destroyed in A.D. 70, as our Lord had predicted. The contruction, then, went far beyond Herod the Great's time. Even in the first year of the Lord's ministry, the Jews said, "Forty and six years was this temple in building . . ." (John 2:20), and many more years would it be before it was completed—only to be destroyed. Of a truth, "Except the Lord build the house, they labour in vain that build it" (Ps. 127:1).

In 6 B.C., Herod the Great killed his wife Mariamne, and his two sons by her, when he found her plotting to kill him and place her sons on the throne. He killed to get on the throne; he killed to stay on the throne, and when the Magi reported that a baby had been born King of the Jews somewhere around Bethlehem, he killed all the children in that area up to two years of age.

When Herod the Great died in 4 B.C., Archelaus ruled in Judea in the place of his father. He was the oldest and worst of Herod's sons. According to the will of Herod the Great, Archelaus was to rule as king in his place, but a delegation of 50 Jews sailed to Rome to protest to the Emperor Augustus. Because of this, Archelaus was only appointed ethnarch over one-half of his father's kingdom—Samaria, Judea and Idumea —with the promise that if he ruled well he would ultimately have both the title king and also the other territories of his father. But well he did not rule. Josephus tells us that he inaugurated his reign with the massacre of 3000 people just to show he was a true son of his father. After ruling nine years, Judea and Samaria could no longer endure his tyranny, and complained to Augustus, who then banished him to Vienne, and placed Palestine under the control of a Roman Procurator which condition remained from this time to A.D. 41. It was Archelaus's reigning in his father's place that caused Joseph, upon returning from Egypt, with Mary and the boy Jesus, not to settle in Bethlehem, or anywhere under his jurisdiction, but to return to Galilee (Matt. 2:22).

Two other sons of Herod the Great are mentioned once

each in the New Testament. Herod Philip I was the son of Mariamne, daughter of Simon the high priest in Israel. Philip was disinherited by Herod the Great, and is only mentioned in Scripture as being the first husband of Herodias (Mark 6:17). It will be Herodias, who will divorce Philip in order to marry Herod Antipas. Under Roman law, the wife could divorce her husband, as well as the husband divorce his wife, and this is what she did. The daughter of Herod Philip I and Herodias was Salome, who will dance before Herod Antipas and be offered up to half of his kingdom. Herod Philip II is another son of Herod the Great and is mentioned because he received, upon the death of his father (Luke 3:1), the tetrarch of Iturea and Tranchonitic (territories in the northeast of Palestine).

Herod Antipas

This brings us to the major Herod of Scripture, Herod Antipas. That is to say, more is said about him, and he is found involved in more incidents that concern Scripture than any other Herod. These incidents give us an insight into what is happening at the trial of the Lord Jesus Christ, and why.

Herod Antipas was the seventh and youngest son of Herod the Great and the Samaritan, Malthace. He was born prior to 20 B.C., and, upon the death of his father, became the tetrarch of Galilee and Perea, which he ruled for some forty-three years (4 B.C.—A.D. 39). Archelaus who ruled over Samaria and Judea, was his full brother. The rest of the tangled events of his life we will unravel as we consider the Scriptural accounts.

The Imprisonment of John the Baptist

The first incident is recorded in Luke 3, "But Herod the tetrarch, being reproved by him for Herodias his brother Philip's wife, and for all the evils which Herod had done, added yet this above all, that he shut up John in prison" (vv. 19-20). Luke leaves the story at this point with John the Baptist in prison, and then takes up the story of the Lord Jesus Christ and His ministry. He shows here, however, that

John was a fearless preacher and prophet. It made no difference whether his audience was one or one thousand. He called it like it was, and rebuked this leader for every evil he had ever done.

The Death of John the Baptist

After this, two of the Gospel writers—Matthew and Mark—record for us, as a flashback, what happened while John was in prison, and how he was beheaded by Herod Antipas (Matt. 14:1-12; Mark 6:14-29; cp. Luke 9:7-9). All the details are very important in understanding the subsequent events in Herod's life and the trial of our Lord before Herod. Mark's Gospel is the fullest account, so we will examine the story as presented in Mark.

"Herod himself had sent forth and laid hold upon John, and bound him in prison for Herodias' sake, his brother Philip's wife: for he had married her. For John had said unto Herod, It is not lawful for thee to have thy brother's wife. Therefore Herodias had a quarrel against him, and would have killed him, but she could not" (Mark 6:17-19). Behind a man often stands a woman either for good or for ill. In this case, as with Ahab, it was for ill.

Herod Antipas was educated at Rome with Archelaus, his full brother, and Philip, his half-brother, son of Mariamne, daughter of Simon. It was here that he acquired the tastes and the vices of the Romans. Herod Antipas was first married to the daughter of Aretas, the Arabian king of Petra. But while visiting in Rome with his half-brother, Philip, he fell in love with Philip's wife, Herodias, who was also niece to both. She left Philip and married Herod Antipas on the condition that Antipas would get rid of his first wife. Antipas' first wife learned of this and fled back to her father.

Here, then, was a ruler of the Jews shamelessly defying the Jewish laws, first by marrying his niece, and, secondly, by marrying his brother's wife. This is the evil relationship that John the Baptist fearlessly denounced: "It is not lawful for thee to have thy brother's wife" (v. 18). For this it eventually cost him his life. Herodias would have gotten rid of John the Baptist right now, but she couldn't get Herod to move any further than to put John in prison. She had the will; Herod had the power.

"For Herod feared John, knowing that he was a just man and an holy, and observed him; and when he heard him, he did many things, and heard him gladly" (v. 20). The attitude of Ahab toward Elijah is remarkably similar. It was Jezebel, not Ahab, who plotted Elijah's death (I Kings 19:2). John the Baptist was both just and holy. He was righteous in all his relations to his fellow men, and holy in all his relations to God.

Now there seems to be much stated here that we dare not miss. It appears that Herodias felt Herod might "get religion" from this Baptiser as he had begun to change certain things about his life and was hearing this John gladly. Now she knew that if he got "converted" she would go, for the Baptiser said it is unlawful for Herod to have her. But she could not go back to her first husband, therefore an evil mind only plots more evil. Herod had commenced to do many things in response to John's preaching to him. It only remained for him to do the one major thing and Herodias would be gone. She felt forced to act.

"And when a convenient day was come," that is, when a convenient day had come for Herodias to act and secure what she wanted, "that Herod on his birthday made a supper to his lords, high captains, and chief estates of Galilee" (Mark 6:21). Everybody that was anybody was there.

"And when the daughter of the said Herodias came in [who was Salome according to Josephus], and danced, and pleased Herod and them that sat with him, the king said unto the damsel, Ask of me whatsoever thou wilt, and I will give it thee" (v. 22). What a contrast. Here was a man who was listening to John preach one day, and throwing off all restraint the next. Here is wine, women and song, and it leads to the silencing of a man of righteousness. You cannot go sin's way without reaping sin's wages. You cannot take fire into your bosom without being burnt by it.

"And he sware unto her, Whatsoever thou shalt ask of me, I will give it thee, unto the half of my kingdom" (v. 23). What a promise of a fool! He has fallen into the trap set by his wife, and soon it will spring shut.

"And she went forth, and said unto her mother, What shall I ask? And she said, The head of John the Baptist" (v. 24). Salome was totally unprepared for knowing what to request, but her mother wasn't. Yet when her mother spoke, she entered right in with the request. She was one with her mother in wickedness else she would not have danced this kind of a dance in the first place, nor gone along with her mother's request in the second place.

"And she came in straightway with haste unto the king, and asked, saying, I will that thou give me by and by [literally, 'at once'] in a charger the head of John the Baptist" (v. 25). She returned immediately while the guests are still present and before the spell of her dancing has passed, and makes her request to be carried out *at once*.

"And the king was exceeding sorry; yet for his oath's sake, and for their sakes which sat with him he would not reject her" (v. 26). This brought him back to reality, and grim reality it was. He felt he could not slight her by treating the oath and promise he had made as a joke. Had she waited until another day, he might have done so.

"And immediately the king sent an executioner, and commanded his head to be brought: and he went and beheaded him in the prison, and brought his head in a charger, and gave it to the damsel: and the damsel gave it to her mother" (vv. 27-28). The deed was done, but the consequences linger on.

Mark is telling us this entire episode because when Herod hears about Jesus, his conscience is so sensitive that he said that John the Baptist was risen from the dead, and "therefore mighty works do show forth themselves in him" (Mark 6:14). His murdering of John the Baptist haunted him, and because he heard Jesus was also righteous, he felt this was John risen from the dead now performing miracles.

This is startling. Herod was Idumean by descent through his father, and Samaritan through his mother, yet by religion was a circumcised Jew and a Sadducee. But Sadducees do not believe in resurrection (Acts 23:8). In reality, they try to convince themselves there is no resurrection when they know better. Every once in a while their true feelings come to the surface under extreme pressure (cp. Rev. 6:15-17).

But how does all this relate to Christ and His appearance before Herod now? Herod knew that he had done wrong in regard to murdering John the Baptist, and so did everyone else. Soon after this event, the father of Herod's first wife, King Aretas, invaded the country to avenge his daughter's wrong, and Herod's forces were totally defeated. The populace considered this as divine punishment for what he had done concerning John the Baptist.

Herod's own mind too was haunted with remorse for this action, and, in order to deaden his piercing conscience, he began to fill his court with constant activity. He had singers, dancers, jugglers, circuses—anything new was welcomed at Tiberias. His constant pursuit was for pleasure and something new with which to amuse himself.

The Pharisees Warn Christ About Herod Antipas

Some considerable time after this event, Dr. Luke records an incident involving Herod Antipas that needs to be considered, found in Luke 13. "The same day there came certain of the Pharisees, saying unto him, Get thee out, and depart hence: for Herod will kill thee" (literally, "for Herod wills to kill thee") (v. 31). Can you imagine the Pharisees being interested in saving the life of Jesus Christ? They were not interested in this at all. What they were interested in is terrifying Jesus from ministering in Galilee under Herod's jurisdiction and so have Him come into Judea and to Jerusalem where their authority could exercise more control over Him. But the Lord Jesus Christ does not terrify.

"And he said unto them, Go ye, and tell that fox, Behold, I cast out devil [demons], and I do cures to day and to morrow, and the third day I shall be perfected" (literally, "I am perfected," present tense action) (v. 32). He is saying, *Since you are the message bearers to Me from him, go and return a message. I am working today and tomorrow, and then I am perfected. That is it. No man is going to do anything to Me before My time has come.* Christ accommodates the message bearers with a message to return. It may be that the Pharisees had picked up a bit of gossip from Herod's courtiers of what Herod expressed once to them (cp.

Mark 6:14). They capitalize upon it for their own ends.

Jesus calls Herod "that fox," and it was a perfect description of his character. But just because He used such an epithet does not mean that we have this right. We are still "not to speak ill of the ruler of thy people." Here is a case when the prophet is not sparing the king in denouncing his actions. Herod was plotting snares as a fox, while Christ was continuing to work His good works. *He can plot all he wants,* Christ says. *It will do him no good. I will finish the work set before me.*

"To day and to morrow" seem to indicate a specific period of time which is very definite, and it will neither be lengthened nor shortened by anyone. In the context, it can neither mean literal days nor stand for years. It is used as a figure of speech for a period of definite duration.

"I am perfected"—What does this phrase mean? The next verse parallels this verse and shows that Christ will be perfected through suffering and death that He will encounter in Jerusalem. This word is the same as that used in Hebrews 2:10, " . . . to make the captain of their salvation perfect through suffering"; and Hebrews 5:9, "Though he were a Son, yet learned he obedience by the things which he suffered; and being made perfect, he became the author of eternal salvation unto all them that obey him."

"Nevertheless I must walk to day, and to morrow, and the day following: for it cannot be that a prophet perish out of Jerusalem" (Luke 13:33). It seems that this verse is addressed not to Herod so much as it is to the Pharisees. Jerusalem has the monopoly of killing the prophets, and the city will not be deprived of its right to kill the Prophet. *When I die, it will be Jerusalem, but I am not there yet, and I have the time until I arrive.*

With the mention of Jerusalem as the executioner of the prophets, His heart breaks forth into what will be a prelude to the tears on Palm Sunday. Here it is anticipation; there it will be realization. Here He cries: "O Jerusalem, Jerusalem, which killest the prophets, and stonest them that are sent unto thee; how often would I have gathered thy children together, as a hen doth gather her brood under her wings, and ye would not! Behold, your house is left unto you desolate:

and verily I say unto you, Ye shall not see me, until the time come when ye shall say, Blessed is he that cometh in the name of the Lord" (vv. 34-35).

Herod's Desire to See Jesus Christ

This brings us to the place of considering the trial of the Lord Jesus Christ before Herod. Once the very mention of the name of Jesus, and the hearing of His deeds, would have filled Herod's heart and soul with terror and trembling, but that time is passed. Now when he saw Jesus, (whether he was coming in chains or not, made no difference) "he was exceeding glad: for he was desirous to see him of a long season, because he had heard many things of him; and he hoped to have seen some miracle done by him" (Luke 23:8). Christ had acquired great fame as a miracle worker, and perhaps he would display His skill before Herod. This would have given great satisfaction to him, for he might out-perform any of the magic Herod had previously seen. Certainly the Lord ought to consider it an honor to display His abilities before the ruler, as all the others that had come to his court. As far as Herod was concerned, this was going to make this day, and his visit to Jerusalem, complete. How wonderful it was to have the opportunity to see Jesus since he had never honored Tiberias, where Herod resided, with a personal visit.

Herod had become like a fat blob of protoplasm, like a spineless jellyfish, without character or stamina. All that entered his mind was his own pleasure. He never allowed it to cross his conscience once that he was trying a man, and that righteousness and justice were at stake. His conscience had been so seared that those things were no longer issues of importance. All that mattered was Herod's enjoyment and pleasure.

No wonder Christ warned His disciples to beware of the leaven of Herod (Mark 8:15). Herod was mad after pleasures. All that Paul states will come in the last days of the church age, and is in truth, here today, is true of Herod. "This know also, that in the last days perilous times shall come. For men shall be lovers of their own selves, covetous, boasters, proud, blasphemers, disobedient to parents, unthankful, unholy, without natural affection, trucebreakers, false accusers, incontinent, fierce, despisers of those that are good, traitors, heady, highminded, lovers of pleasures more than lovers of God, having a form of godliness, but denying the power thereof" (II Tim. 3:1-5). This is the leaven of Herod and "from such turn away," child of God, or it will corrupt your character likewise.

Christ is now standing before Herod in the ancient palace of the Maccabees where Herod resided when he was in Jerusalem. Herod had never before seen the face of Jesus, though most of the Lord's life and ministry was in Herod's territory of Galilee, nor had he heard a word from the Savior's lips. But "he had heard many things of him," perhaps from his steward Chuza, whose wife Joanna was one of our Lord's disciples (Luke 8:3).

Herod's highest hopes were "to have seen some miracle done by him." Christ was to Herod just as another juggler or magician that came to his court. His only interest was that which satisfied the flesh. He was looking for the pleasure of a moment, but to this Christ did not respond. He had not come to be a miracle-worker. He said, "An evil and adulterous generation seeketh after a sign; and there shall no sign be given it, but the sign of the prophet Jonas" (Matt. 12:39). The sign He will give Herod, and the world, will be His resurrection. This is His sign; this is His vindication for His claims.

There are men like this in every age who desire to see and hear God's servant, not to be changed in life, but to be entertained and to reveal their broadmindedness. They will marvel at the Lord's power and even seek to hear what He has to say, but that is as far as they will ever go. They are a part of this world system, and they love it. They are not about to change. They will die in it, and will die in their sins. Woe be to the man of God that will do anything to satisfy their flesh. We are only to reason with them in reference to righteousness, temperance, and judgment to come (Acts 24:25).

The Silence of Christ Before Herod

"Then he questioned with him in many words; but he answered him nothing" (Luke 23:9). Concerning the subject of Herod's questions, Scripture is completely silent. Many a man would have considered this the opportunity of a lifetime, and would have used it to give forth the truths of God. But the Lord's ways are not our ways, and His thoughts are not our thoughts (Isa. 55:8). He does not cast pearls before swine.

But why did the Lord answer not even one word? Herod had heard the truth over and over again from John the Baptist. Herod's need was not more knowledge, but to act upon what he already knew. Until he did this, no more truth would be given him.

Kings and rulers came to Solomon to hear his wisdom. Yet a greater than Solomon was present, and by the very fact that He was greater, He spoke not a word. Here, in this instance, the Lord's silence hurts far worse than speaking could have. I feel we are thoroughly justified to complete the picture. Christ is standing before Herod and looking straight at the murderer of John the Baptist. The Lord's eyes were piercing into the very innermost secrets of Herod's heart. There was another voice that was speaking still to Herod. Long had Herod sought to put out of his consciousness the voice of John the Baptist, but "he being dead yet speaketh." Christ was silent to allow His voice to be heard.

Herod becomes all the more uncomfortable because Christ would not break His silence. The air is electrified with tension. Again the king is on trial, and the Prisoner is the Judge. Now the Creator stands before the creature, who sits in sinful splendor, but there is another day and another place when the Lord will sit upon a great white throne, and it will be in truth a throne of righteousness and purity. Before Him the dead, small and great, will stand. There the books will be opened, and every man will be judged according to the atrocities that he has done against the truth, which are recorded in the books. Then they will be cast into the lake of fire for ever and ever (Rev. 20:11-15).

The Accusations of the Sanhedrin

Finally the silence is broken, not by our Lord, but by His enemies that accompanied Him to this trial for the purpose of accusing Him before Herod. "And the chief priests and scribes stood and vehemently accused him" (Luke 23:10). These bitter enemies of our Lord had seated themselves to watch the show, but when it failed to materialize they stood to their feet vehemently accusing Him. Their last accusation before Pilate had been sedition, and this charge was now brought before Herod. The acts of sedition had supposedly taken place in Herod's province.

The Mockery and the White Robe

Herod finally had enough. "And Herod with his men of war set him at nought, and mocked him, and arrayed him in a gorgeous robe, and sent him again to Pilate" (v. 11). Here is Herod's verdict. It is acted out by him and his bodyguard that had accompanied Herod to Jerusalem. Herod indicates by this that he regards Jesus as a foolish and contemptible person. He is to be mocked and ridiculed, not to be feared.

So calloused of conscience, Herod makes as if Christ's silence manifested His stupidity, and that the reason why He did no miracle was because He was powerless. It is either this or fall down before the Lord Jesus and confess his sins, but Herod is not about to do this. He has traveled the road of sin too far to retreat now. He had set his course and hardened his heart before, and now he was reaping the consequences of that hardened heart.

Christ would not put on a show for them, so they will make their own. Herod, with his bodyguard, set Him at nought, i.e., they treated Him with contempt and ridicule. In their mocking, Christ is arrayed "in a gorgeous robe." This is significant and deserves our attention. The expression means "bright" and it signifies a glistening white robe. This adjective comes from the verb "to shine." Another related word signifies a "torch," "lamp." The same word used here is used in Acts 10:30 and Revelation 15:6 of the glistening garments of angels.

Roman princes wore purple robes, and this is why the Roman soldiers put on Christ a purple robe when they mocked Him as King. The Jewish kings, however, wore a white robe, which was often rendered shining or gorgeous by interweaving silver in the cloth. Josephus tells us that the robe which Agrippa wore was so bright with silver that when the sun shone on it, it so dazzled the eyes that it was difficult to look upon. Such a robe was probably worn by Herod Agrippa I when, Dr. Luke tells us in the book of Acts, he went to the people of Tyre and Sidon. "And upon a set day Herod, arrayed in royal apparel, sat upon his throne, and made an oration unto them. And the people gave a shout, saying, It is the voice of a god, and not of a man" (Acts 12:21-22). Because Herod accepted their worship and did not reprove them for their action, God struck him with a dreadful disease, and he died (12:23). It seems that what started the whole thing was that royal robe he wore which glistened in the sun.

Now one does not have a robe around like this just anywhere. How was it that one was available here in Jerusalem? Josephus tells us that Herod Antipas' full brother, Archelaus, after mourning seven days at his father's funeral feast, i.e., of Herod the Great, "put on a white garment and went up to the temple" (Wars, II, i,i). There the people were wont to make him king, but he wanted, from the Roman's first, the complete title to the kingdom. When the Jews complained to Caesar that they would rather be subject to Roman governors, Caesar divided Herod the Great's kingdom into two parts, giving "the one half of Herod's kingdom to Archelaus, by the name of Ethnarch, and promised to make him king also afterwards, if he rendered himself worthy of that dignity; but as to the other half, he divided it into two tetrarchies, and gave them to two other sons of Herod, the one of them Philip, and the other to that Antipas who contested the kingdom with Archelaus" (II, vi, 3). Archelaus did anything but render himself worthy of this dignity, and was finally banished by Caesar. Archelaus's ethnarcy is reduced into a Roman province, and in time Pilate was sent as Procurator.

Through the misrule of Archelaus, the Herod family

loses half of their territory, and this may be the personal problem between Herod and Pilate spoken about in Luke 23:12. Herod Antipas, ruling over Galilee, wanted the territory awarded to Pilate. He had contested it even when it was given to his brother. But now, through the politeness of Pilate sending Jesus to Herod this day because Jesus belonged to Herod's territory, that enmity of long standing was cleared up. Herod Antipas and Pilate became friends. Luke gives us both the day and the occasion by which it|occurred.

The white robe—the gorgeous robe—was then probably that worn by Archelaus, and had been left in Jerusalem where he lived. Someone thought about it—perhaps even Herod himself—and placed it on Jesus to ridicule His claim to be a King. Herod thought such a claim to be absurd. At this gesture, Herod and those present must have doubled over with laughter. And it is while the assembly is in such a state that Herod orders Jesus sent back to Pilate.

But we cannot so soon leave this white robe. This is the only robe Luke mentions in connection with Christ, and if he mentions any, it has to be the white one. The reason is that the Gospel of Luke presents Christ as the Man, the Perfect Man. He is sinless and spotless. He is intrinsically white.

If the Father will clothe the sinner who has returned to Him with the best robe (Luke 15:22), how much more will He so clothe the Son. When Christ was transfigured before the three disciples, Luke tells us "the fashion of his countenence was altered, and his raiment was white and glistering" (Luke 9:29). This word glistering means "to send forth lightning, to lighten; to flash out like lightning, to shine, be radiant" (Thayer). The same word is used of the glittering of armor in the Septuagint of Nahum 3:3 and Ezekiel 1:7. This was our Lord's raiment, and the disciples "saw his glory" (Luke 9:32). The Lord is now crowned with glory and honor (Heb. 2:9), and someday "He shall come in his own glory, and in his Father's and of the holy angels" (Luke 9:26).

When David brought the ark of the covenant into the Holy City, he was "clothed with a robe of fine linen" and "David also had upon him an ephod of linen" (1 Chron. 15:27). The white linen all through Scripture speaks of purity and righteousness (cp. Ezek. 9:3). It is thus used in the tabernacle, and in the book of Revelation where the bride is "arrayed in fine linen, clean and white" and where the armies in heaven which follow the Lord are "upon white horses, clothed in fine linen, white and clean" (Rev. 19:8, 14).

When Eliakim is given the government of David, he is seen wearing the robe of that government (Isa. 22:20-22). Here is a picture of the true Messiah whom God will make as "a nail in a sure place; and he shall be for a glorious throne to his father's house. And they shall hang upon him all the glory of his father's house" (22:23-24). But the nail that was there previously—the antichrist—shall be removed completely out of his place (22:25). Here is the picture, and in the Gospel we have a pre-picture of the future fulfillment. Archelaus was unrighteous and was removed, and the robe of the house of David and of its glory was laid upon the Lord Jesus Christ. Archelaus was not the nail, but was an impostor.

Little did these unbelievers, acting in mockery and ridicule, realize the significance of their actions. But the robe was His to wear, and someday He will wear it in His glory. But not only will the Lord be wearing that white robe someday, also we have the privilege of being clothed in His righteousness and whiteness. Isaiah 61:10 says, "I will greatly rejoice in the Lord, my soul shall be joyful in my God; for he hath clothed me with the garments of salvation, he hath covered me with the robe of righteousness . . . ." That robe which Adam lost, we gain in Christ. We are to put on the Lord Jesus Christ (Rom. 13:14), and be clothed with humility (I Pet. 5:5). We are continually to be transfigured even as Christ was (Rom. 12:2, Greek) with the very glory of God.

Jesus is sent back to Pilate wearing this white, royal robe as He returns, for this is the meaning of the original, "and arraying him in gorgeous apparel, sent him back to Pilate" (R.V.). Christ is wearing this white robe through the streets of Jerusalem, but He is wearing it bound and led as a prisoner of men. How different it will be when He comes again. His wearing it was intended to be a parody of His royalty, but at the very same time it was an indirect declaration of His innocence. Though the Lord had spent most of His earthly life and public ministry in the territory of Galilee, yet the ruler of Galilee had nothing to lay to His charge. He was "without blemish, and without spot." He, therefore, can become God's Lamb that taketh away the sin of the world.

Chapter 12

The Second Trial
Before Pilate

We now begin the sixth and last trial for the Lord Jesus Christ. It is the second time that Christ appears before Pilate. The previous trial before him ended in acquittal, and Pilate will state this himself as he reviews the proceedings. This trial, that ultimately ends in the Lord's crucifixion in spite of the fact of His complete innocence, is very extensive and is covered by all four evangelists (Matt. 27:15-26; Mark 15:6-15; Luke 23:13-25; John 18:39—19:16). It should be kept in mind that only Luke gives us the true sequence of two trials before Pilate with the trial before Herod between them, while the other writers merely record the events before Pilate as one continuous, unbroken series of incidents.

At this point, all four reporters join together to give us various aspects of what went on. Each is reporting what in truth he saw and heard, but each looks at the events in the light of his own personality and purpose for reporting. Each hears these things in the Aramaic language, but is forced to translate them into the language of international communication, which is Greek, and this accounts for some slight variations. Let us, as nearly as possible, piece together the complete picture.

Pilate Summons the Sanhedrin

Not all of the Sanhedrin had accompanied Christ to Herod's residence, so as they return, the entire Sanhedrin must be summoned. It appears that they were together in one place, presumably at the Temple, and they quickly came. Luke 23:13 reads, "And Pilate, when he had called together the chief priests and the rulers of the people, said unto them . . . ." With all the members of the Sanhedrin assembled, Pilate takes his position on the tribunal which was the official seat carried to the Pavement before the Praetorium since the people would not enter therein (Matt. 27:19). He then addresses them, rehearsing the decision of the two civil trials.

"Ye have brought this man unto me, as one that perverteth the people: and, behold, I, having examined him before you, have found no fault in this man touching those things whereof ye accuse him" (Luke 23:14). My own verdict was for acquittal.

"No, not yet Herod: for I sent you to him; and, lo, nothing worthy of death is done unto him" (v. 15). Herod's verdict was that the case was too ridiculous even to try. It was a joke, and was so treated.

What did Pilate expect of Herod and want him to do? Pilate did not look to Herod merely for a fellow judge's opinion. He had hoped Herod would dispose of the case. It appears that Pilate wanted Herod to examine Jesus, and, if he found him innocent, let Him go. And if He was guilty, take Him to Galilee for trial and judgment, or judge Him right now while in Jerusalem. The fact that Jesus was sent to Herod gave him authority from Pilate to handle the case completely even while in Jerusalem.

However, it appears that Pilate did not expect Herod to find the Lord guilty of any crime, for if Jesus were really a dangerous agitator, certainly Herod would not have permitted Him to function in Galilee for the length of time that He had, but would have disposed of Him long ago. Moreover, Pilate himself found Christ innocent of leading any insurrection, and knew it was for envy that the Jewish leaders had brought Him to Pilate for trial. The important point is that Herod did have the power himself to release Christ if he found Him innocent. This is seen from Acts 4:27 where both Herod and Pilate are seen responsible for the death of the Lord Jesus. Had Herod disposed of the case, Pilate would have been freed from making a decision concerning the Lord Jesus Christ. But this did not happen, for the Prisoner is brought back to Pilate for his ultimate verdict.

Pilate had unquestionably hoped that the case had been settled by Herod, for this would have gotten him off the hook from making a decision concerning Jesus Christ before the Sanhedrin and this multitude. With the populace of the city gathered before him now, conditions were even worse for Pilate than before.

We must realize too, that Pilate was technically justified in sending Jesus to be tried by Herod, as well as suspending His release until He returned from him. Even though Pilate had found no fault with this man, yet he could have been ignorant of the customs and laws of the nation and the interrelation of these laws with Roman laws. Herod would have been thoroughly acquainted with both.

The very fact that Dr. Luke records that this "same day Pilate and Herod were made friends together: for before they were at enmity between themselves" (23:12), is worthy of even further meditation. All through Scripture we find the history of nations as well as individuals hanging on one little thing. It was true in Esther, as it was true of the birth of Christ, and it is true here. Had Pilate and Herod retained their enmity this day and not have been reconciled by this event, Herod would have tried to give a different verdict from what Pilate had rendered. But such was not the case. Pilate announces Herod found him innocent also.

His Release of One at the Passover

We read in Mark 15:6-8, "Now at that feast he released unto them one prisoner, whomsoever they desired. And there was one named Barabbas, which lay bound with them that had made insurrection with him, who had committed murder in the insurrection. And the multitude crying aloud [the better reading is 'went up'] began to desire him to do as he had ever done unto them." The crowd gathered before Pilate at this time was different from that gathered in the early morning hour of the first trial before Pilate. Then it was mostly the Sanhedrin, but now the city was beginning to awaken from its slumber of the night, unaware of the events that had transpired while they slept. They begin to congregate together before the Praetorium because it seems Pilate had established a precedent each year previously of releasing a prisoner to them on this feast day.

While this certainly was not justice, it was mercy, and was loved by a people who were bitterly opposed to the yoke of Rome over them. It was also much like the very birth of the nation itself for which they commemorated the Passover days. The nation had been guilty of gross sins in Egypt (Ezek. 20:6-10), and were in the place of bondage. They were not redeemed because of any righteousness of their own part, but merely because of the mercy of God (Deut. 9:4-6). Once delivered, they were permanently free from their former bondage.

The people, who had each year secured this act from Pilate, do not want to let it die, but will vigorously clamor to have it done again. But Pilate wants, because Jesus is innocent of any crime, to release Him to them. "I will therefore chastise him and release him." And Luke then adds why he said this: "(For of necessity he must release one unto them at the feast)" (Luke 23:16-17). Pilate was seeking to use this custom for his own benefit. He saw in this a way to get himself out of the dilemma in which he found himself.

We dare not pass over this hurriedly. Pilate has just pronounced the verdict of both himself and Herod. Jesus has been tried and is acquitted. Justice demands that the case be immediately ended and the prisoner be released at once; and, further, that He be protected by Rome from all harm or violence, should the need arise. But this is not what we read. Pilate, having rendered the dual verdicts of acquittal, now ceases to act as judge, and acts as politician. He will seek to appease the Sanhedrin's wrath by scourging Christ, and yet release Him because He is innocent.

Gerhard wrote in 1889 concerning Pilate's actions: "Be consistent with thyself, Pilate, for, if Christ is innocent, why dost thou not send him away acquitted? And if thou believest him deserving of chastisement with rods, why dost thou proclaim him to be innocent?''

Pilate has just put Jesus up for auction to His own people who are gathered before Him. Whether he, Pilate, releases Jesus at all is now no longer a decision of justice, but a decision which Israel will make. Here is Pilate's statement of intent—"I will therefore chastise him, and release him" (Luke 23:16)—and with it his whole plan was exposed to his opposition. It now was only a matter of time for the Lord's enemies to rally their forces and defeat Pilate's plan.

The protest against this was immediate from the Sanhedrin. This would not satisfy them whatever. They had come for His death—nothing else would appease them. With Pilate's original plan thwarted, he is forced to go one step further. He knows that Rome has one prisoner that is "notorious," named Barabbas. His crimes are listed by the evangelists as robbery (John 18:40), high treason (Luke 23:19) and murder (Luke 23:19). The penalty for these crimes against Rome was death by crucifixion. A cross was in the process of being prepared for this "notable prisoner" (Matt. 27:16) along with two other lesser personages. These were to be crucified as an example of what will happen to any others that would commit such crimes against Rome.

Having placed the destiny of Jesus in the hands of the people, Pilate decides to give them the choice between two men. He will release either Barabbas or Jesus. So "Pilate said unto them, Whom will ye that I release unto you? Barabbas, or Jesus which is called Christ?" (Matt. 27:17). For Pilate, the decision was obvious. There was no logical comparison between the two. "He knew that for envy they had delivered him," Christ, to him (Matt. 27:18). All reason and logic demanded that they select Jesus, who is called the Christ. Their immediate response was, "Not this man but Barabbas" (John 18:40; Luke 23:18-19).

Word From His Wife

As Pilate sat there on the judgment seat at this very moment, an important event occurs. "When he was set down on the judgment seat" [Greek: 'While he was sitting on the judgment seat'], "his wife sent unto him, saying, Have thou nothing to do with that just man: for I have suffered many things this day in a dream because of him" (Matt. 27:19).

Matthew alone records this event. As such, it is another indictment against His own people. Just as earlier in the Gospel, wise men from afar came to worship the young child, while Israel did not, so here a Gentile, heathen woman knows concerning His person and character, but Israel does not know.

God has often used dreams in making known Himself to man. He did so with Pharaoh and with Nebuchadnezzar, and so He does with Pilate's wife. It seems that it was only during the reign of Tiberius that the governors of provinces had been permitted to take their wives with them. For Pilate's wife, who tradition names Claudia Procula, to send a messenger to her husband while he was occupied with official business, shows something of the impression the dream had upon her. She knew it was supernatural. Upon arising and finding her husband gone, she must have inquired as to the nature of his business at such an early hour. Learning that it concerned the very One of whom she had dreamed and had suffered many things in her dream, she felt compelled to warn her husband. It could not wait! The Lord in His compassion was in this, giving Pilate himself a warning. What Pilate does now will be against increased light. He himself knows Jesus is innocent. There has come the confirmation of this through his wife from heaven itself.

Her message to her husband was short and to the point. It is literally, *Nothing between you and that Righteous Man . . . .* No one can prosper who allows anything to come in between himself and the Lord. Pilate did not prosper, even though he sought to wash his hands of the affair and to make the Nation bear the entire guilt. He was soon to be banished from his office, and the historian Eusebius says that soon afterward, "wearied with misfortunes," he killed himself. How can we hope to prosper if we allow something between us and this Man who is infinitely righteous? Since He is righteous, to the extent something is between ourselves and Him, it only indicates our unrighteousness.

"Nothing between, e'en many hard trials,

Tho' the whole world against me convene;
Watching with prayer and much self-denial,
I'll triumph at last, with nothing between.
"Nothing between my soul and the Savior,
So that His blessed face may be seen;
Nothing preventing the least of His favor,
Keep the way clear! Let nothing between."
—C. A. Tindley

The Decision of the Multitude

While Pilate was receiving the messenger with the urgent appeal from his wife, probably no more than 30 seconds went by. He had previously committed the case into their hands. The mob gathered before him had been empowered with the verdict. They have the choice between two men: Barabbas and Jesus. This short space of time was enough to allow the members of the Sanhedrin to disperse among the crowd to persuade them to ask for Barabbas.

"Now the chief priests and the elders persuaded the multitude that they should ask Barabbas, and destroy Jesus " (Matt. 27:20). "But the chief priests moved the people that he should rather release Barabbas unto them" (Mark 15:11). Having mingled with the crowd, the entire Sanhedrin will be united as one voice for Barabbas to be released and for Jesus to be crucified. Coming from every section of the crowd and with others joining in with them, when the question is asked, it will appear as it if the whole were united.

The governor, having regained his composure after this message from his wife, is now ready to ask them again for their decision. "The governor answered and said unto them, Whether of the twain will ye that I release unto you? They said, Barabbas. Pilate saith unto them, What shall I do then with Jesus which is called Christ? They all say unto him, Let him be crucified. And the governor said, Why, what evil hath he done? But they cried out the more, saying, Let him be crucified" (Matt. 27:21-23). Mark's account (15:12-14) is almost identical. Luke only enlarges on a few statements: "Pilate therefore, willing to release Jesus, spake again to them. But they cried, saying, Crucify him, crucify him. And he said unto them the third time, Why, what evil hath he done? I have found no cause of death in him: I will therefore chastise him, and let him go. And they were instant with loud voices, requiring that he might be crucified" (Luke 23:20-23a).

Pilate had placed the decision in their hands, thinking he knew which way they would go; but he was wrong. He is trying desperately to change their course of action, but to no avail.

"And the voices of them and of the chief priests prevailed" (Luke 23:23b). Luke is telling us that the verdict was very definitely one-sided, but by no means unanimous. These gathered before Pilate were mainly the people of the city and area of Jerusalem. They were not the same as the Galileans who had accompanied Jesus into the city with shouts of "Hosanna to the son of David: Blessed is he that cometh in the name of the Lord; Hosanna in the highest" (Matt. 21:9). This present assembly was mainly the people of Jerusalem, who were under the complete control of the Sanhedrin. The common statement that the fickle crowd shouted "Hosanna" at the first of the week, and "Crucify" toward the last of the week, is entirely unwarranted.

Pilate Washes His Hands

"When Pilate saw that he could prevail nothing, but that rather a tumult was made, he took water, and washed his hands before the multitude, saying, I am innocent of the blood of this just person: see ye to it" (Matt. 27:24).

Notice that this act was done, not at the very end of Pilate's dealings before the crowd, as has been supposed by many, but actually midway in them. Even after Christ has been scourged, He is brought forth to the crowd, and Pilate's hope is that they will say it is enough and change their verdict. The point we are making is this: Though Pilate is washing his hands, he is still not through in seeking to get Jesus Christ freed, but will try twice more to attain this decision, yet to no avail.

What is Pilate seeking to do in washing his hands before the people? This action by Pilate has been greatly misunderstood, mainly from a lack of understanding of the culture of the nation. It is poor and faulty exegesis to read into this event what it would signify in our culture. We must come to understand what it signified in the culture of the day.

The entire rite and the words used were Jewish, not Roman. Under the Law in Deuteronomy 21:6-9, the elders of a city would wash their hands with water when they were free from the murder of a person and they were unable to find the guilty person.

David the king cried out when Joab killed Abner, "I and my kingdom are guiltless before the Lord for ever from the blood of Abner the son of Ner" (II Sam. 3:28). The judgment was to rest on Joab and his seed from that moment on (3:29), and it did.

Psalm 26:6 and 73:13 (LXX) speak of the same language. Edersheim informs us: "The Mishnah bears witness that this rite was continued. As administering justice in Israel, Pilate must have been aware of this rite. It does not affect the question, whether or not a judge could, especially in the circumstances recorded, free himself from guilt. Certainly, he could not . . ." (II, 578).

Pilate is unable to reason with the people who are now given to their emotions. He has only one recourse that he knows at present. Normally, this would have been effective to bring the people back to complete sobriety. "When a Judge, after having declared the innocence of the accused, actually rises from the Judgment-Seat, and by a symbolic act pronounces the execution of the accused a judicial murder, from all participation in which he wishes solemnly to clear himself, surely no jury would persist in demanding sentence of death" (II, 577-8).

The Request for His Blood

This is what Pilate is doing. Did it have the desired effect upon the nation which Pilate wished? Not at all. Nothing Pilate is trying is working. When the Elders performed this rite, the prayer response was: "Be merciful O Lord, unto thy people Israel, whom thou has redeemed, and lay not innocent blood unto thy people of Israel's charge"

(Deut. 21:8). Then God says: "The blood shall be forgiven them." In this case there is no request for mercy whatever, but, on the contrary, a brazen request for His blood. "Then answered all the people, and said, His blood be on us, and on our children" (Matt. 27:25). How calloused; how defiant.

Pilate, in the providence of God, uses the very words— "See ye to it"—that the Sanhedrin had said to Judas which broke him with such grief because he had betrayed the innocent blood (Matt. 27:4) that he went out and hanged himself. Yet it didn't phase these people.

Just as they asked, they received. God granted their request. These people began to suffer mercilessly after God gave them space to repent under the Apostles, and still they hardened their hearts even more (Acts 7:51). Then in A.D. 70, 38 years as God reckoneth the generation in the wilderness, it came upon their children who were just like their fathers, and it came upon themselves (Luke 21:18-24). Still they suffer and will continue to do so until in the great tribulation they acknowledge their sin and seek His face (Hos. 5:15—6:3).

Little did the people or the Sanhedrin even remember their words, for in Acts 5, when the Apostles were brought before the Sanhedrin, "the high priests asked them, Saying, Did not we straitly command you that ye should not teach in this name? and, behold, ye have filled Jerusalem with your doctrine, and intend to bring this man's blood upon us" (Acts 5:28).

No, the Apostles were not motivated with the purpose of bringing upon the city the innocent blood of the Son of God, whom the nation and leaders murdered. The Sanhedrin had already brought it upon themselves and their city. The Apostles were proclaiming that there was salvation for them individually and collectively in no other name (Acts 3:23; 4:12; 5:31) than the name of the Son of God, whom they crucified, and whom God raised from the dead and exalted at His own right hand.

The nation, who had been judicially blinded (Matt. 23:39; Luke 19:42-44), willingly accepted the judicial guilt for the murder of Christ. Pilate's guilt will be personal and moral. He was wrong because he was willing to gamble with an innocent man's life. He gambled and lost. He in no way goes free of responsibility, but our Lord's words are very exact in this regard: "he that delivered me unto thee hath the greater sin" (John 19:11).

Pilate Submits to Their Will

After washing his hands, and the people responded to take the guilt of it to themselves and their children, Pilate issues two orders to his soldiers: the release of Barabbas and the scourging of Jesus. "Then released he Barabbas unto them" (Matt. 27:26a), "but Jesus he scourged (27:26b R.V.). "And Pilate gave sentence that it should be as they required. And he released unto them him that for sedition and murder was cast into prison, whom they had desired; but he delivered Jesus to their will" (Luke 23:24-25).

The six trials of the Lord Jesus Christ are officially over. Pilate has yielded to the clamor and pressure of the mob. Jesus Christ is being scourged, not because He did any wrong, but because men and men's hearts were wrong. So Peter will write, "It is better, if the will of God be so, that ye suffer for well doing, than for evil doing. For Christ also hath once suffered for sins, the just for the unjust, that he might bring us to God . . ." (I Pet. 3:17-18). One who is guilty goes free, while the One who was innocent now begins to suffer. He will be taking the guilty one's cross and, literally, dying in his place.

Chapter 13

Barabbas' View of the Atonement

The Story of Barabbas

I want you to imagine that the year is A.D. 32, and you are being held in a Roman prison in the city of Jerusalem. You have been tried, and condemned to die because you were involved in insurrection against Rome. In this insurrection, you commited murder against a Roman officer. You also plundered—and, therefore, were a robber. Because of these crimes involving high treason against Rome, a cross is being prepared for you and two others of your buddies that were captured with you. Insurrection against Rome was always met by crucifixion for any who were involved and caught, in order that Rome might publicly demonstrate the price that was paid for this crime. You knew what the penalty was even before you acted, and you knew you were guilty of these crimes, even as one of your fellow insurrectionists will later testify: "We are receiving justly what we have done." Thus, you stand condemned righteously under the law. Your name is recorded in the annals of all four Gospels. Your name is Barabbas. Tradition says that your full name is Jesus Barabbas, "Jesus," or Joshua as it would have been in the Old Testament, "Barabbas" i.e., son of Abbas, or son of Father.

Incarcerated, you are waiting your execution. Already, three crosses are being prepared, and, because you are the ringleader, you are going to die on that center cross. But news begins to come to you that at the Passover—the very season it is now—Pilate has previously released one prisoner whomever the people wanted. And the wonder of it all is that the crowd is yelling out that they want released unto them Barabbas. That's you! If this is what Pilate will do, then it may be that you won't have to go to a cross; you won't have to die after all. Could it be that you will escape this death?

Oh, you have already felt the agony of such a death, for you had seen what others went through as they died by crucifixion. You have anticipated what would be involved, for you know that before the Romans ever crucify anyone, they always scourged him. They take that whip with leather straps to which metal or sharp pieces of bone have been tied, and they beat you with it. While the Jews only give thirty-nine stripes in order to adhere to the Law, the Romans never count the scourges. When one man got tired, he turned the whip over to another and another. Many a man never went beyond the scourging, but died right there. Each scourge tore into the flesh, and sometimes they would not only beat the back, but let it wrap around the body to the front and around the face, as it was said of one, that his countenance was so marred that he was beyond recognition.

After the scourging, the agony of having the spikes driven through your hands and feet did not seem so intense. But they would give you some strong wine that would kind of anesthetize you so that you would not feel the agony so greatly. Yet you know that many times a person would linger in this agony—for you have seen many others in your day crucified, as Rome did it quite frequently—for two or even three days before they died. And there hanging on a cross, every bone would be out of joint in your body, and fever would take over so that it would seem you would die of thirst, as you were suspended between heaven and earth, touching neither. This is what you had to look forward to as you righteously died on that center cross.

But then the word comes, and it is official—the crowd has asked for you, and Pilate has given the order for you to be released. You are going free, Barabbas, you are going free!

Yet, you hear in the midst of the commotion that while you are being set free, there is another man that is going to take the cross which had been made for you—someone by the name of Jesus who is called the Christ. From what you hear, He had done nothing wrong, yet He is taking your scourging right now, and later He will be bearing that cross out to a hill called Golgatha, and there they will crucify Him. Yet what difference does it make, you are a free man. Barabbas, you are free!

But you cannot so easily dismiss this other One from your mind. You begin to realize this One is a substitute for you. Had you died, the guilty one, He would have gone free; but since you go free, He must die. He is taking the stripes due you and is going to die in agony and suffering. You realize, further, that there is no merit on your part; you were not released because of any good works or because of a righteous standing or because you were such a good and fine individual at all. You had no merit or righteousness that you can claim whereby someone else would be willing to die in your place. But the wonder of it all is that when this One dies on the cross, the law is never going to be able to touch you again. The Romans who condemned you to die have a maxim that no man shall be put twice in jeopardy. So it is that as Jesus dies, you, Barabbas, are going to go free forever. And those crimes that were due you are never going to be able to be justly brought out; you will never come under condemnation to them again. You, Barabbas, are absolutely and forever free!

Prophecy and Typology

What an amazing truth this is that Jesus Christ actually died in Barabbas' place. What we have in the Gospel accounts is where type and antitype come together in the persons of Jesus Christ and Barabbas.

Through the Old Testament there are two separate threads of proof of the divine inspiration of all Scripture.

This is a book that man could not have written even if he wanted to, and would not have written even if he could. The one line of proof is specific, detailed prophecies predicted years before they could have been known, which have been fulfilled in exact detail. Only God could give these and cause them to be fulfilled. The major theme of prophecy is the person and work of the Lord Jesus Christ.

There are no less than 60 different Old Testament prophecies which have been fulfilled this last day of 24 hours of Jesus Christ's life in human history. These prophecies are in addition to the predictions Christ made Himself which were given at the very beginning of this study.

There never was a day like this before in human history, and there will never be another to equal it. All history is moving toward it, and all history moves from it. It stands as the very center of history. History is actually HIS-story. As Jesus Christ is sent to be scourged, Psalm 129:3 is being fulfilled, "The plowers plowed upon my back: they made long their furrows," as well as many other passages.

But there is another line of proof of the inspiration of Scripture, and that is type with its counterpart of antitype in the New Testament. The antitype is the fulfillment of the truth of which the type is the picture. No other writing in all of the world has type and antitype, and the reason is because God alone can give it. It is this that comes into living reality in the story of Barabbas. It is in no way by accident that a man, identified as Barabbas, is at this very time being released and set free. He stands in the providence of God as a picture of the sinner set free because another, who was innocent, is taking his stripes and will die on his cross in his place.

This theme of Scripture that ends with Barabbas started in the Garden of Eden. There innocent animals were sacrificed by God in order to provide for Adam and Eve an acceptable covering before God (Gen. 3:21). It is seen in every animal sacrifice made in the Old Testament, each one portraying a different aspect of the one infinite sacrifice of God's perfect Lamb.

Sometimes one animal was sacrificed while another animal went free. This happened on the Day of Atonement when, in reference to the two goats, one dies and the other became a scapegoat that was to be led out into the wilderness and released, never to be seen again (Lev. 16). In the cleansing of leprosy, two birds were used. One was killed, and the live bird dipped in the blood of the dead bird, and then he was allowed to go free in an open field (Lev. 14). This signified not only the sacrifice of our Lord for our sins, but of their complete removal from us.

In some cases there were no animals involved at all. It might be an inanimate object like a rock that was struck and out from it flowed a stream of lifegiving water (Ex. 17:1-7; John 7:37-39; etc.). Or it could be a brass metalic serpent which was raised up on a pole that the Lord Jesus Christ Himself likens as a divine illustration of the believer's personal appropriation of the sacrifice of Christ to himself (Num. 21:4-9; John 3:14-16).

Sometimes typology has used the life or the death of men as an example of Christ's sacrifice. The kinsman redeemer portrayed in Ruth is a type of our Great Kinsman Redeemer, the Lord Jesus Christ, according to the prediction of Isaiah 59:20. The death of the High Priest in Israel freed all in the cities of refuge (Num. 35:28), and in this the High Priest stands as a picture of Christ, our Great High Priest, who by His death freed all who were held in bondage. In certain incidences it was actually portrayed by a man as Abraham who took his beloved son up Mt. Moriah, there to give and sacrifice him as a burnt offering to the Lord (Gen. 22:1-19).

However, with Christ and Barabbas, type and antitype meet. Christ is the antitype of all the types, pictures, figures, symbols and illustrations that foretold of Him. But Barabbas is a picture, a divine picture, a picture planned and arranged in the providence of God of you and of me. Barabbas is the type, and we are the antitype. It is not by mere chance that Barabbas was available this day of all days to be traded for Jesus Christ. He was there in prison under the sentence of death by crucifixion that the Gospel message to my heart and yours might be a personal relationship with Jesus Christ. Here is the story.

The Gospel According to Barabbas

First, Barabbas stood under the righteous condemnation of the law. Justice demanded his punishment. This is acknowledged even by one of the lesser personages in this threesome who admitted to his own fellow as he hung on a cross, "Dost not thou fear God, seeing thou art in the same condemnation? And we indeed justly; for we received the due reward of our deeds . . ." (Luke 23:40-41).

If Barabbas had received justice, he would have died on the center cross. It had been prepared for him. He was to have the center cross because he was the ringleader and the most notorious of those being crucified this day. He was a sinner that had knowingly broken the law, and knew that the demands of that broken law must be met. He was to die justly.

Secondly, Barabbas knew the One who was to take his cross and take his place was innocent. Pilate had so declared Him to be innocent over and over again. The one member of the trio testifies that he knew it: "but this man hath done nothing amiss" (Luke 23:41). He rebukes his fellow because he also knew it, and yet was mocking. If both of these knew it, we can know that Barabbas knew it also.

Thirdly, Barabbas knew that Jesus Christ was for him a true substitute. There was in truth One dying in his place and stead. Pilate had given the people of Israel their choice; it was Barabbas or Jesus. If one was freed, the other suffered. If Jesus had been freed, Barabbas would suffer justly. If Barabbas is freed, Jesus must suffer unjustly—the just for the unjust.

Fourthly, Barabbas knew that he had done nothing to merit going free while another took his place. There were no good works or deeds of righteousness to which he could cling as a hope to merit salvation. He had no worthiness; he stood with no merit; he could claim no righteousness. He was saved by a divine act of mercy and grace. None other than God Himself was working to have Jesus crucified and Barabbas freed. God was working in the one as much as the other, yet the people themselves were doing just what they wanted to do and were totally responsible for their actions.

Peter will testify on the day of Pentecost: "Him, being delivered by the determinate counsel and foreknowledge of God, ye have taken, and by wicked hands have crucified and slain" (Acts 2:23). Then later he will further proclaim, "The God of Abraham, and of Isaac, and of Jacob, the God of our Fathers, hath glorified His Son Jesus; whom ye delivered up, and denied him in the presence of Pilate, when he was determined to let him go. But ye denied the Holy One and the Just, and desired a murderer to be granted unto you, And killed the Prince of life . . ." (Acts 3:13-15).

Fifthly, Barabbas knew Christ's death was for him perfectly efficacious. He was forever free from the law that condemned him, because another died in his place. *Non bias in idem*, no man shall be put twice in jeopardy is a maxim which has come down to us from the Romans. The law could never touch Barabbas again.

Krummacher has penned it well: "Observe now the result of the decision. Barabbas and Jesus change places. The murderer's bonds, curse, disgrace, and mortal agony are transferred to the righteous Jesus; while the liberty, inno-cence, safety, and well-being of the immaculate Nazarene become the lot of the murderer. Jesus Barabbas is installed in all the rights and privileges of Jesus Christ; while the latter enters upon all the infamy and horror of the rebel's position. Both mutually inherit each other's situation and what they possess: The delinquent's guilt and cross become the lot of the Just One, and all the civil rights and immunities of the latter are the property of the delinquent."

The Good News According to Scripture

When Jesus Christ died, He died for Barabbas—no, He died for me and He died for you. Had He been only an innocent man among men, He could have died for only one man—Barabbas. Had He been only God, He could have died for no man, for God cannot die. Since He was the sinless God-man, He could taste death in a point in time for every man (Heb. 2:9).

"In due time Christ died for the ungodly . . . while we were yet sinners, Christ died for us" (Rom. 5:6, 8). "Christ died for our sins" (I Cor. 15:3). "Jesus Christ, who gave himself for our sins, that he might deliver us from this present evil world, according to the will of God and our Father" (Gal. 1:4). "The Son of God, who loved me and gave himself for me" (Gal. 2:20). "Christ hath redeemed us from the curse of the law, being made a curse for us . . ." (Gal. 3:13). "Stand fast therefore in the liberty wherewith Christ hath made us free . . ." (Gal. 5:1).

We were sinners, having broken the Law, and so under the curse (Gal. 3:10). We were legally dead in trespasses and sins (Eph. 2:1-3). But God, through mercy and grace and for His great love wherein He loved us, did something we couldn't do for ourselves (Eph. 2:4-7). He did it all through Jesus Christ, and not because of any works or merit wherein we could boast (Eph. 2:8-9). He took all the crimes against us, and the handwriting of ordinances "which was contrary to us, and took it out of the way, nailing it to his cross" (Col. 2:14).

The picture is vivid. When a man was in prison under Roman law, his crimes were written out and nailed to his cell door (cp. Gal. 3:23). When a prisoner was set free, he would be handed this indictment having it cancelled by writing that it was fulfilled. He would then nail this to his own front door showing his right to be free. When a criminal was executed, this indictment, was taken from his cell door and was nailed over his cross. Jesus Christ took that which was against us and paid its price, nailing it to His cross. He had no crimes, so He died for mine.

He "died for us, that whether we wake or sleep, we should live together with him" (I Thess. 5:10). "This is a faithful saying, and worthy of all acceptation, that Christ Jesus came into the world to save sinners; of whom I am chief" (I Tim. 1:15). Barabbas was one sinner; Paul was—he himself says he is chief—I am one; you are one. Christ died for you too.

The Scriptures abound that this is the Gospel. "For even the Son of man came not to be ministered unto, but to minister, and to give his life a ransom for many" (Mark 10:45). "For there is one God, and one mediator between God and men, the man Christ Jesus; who gave himself a ransom for all, to be testified in due time" (I Tim. 2:5-6). Then there is Titus 2:11-14; 3:5-7; Philemon 18; Hebrews 9:26-28; 10:10-14; I Peter 2:24-25; 3:18; I John 2:2; 4:9-10; Rev. 1:5 (Greek); 5:9; etc.

And still there is more. "For the Son of man is come to seek and to save that which was lost" (Luke 19:10). "They that are whole need not a physician; but they that are sick. I come not to call the righteous, but sinners to repentance" (Luke 5:21-32). Not until you realize your terrible state under condemnation and death, with no way out but Jesus Christ, is there any hope for you to be saved. If you have any hope of making it any other way, then Jesus Christ died in vain as far as you are concerned (cp. Gal. 2:21).

But He who knew no sin was made sin for us that we might be made the righteousness of God in Him (II Cor. 5:21). Our part is to believe in Him. We must believe the good news as it comes to us just as we are—in sin. It isn't a matter of cleaning up our lives first; it isn't a matter of self-reformation. Jesus Christ is dying in our place, just as we are.

The Need for Personal Acceptance of a Pardon

Could you imagine Barabbas saying, "I don't believe it," or "I won't accept it"? Not on your life! This was good news; he accepted it and was delivered, forever free. Would a Barabbas today refuse such an offer? It is not very likely in the legal realm that a man would, but there have been some.

Martin Dalton died March 23, 1960 at the age of 91. He had been 63 years behind the bars of Rhode Island State Prison. He murdered a New York business man in East Providence, Rhode Island in 1897, was found guilty and sentenced at the age of 28. In 1930 his case was reviewed. He was granted a full pardon and could go free being 61 years old. But he refused. He chose to remain in prison. Could he refuse a pardon? Yes. According to a decision made by the Supreme Court of the United States in 1830.

The Supreme Court ruling of 1830 came during the presidency of Andrew Jackson. A George Wilson was sentenced in the Pennsylvania courts to be hanged for robbing the United States mails and murder. When pardoned by President Jackson, Wilson refused to accept pardon, insisting that it was no pardon if he did not accept it. The sheriff was perplexed and asked that the matter be settled, for he did not know what was to be done with his prisoner. The Attorney General declared that the law was silent on this point. The case was finally taken to the Supreme Court of the United States. The following is part of the decision handed down by Chief Justice John Marshall, one of America's great lawgivers: "A pardon is a paper, the value of which depends upon its acceptance by the person implicated. It is hardly to be supposed that one under sentence of death would refuse to accept pardon, but if it is refused, it is no pardon. George Wilson must hang."

While few today may refuse this pardon in the legal realm, this same offer in the spiritual realm is being refused by one Barabbas after another. Why? It is because "the god of this world has blinded the minds of them which believe not, lest the light of the glorious gospel of Christ . . . should shine unto them" (II Cor. 4:4). May, by the grace of God and the working of the Spirit of God, your eyes be opened to see your personal Savior who loved you and gave Himself for you. May you not spurn the Lord's pardon. "The Lord is . . . not willing that any should perish, but that all should come to repentance" (II Pet. 3:9).

Jesus Christ has died for you; He can do nothing more. The decision is yours. What will you do with Him?

Chapter 14

The Beginning
of the End

Pilate offered the crowd their choice. They could have one man released to them at this Passover season. They yelled out for Pilate to release to them Barabbas. Pilate then said to them, "What shall I do then with Jesus which is called Christ?" They all said unto him, "Let him be crucified." Though Pilate tried to change their decision, it was to no avail; and when he saw that he could prevail nothing, but that rather a tumult was made, he released Barabbas to them, and scourged the Lord Jesus.

Leaving Barabbas, we now follow the steps of the Lord Jesus Christ. John alone, at this point, gives us the true sequence of events. He shows that after the scourging, Jesus is brought back again before the people as Pilate seeks once again to have Him released, but to no avail. Matthew and Mark give the account of the scourging and mocking but do not record Pilate's last efforts to free Jesus since these efforts were fruitless. Luke goes from the trial right to the road that leads to Calvary.

The Scourging of Jesus Christ

"Then Pilate therefore took Jesus, and scourged him" (John 19:1). Like the crucifixion itself, where the Scriptures are silent except for the words, "They crucified him," so here. A veil is drawn over this scene, and it is done purposely. We should, therefore, be content with only a few comments and then move on.

The scourging and mocking by the soldiers takes place within the palace itself, and was not seen by the people. After it was all over, Pilate brings Jesus back before the crowd, and they see Him for the first time in this condition.

The scourge consisted of a handle to which several leather thongs were affixed. These were weighted on the ends with jagged pieces of bone or metal. This would help tear the flesh and make each blow more effective.

The victim was stripped, and usually tied to a post with his hands also bound (Acts. 22:25) so as not to be able to defend himself. The blows were normally applied to the back and loins, but sometimes to the whole body. We shall see shortly, reasons for believing that the face and whole body of Christ was scourged. The punishment by scourging was so severe that the victim usually fainted, and not rarely died.

According to Jewish law, a man could receive no more than forty stripes (Deut. 25:3). For this reason the Jews limited their scourgings from either rods or whips to 39 stripes so as never to break this law if perchance they have miscounted (cp. II Cor. 11:23-25). With the Romans, however, no such limitation was observed; it depended entirely on the commander in charge. The implication of the text is that Jesus Christ received a Roman scourging, and it was by no means limited to 39 stripes.

Pilate had a reason for the severity of this flogging. He was seeking to present Jesus Christ to the crowd once again and hoped that the severity of His sufferings would suffice. The very fact that later on Jesus Christ is unable to carry His cross is another indication of the suffering He previously encountered. It is not a case that the Lord *would not* carry His cross; He *could not* carry it, and the soldiers knew it, and knew why this was the case.

The Mockery

The soldiers have finished the scourging, and now they enter into a little sport with this One who is before them. Though it is a breach of military discipline, their own hostility toward the Jews is taken out on the Lord. Not wanting any of their buddies to miss this, "they call together the whole band" or cohort of soldiers (Mark 15:16), perhaps the same that were used to capture Him in the early morning. They now give a mock coronation to the King. "And they clothed him with purple, and platted a crown of thorns, and put it about his head, and began to salute him, Hail, King of the Jews! And they smote him [kept on smiting Him] on the head with a reed, and did spit upon him [kept on spitting upon Him], and bowing their knees worshipped him. And when they had mocked him, they took off the purple from him, and put his own clothes on him, and led him out to crucify him" (Mark 15:17-20).

Once the direction of mocking Him was started by the soldiers, it continued until it was a full dress occasion. A king must have a robe. They found an old military cloak of purple color. This they threw over His bleeding form and clasped it on the right shoulder. This robe was one probably worn by Roman generals and sometimes presented by Rome to foreign kings. A king needs also a crown. This was supplied by intertwining the twigs into a crown from the long-spiked thorn bush which grows in Palestine. This was put upon His head. One thing still was lacking. A king needs a sceptor, and finding a reed, they placed it into His right hand (Matt. 27:29). Now the picture is complete, and they begin their derision. "And they bowed the knee before him, and mocked him, saying, Hail, King of the Jews! And they spit upon him, and took the reed, and smote him on the head" (Matt. 27:29-30). Literally the Greek says, "They kept on smiting Him on the head."

Let us not think of this reed as some little thing that bends every time it is used. This is not the case. The most common reed in Palestine grows in immense quantities in the Jordan valley along the Jordan and its tributaries. It is a lofty reed often 20 feet high. It would be something like what we know as bamboo. This was what they first used as a scepter in His right hand, but then took and smote Him on His thorn-crowned head, over and over again.

John adds one other detail: "and they smote him with their hands" (John 19:3). Again it is imperfect tense: "They kept on smiting Him." All their mockery was in reference to Christ being *King*, while that given before Caiaphas and the Sanhedrin was in reference to His being *Prophet*.

This is still the hour when all that they willed to do was done, but all who had dealings with Him merely revealed the baseness and depravity of the human heart. *The heart is deceitful above all things and incurably wicked; who can know it? (Jer. 17:9)*. Since the human heart is being revealed, it is any human heart. It is my heart; it is your heart. Here is a picture of what I would have done had I been there.

The Man Before Men

"Pilate therefore went forth again, and saith unto them, Behold, I bring him forth to you that ye may know that I find no fault in him. Then came Jesus forth, wearing the crown of thorns, and the purple robe. And Pilate said unto them, Behold the man!" (John 19:4-5).

Even though Pilate ordered Jesus to be scourged as the preparation for crucifixion, and this was carried out, Pilate still wants to release Him. He previously had said: "I will chastise him and release him." He comes back to the crowd now, saying to them, "Look, the man." Is not this enough?

Little did Pilate realize that by this very act he was fulfilling Scripture. We have not examined many of the passages that have been fulfilled during these trials, because this has been outside the scope of our present study, but there is one which is significant to this occasion. We need to look closely at Isaiah 52:13-15.

The Hebrew is a very descriptive language, and a very careful translation of these verses reveals previous truths, "Behold, my servant shall act prudently. He shall be exalted and lifted up and He shall be very high. Just as many will be astonished at Him (so disfigured in His appearance from man and His beauty from the sons of men) so He shall startle many Gentiles. Kings shall close their mouths before Him, because they shall see that which was not revealed to them, and they shall come to perceive that which they have not heard." In these verses we have an overview of Jesus Christ as the true servant of the Lord, followed in chapter 53 by the detailed examination of this One under three categories: (1) the cross, 53:1-3; (2) the tomb, 53:4-9; (3) the resurrection, 53:10-12. It was Philip who was led by the Spirit of God to join the chariot of the Ethiopian eunuch who was reading the prophet Isaiah (Acts 8:26-31). The passage he was reading was from Isaiah 53. "And the eunuch answered Philip, and said, I pray thee, of whom speaketh the prophet this? of himself, or of some other man? Then Philip opened his mouth, and began at the same scripture, and preached unto him Jesus" (Acts 8:34-35). This passage speaks of Israel's Messiah.

Using a brief outline, let us meditate upon the three verses of Isaiah 52:13-15.

A. The Servant and His Position, 52:13
    1. The Exclamation: "Behold," "Lo," "Look."
        Something of the utmost importance is going to be stated.
    2. The Subject: "My Servant."
        It is not a king that is introduced, but a servant. He is One who is sent by God to accomplish a work and to fulfill a mission (cp. Isaiah 42:1-4). God says, "Behold my servant" (Isa. 52:13). Pilate says, "Behold the man" (John 19:5), and "Behold your king" (John 19:15).
    3. The Action
        a. The perfect obedience of His entire life
            "Shall act prudently."
        b. The resultant exaltation by the Father
            "He shall be exalted and lifted up and he shall be very high." These three expressions are not synonymous, but progressive, and are a result of the life He lived. They refer to (1) the resurrection; (2) the ascension; and (3) the seating (Eph. 1:20-22).
    4. The Astonishment

"Just as many will be astonished at Him . . ."
- a. The object of the astonishment: The Messiah
- b. The subjects of the astonishment: the believing remnant who will come to believe in Him when He comes again, and they see Him whom they have pierced.

B. The Messiah and His Sufferings, 52:14
1. His Face
"(so disfigured in His appearance from man . . ."
It was His face that was marred more than that of any man.
2. His Physical Form
"and His beauty from the sons of men)"
His form was disfigured more than the sons of Adam. The Hebrew scholar, Delitzsch, translates this, "His appearance and His form were altogether distortion . . . ."

C. The King and His Glory, 52:15
1. His Objective Ministry: The Action Caused by Him
"so He shall startle many Gentiles."
He is going to startle the Gentiles as well as Israel that He was in truth the Messiah.
2. His Subjective Ministry: The Action of the Kings toward Him
"Kings shall close their mouths before Him."
They will do this because of astonishment and reverence. "Because they shall see that which was not revealed to them, and they shall come to perceive that which they have not heard."
What could not have been told them by any man and was previously unheard of, they shall see and shall understand when they see Him in all of His glory, yet with nail scarred hands.

Let us return to this very significant verse of Isaiah 52:14. The first word is a reference to His face. In the Hebrew it signifies the disfiguring of the face. The second word is a reference to His physical form. When they looked at the Son, what did they see at this time? Isaiah 53:2b tells us, "He hath no form nor comeliness: and when we shall see him, there is no beauty that we should desire him." Three

things are involved in these words:
(1) *No form* refers to His being, showed His body was beyond recognition.
(2) *No honor* is due to the fact that He is rejected by His own people, crowned with thorns as a symbol of the curse, and partakes of a rebel's scourging and death. Hanging on a tree makes Him, according to the law, an accursed thing (Gal. 3:13).
(3) *No sight* (Literally: "There is no sight so that we should desire Him"). There are no reasons why we should look on Him. The sight is repugnant to our esthetic nature. Israel did not want a suffering savior; they wanted a conquering deliverer. He did not answer to their ideal. Barabbas did. They did not want someone spiritual, but, someone political. Sin was troubling them; therefore a Savior from sin could not delight them.

Why was Jesus in such a condition that both His face and physical form were disfigured from that of man? Let us review the Savior's sufferings.

The trial before Annas:
   1. John 18:22, "The servant struck Jesus with the palm of his hand."
The trial before Caiaphas:
   2. Mark 14:65; Matt. 26:67; Luke 22:64.
       They buffet Him, which is "to strike with the fist" from the Greek word, "the knuckles."
   3. They smote Him with the palms of their hands.
The trial before Pilate:
   4. Matt. 27:26; John 19:2.
       They scourged Him. This must have been all over His body.
   5. Mark 15:17; John 19:3.
       They plaited a crown of thorns and put it about His head.
   6. Mark 15:19.
       They kept on smiting Him on the head with a reed (rod).
   7. John 19:3.
       They smote Him with their hands.

After the trials:
    8.   Matt. 27:35; John 19:18.
          They crucified Him.

It is because of our Lord's great disfiguring that He sought all the more to prove to His disciples that it was He who was alive after His resurrection (Luke 24:39-43), and His disciples required all the more proof to be sure it was He (John 20:25-29).

The world, still in their unbelief, sees Jesus as the object of ridicule and mockery. They still would crown Him with a crown of thorns in their hatred for Him.

By faith we who believe see Jesus crowned with glory and honor (Heb. 2:9). He who once was crowned with the symbol of the curse, now wears the garland of the highest honor. As the perfect servant of Jehovah, God has supremely exalted Him, and given Him a name which is above every name: that at the name of Jesus every knee should bow, of things in heaven, and things in earth, and things under the earth; and that every tongue should confess that Jesus Christ is Lord, to the glory of God the Father (Phil. 2:9-10).

Someday He shall appear wearing many crowns or diadems (Rev. 19:12). These crowns were ribbons or bands which indicate rulership and authority. In that day all shall know He is KING OF KINGS AND LORD OF LORDS (Rev. 19:16). The fact that He is who He is will startle many Gentiles as well as the whole nation of Israel. By faith we know who He is today.

The Response of the Sanhedrin

What was the reaction of the Sanhedrin at the sight of Jesus, the Man? "When the chief priests therefore and officers saw him, they cried out, saying, Crucify him, crucify him" (John 19:6a). The sufferings Christ had endured might have been enough for the people, but this was not enough for the Sanhedrin. Nothing but His death would suffice. His wounds would heal, they felt; His death would not. How wrong they were.

Pilate has reached the end. He is exasperated that they will not listen to reason. "Pilate saith unto them, Take ye him, and crucify him: for I find no fault in him" (John 19:6b).

Even though Pilate says this, yet this action is impossible for the Jews to do. Pilate has gone around in a circle. He started out with the statement, "Take ye him, and judge him according to your law" (John 18:31). This did not satisfy because the Jews wanted death. Now Pilate refers the entire case to their own actions. He will not simply ratify their decision. If they want crucifixion, let them do it. Pilate now is controlled also by emotion. The fact that they cannot crucify anyone seemingly does not enter his mind.

"I find no fault with him." It might do us well to gather together at this closing declaration, just how many times Pilate has rendered this verdict.

1. Luke 23:4; John 18:38 — 1st Trial before Pilate.
2. Luke 23:14 — 2nd Trial before Pilate
   (Luke 23:15 — Trial before Herod).
   (Matt. 27:19 — Pilate's wife's statement).
3. Matt. 27:23; Mark 15:14; Luke 23:22 — After the crowd renders their decision for the release of Barabbas.
4. Matt. 27:24 — The washing of Pilate's hands.
5. John 19:6 — After scourging.

He is the Holy One and the Just (Acts 3:14).

With Pilate referring the case to them, The Sanhedrin bring out to Pilate the real reason for their bringing Jesus to him asking for crucifixion. This is an entirely new complaint requiring new examination.

A New Charge

"The Jews answered him, We have a law, and by our law he ought to die, because he made himself the Son of God" (John 19:7).

But the Sanhedrin never examined the evidence concerning His deity. No man makes himself the Son of God. He either is or he is not. Since they would not take the evidence of His miracles, He Himself said there would be no sign but the sign of the prophet Jonah—death, burial, resurrection and the Gospel going to the Gentiles.

For being Prophet, Christ suffered the mockery following the trial of Caiaphas and the Sanhedrin. For being King,
Christ suffered the mockery of the Roman soldiers. For being
the Son of God, He suffered the mockery on the cross.

No longer is the Sanhedrin appealing to Roman law or a
Roman crime. They are appealing now to their own law and
to crime against that law, which, they feel, is Pilate's duty to
uphold since he is their governor.

"When Pilate therefore heard that saying, he was the
more afraid" (John 19:8). Up to this point Pilate had been
quite apprehensive about the entire proceedings. He had
heard of Jesus before, and everything he heard was good. He
knew that for envy the Sanhedrin had brought Jesus to him.
He had received his wife's stirring message. Above all of these
things, he had observed the composure of Jesus Christ during
the entire time, and this could not but have strongly
impressed Pilate. His prisoner was not like other men.

We must remember that Pilate is a Roman, and when he
hears of Jesus' claim of being the Son of God, he would
understand this according to his own background. Among the
various religions and traditions of the nations, the gods had
sons, and some of them appeared on earth. In Acts 14, when
the people saw what Paul and Barnabas had done in their
city, they thought, "The gods are come down to us in the
likeness of men" (v. 11).

In light of this new development, Pilate wants to speak
to Jesus one more time.

Further Investigation

"And went again into the judgment hall, and saith unto
Jesus, Whence art thou?" (John 19:9). When Pilate asked
Jesus, "Whence art thou," he is not asking for his earthly
origin, because Pilate already had sent Jesus to Herod when

he learned that He was a Galilean. He is asking in effect, "Are you from earth or from heaven?"

"But Jesus gave him no answer." This is the fourth time we have seen the silence of Jesus Christ before His enemies.

1. Before Caiaphas and the Sanhedrin.
   Matt. 26:62-63; Mark 14:61
2. Before Pilate in the first Trial.
   Matt. 27:12-14; Mark 15:3-5
3. Before Herod.
   Luke 23:9
4. Before Pilate in the second Trial.
   John 19:9.

In each case His silence was far more eloquent than any word He could have spoken. It is a mark of wisdom not only to speak but also to be silent.

Why was Christ silent at this point? Some have felt it was a question He could not answer with a "yes" or "no" to Pilate. Had He answered "yes," Pilate would have understood it in a pagan idea which would not have been right. He could not say that He was not the Son of God and, therefore, He said nothing. Certainly this cannot be the full explanation, because He who is truth surely could have witnessed and conveyed truth to Pilate so he could have understood.

Remember, however, what we have already discussed. When Pilate left speaking to Jesus Christ before in the Praetorium, he left asking the question: "What is truth." He never waited for the answer. Pilate at that time rejected truth, and he is not given any more truth with the exception of the fact he will be told of his sin and the reason for it (John 19:11). Christ broke his silence to Pilate for this one thing alone.

Stalker adds also, "Jesus would say nothing about whether He was the Son of God or not, because He did not wish to be released on this ground. Not as a Son of God, but as an innocent man, which Pilate had again and again acknowledged Him to be, was He entitled to be set free; and His silence called upon Pilate to act on this acknowledgement."

Krummacher states that had Christ disclosed His true person and nature to Pilate, it would only have increased

Pilate's responsibility and judgment. His act of silence was, therefore, an act of compassion and mercy.

Before we leave this, we need to realize even a further significance. Had Jesus Christ not have been the Son of God, He was duty-bound to stop such a thing right here. This is the only way He could have been a good man. Had He made the statement, "I am not the Son of God," the charges would have been dropped by the Sanhedrin, and the case dismissed. Since He did not make that statement, He will die. He will die, not because He made Himself the Son of God, but because He was in fact the Son of God. He will prove that He was by His resurrection from the dead.

Pilate is upset because Christ will not reply to his question. "Then saith Pilate unto him, Speakest thou not unto me? knowest thou not that I have power to crucify thee, and have power to release thee?" (John 19:10). The "me" is emphatic in the whole sentence. Oh how haughty is a little man in a big place. The only way he can show his importance is with words. Yet Pilate was speaking the truth in one respect. He could have released Christ, and because he did not, the responsibility for failing to do so was his.

Christ now breaks his silence to judge His judge.

Jesus Judges His Judge

"Jesus answered, Thou couldest have no power at all against me, except it were given thee from above: therefore he who delivered me unto thee hath the greater sin" (John 19:11).

Think of the dignity with which He speaks in such a situation as He was, with the intense pain in His body from the scourging. Christ judges the entire situation. It is not Pilate who is the judge, but He is the judge. Pilate is on trial. And here is the verdict of the righteous Judge. The Sanhedrin has the greater sin because they have sinned through wickedness, while Pilate is sinning through weakness. They have full knowledge, while Pilate does not. Pilate has been forced to try the case, while the Sanhedrin has been responsible for the indictment.

All the power Pilate has is that which is given "from

above." The Lord Himself has delegated that authority to men even though it would be used against Himself. He is the Creator of the ages (Heb. 1:3) and all that occurs in the various ages.

Notice also that sin is not the same. There are degrees in reference to sinning, and therefore, there are degrees in regard to punishment. Every man will be rewarded according to his works against the Truth at the Great White Throne Judgment, and that is why the books will be opened (Rev. 20:12-13).

The answer greatly impressed Pilate. It causes him to think rationally again, rather than emotionally. He returns, determined to release Jesus Christ.

Move and Countermove

"And from thenceforth Pilate sought to release him: but the Jews cried out, saying, If thou let this man go, thou art not Caesar's friend: whosoever maketh himself a king speaketh against Caesar" (John 19:12).

For every move Pilate makes, the Sanhedrin had a countermove, and a more effective move. Pilate was being backed into a corner. Being "Caesar's friend" was the most coveted position a politician could have, while to incur Caesar's wrath was always feared. Pilate was even now being investigated by the imperial throne, and to have a new charge brought against his administration was the last thing Pilate wanted. The Sanhedrin knew this, and they played it for all they could.

One of the last proverbs recorded of the wisest man in the Old Testament was "The fear of man bringeth a snare" (Prov. 29:25). It is always true. Pilate feared to do the right thing—the just thing—which his conscience told him he should do, because he feared for the consequences. A charge brought against him of releasing a man who claimed to be king over Israel, when such release brought a tumult among the Jews, would certainly be hard to explain. Furthermore, any local king would, in the eyes of Caesar, be in competition against him; and for a Roman governor to uphold such a one, would be a charge of high treason. If Pilate were convicted of malfeasance in office, it would mean banishment and perhaps even execution. The Emperor Tiberius was a despot who only too well enjoyed humiliating subordinates, particularly those who manifested any threat to himself. Philo, who lived at this time, tells us that the Sanhedrin had once before held this same threat over Pilate's head to secure what they wanted.

Pilate feared men, and it ensnared him. In place of doing what was right, and letting the chips fall where they will even if it be his own life, he sought to save his own neck, and to do so he had ultimately to sacrifice Christ. He sought to save his own life, but he lost it. The very thing that Pilate feared, occurred. It was not long before these same men did lodge a complaint against his administration to Rome. Pilate was recalled from office, banished, and took his own life. The Sanhedrin were engaged in political blackmail, and Pilate became a mere puppet in their hands. When they had had enough of him, they pulled the strings to have him removed in spite of his compromises with them. Pilate was too weak a person to say, "Here I stand," and so he yielded to their demands.

You will observe that the Sanhedrin began their proceedings before Pilate against Christ with the charge of treason against Rome, then sedition against Rome, then blasphemy according to their own law. Now if they do not get what they want, their charge will be against Pilate for high treason.

The Final Verdict

"When Pilate therefore heard that saying, he brought Jesus forth, and sat down in the judgment seat in place that is called the Pavement, but in the Hebrew, Gabbatha" (John 19:13).

Jesus is brought out once again to the crowd after having been privately interviewed by Pilate. Pilate sat down on the Bema seat so that what action he now takes will be official. The sentence must be pronounced in the presence of the accused.

The incident is so important for the whole world that John marks the exact place, day and approximate time in the

Roman world. "And it was the preparation of the passover, and about the sixth hour: and he saith unto the Jews, Behold your King!" (John 19:14).

Some hold that it is impossible for it to be "about the sixth hour," but this is not so. The events of the trials, particularly before Pilate, are given by the four evangelists in great detail because of the importance of what was occurring, while the actual time involved could have been very short. If it were about 6:30, it would still only leave two and one half hours for moving out to Mount Calvary, digging the holes for the crosses, crucifying each prisoner, with probably Jesus crucified last. John records it was—about the sixth hour Roman time.

From all indications, Pilate knows Jesus will not be released, but perhaps there is one ray of hope still left in the back of Pilate's mind, "I want to give them one more chance." For this reason, he says, "Behold your King!" Moreover, because he is seated on the Judgment Seat, their decision, as well as his, is official.

"But they cried out, Away with him, away with him, crucify him. Pilate saith unto them, Shall I crucify your King?" (John 19:15).

This is the last Pilate will say to them. The response of the chief priest is the record of history: "The chief priests answered, We have no king but Caesar."

The nation has just officially committed national suicide. They not only reject their true Messiah, they accept the head of the nation from whom will arise the Man of Sin. For the rejection of Jesus Christ, the nation will suffer the destruction of their City and those within it, and will be in exile among the nations; for their making Caesar their king, they shall suffer the period our Lord called "the great tribulation."

"Then delivered he him therefore unto them to be crucified" (John 19:16). The Sanhedrin won the case, not by justice but by craft and the clamour of the populace. This was true in spite of the fact that one of the finest laws of the Romans at this time, or may have come into existence because of this incident was, "The idle clamour of the populace is not to be regarded, when they call for a guilty man to be acquitted, or an innocent one to be condemned" (*Law* 12, *Code de Poenis*).

Pilate signed the sentence for the crucifixion of Jesus Christ, and with it gave in writing an extract of the crime He had committed which was to be placed over the head of the condemned criminal so that the public might know for what crime He died. Since there was only one crime and there was ample space, Pilate wrote the crime in three languages: Hebrew (Aramaic) and Greek and Latin (John 19:20).

Jesus of Nazareth the King of the Jews

The chief priests went to Pilate and objected, but on this Pilate would not concede (John 19:21-22). From this we know that Pilate was in charge of the crucifixion, not the Sanhedrin, for in that case they would have written what they wanted. This way they could not change what Pilate had written even though it galled them.

Why Jesus Christ Will Die

Jesus Christ will die, but on what grounds will He die? It is not that He has done anything wrong in any point, or because He has been guilty of any sin. No one brought any accusation before Him that was at all substantiated by fact, nor was He to die because He was convicted of any transgression. On the contrary, on five different occasions Pilate pronounced the Lord innocent, and yet He will die.

But why?

He will die because the Jews rejected Him through their leaders—the Sanhedrin—and the Gentiles rejected Him through their leaders—Herod and Pilate.

The Lord Jesus Christ came into the midst of His own creation, but His own people, Israel, received Him not (John 1:11). Therefore, He made it possible that any, whoever they may be, who receives Him, to them He gives the right to be the direct, immediate creation of God (John 1:12).

The Lord Jesus Christ will die as the Lamb of God that takes away the sin of the world (John 1:29). He had no sin (Heb. 7:26), so He can bear the sins of many (Heb. 9:28). He will become God's answer to the sin problem—*and His only answer.* "And as Moses lifted up the serpent in the wilderness, even so must the Son of man be lifted up that whosoever believeth in Him should not perish but have eternal life. For God so loved the world that He gave His only begotten Son, that whosoever believeth in Him should not perish, but have everlasting life. For God sent not His Son into the world to condemn the world; but that the world through Him might be saved. He that believeth on Him is not condemned: but he that believeth not is condemned already, because he hath not believed on the name of the only begotten Son of God" (John 3:15-18).

Jesus Christ died in the plan and program of God that whoever believes in Him might have heaven as a free gift without works or merit. If salvation could have come to anyone in any other way, then Christ's death was in vain (Gal. 2:21). But it could not, "for there is none other name under heaven given among men, whereby we must be saved" (Acts 4:12). Jesus Christ is not a Savior; He is "the Savior of the world" (John 4:42). It is the Son, and only the Son, who is the propitiation, or satisfaction before the Father, for our sins (I John 2:2). There is no other substitute, no other mercy seat. The Father is satisfied with *nothing* else than His Son.

Jesus is not on trial; *you* are on trial. Not only so, but you are the judge. What will *you* do now with the Lord Jesus Christ? Will you accept Him as your substitute, and His death as your death before a holy and righteous Father? Or will you, like Pilate, seek to get around making a decision, seeking to postpone the issue and doing that which is right until it is too late, and you are trapped by your own scheming? The issue no longer is what will Pilate do with Him, but what will *you* do with the Savior? You are now on trial. Render your verdict of Him!

Chapter 15

Spiritual Truths from the Study of the Trials

While going through the trials, an attempt has been made to bring out a few of the more significant applications that may be drawn from the various episodes, but it will be well now to stand back and look at the entire six trials and appropriate the spiritual truths gained from an understanding of the whole. It is always true in Scripture that the whole is greater than the sum of the individual parts. It is not the purpose here specifically to review any of the previous lessons or truths, but rather to seek to answer why more space has been devoted by the Holy Spirit of God to this segment of Christ's life than to any other portion. What are the lessons to us as we examine the totality of the six trials? Knowing the facts of what has occurred is only the means of answering this final and important question.

The Sinlessness of the Lord Jesus Christ

It appears there is one major truth the Holy Spirit is seeking to establish, namely, that the Lord Jesus Christ is sinless. All during the trials, He never sinned. Moreover, His whole life was examined, and no one accused Him of one wrong word or act—just as He said, "which of you convinceth me of sin" (John 8:46). His enemies scrutinized every aspect of His life in order to try to find some accusation or some means by which they might accuse Him, but they found nothing.

You will remember that Daniel's life was also searched in order to try to find an accusation (Dan. 6:4), yet men could find nothing except his piety and devotion to his God. Our Lord is greater than Daniel. He had enemies that listened to every word He spoke, seeking to trap Him in His speech or by His actions, but they found nothing (cp. John 7:45-52). The examination given Christ was far more extensive and intensive than that of Daniel, and it existed, furthermore, over His entire ministry, yet they found nothing.

The trials witness that Jesus Christ did not sin before the trials and that He did not sin in the trials. As we follow His life after this, we find that He did not sin either on the way to the cross or on the cross itself. Therefore the Lord Jesus Christ died sinless. That is why the Epistles testify so emphatically, "He did no sin" (I Pet. 2:22); "He knew no sin" (II Cor. 5:21); and "in Him is no sin" (I John 3:5). Peter addresses Him as the Holy One and the just (Acts 3:14). The writer of Hebrews attests that He was sinless (Heb. 7:26). The angel Gabriel, who stands in the presence of God, called Him "Holy" (Luke 1:35). The trials reveal, then, first and foremost, this one basic truth: Jesus Christ is the sinless Son of God.

As the historical account continues, the cross that follows reveals the second significant and vital truth: He is our substitute. His death is vicarious; He died that we do not have to die.

The one truth is as important as the other. You must have a sinless Savior or you have no Savior at all. His death could have meant nothing more than what modernism says of it, had Jesus Christ not been sinless. This is what changes Calvary and the doctrine of the atonement from being merely the death of a martyr dying for a principle that he held, or any other such inadequate or erroneous concept, into a vicarious, propitiatory death. Vicarious means He died in the place of the sinner; He was the sinner's substitute. Propitiatory means that He made complete satisfaction for sins to the Father. What changes Calvary to become a place of propitiation, and the Lord's death vicarious, is *who He is*. We all know what He did. He died on a cross. This is not in question. *Who* died on that cross makes the difference in what happened. As Peter expresses it, "Christ also hath once suffered for sins, the just for the unjust, that he might bring us to God" (I Pet. 3:18).

Since God was in Christ and sinless, He could taste death for every man on the cross so that all can be saved (cp. Heb. 2:9). He makes reconciliation possible between God and man (II Cor. 5:18-19), but it all goes back to whom the Person is. The trials reveal the Person, His character and nature, and so establish the nature of His work on the cross.

It needs to be stressed emphatically that if Christ is going to die for others, He has to be sinless. There is no other way that He may be the Savior of the world. If He were not sinless, He would have had to die for His own sins; because He was sinless, He can die for the sins of others. Since this is so very important, the Scriptures devote much space to it. Thus the trials examine and re-examine Christ from every angle, but find nothing. He, through it all, exposes His enemies' sins, but manifests that He Himself is "holy, harmless, undefiled, separate from sinners" (Heb. 7:26). He did not need "to offer up sacrifice, first for his own sins, and then for the people's" (Heb. 7:27). He could offer up Himself as the one sacrifice for sins forever because He was sinless.

What more could be said or done to prove the sinlessness of Jesus Christ that has not been done in these trials? The answer is nothing. The Holy Spirit has labored to prove this point simply because it is so essential to our salvation. All the rest of the instruction and lessons that we derive from these trials is subordinate to this theme. This is primary; all others are secondary. It is this truth that Peter takes and expounds so pointedly when he says, "Who did no sin, neither was guile found in his mouth: who, when he was reviled, reviled not again; when he suffered, he threatened not; but committed himself to him that judgeth righteously: who his own self bare our sins in his own body on the tree, that we, being dead to sins, should live unto righteousness: by whose stripes ye were healed" (I Pet. 2:22-24).

The Perfection of the Lord Jesus Christ

Beside the sinlessness of the Lord Jesus Christ stands the complement of this truth—His perfection. His sinlessness is the negative approach, while His perfection is the positive approach. It is not merely the fact that He did not break the law at any point, but the truth that He kept the law in all points. He is the One who loved the Lord His God with all of His heart, and with all of His soul, and with all of His mind. He it was who also loved His neighbor as Himself (cp. Matt. 22:37-39). It is this positive aspect of righteousness He possessed whereby He is called "Holy" and "Righteous" (Acts 3:14).

Just as in salvation of the sinner, it is not enough to have his sins forgiven and removed, since this only makes a person neutral. God's program is to justify the sinner, or legally declare him righteous, having clothed him with the righteousness of the Lord Jesus Christ Himself. Thus the sinner not only has the sin issue taken care of by God, but he is accepted by the Father because he has been given the positive standing of the very righteousness of Jesus Christ. Likewise, the trials show that Jesus Christ is sinless, but they reveal far more than this. In them we see the perfection of perfect humanity. This is what true man should be and how he should act under stress and duress. In the Lord alone we see One completely devoted to the will of the Father. Having prayed in the Garden and thus known the Father's will, He traveled the road set before Him without questioning the Father's plan.

When our lives are put beside His life, we see all the more our imperfection and sinfulness, for we have never lived such a life; and, moreover, we cannot live such a life. If the Lord Jesus Christ had only lived His life among us—and that was all—He would have condemned all of us who have fallen short of the perfect standard of righteousness which is seen in Jesus Christ. Our lives, compared to His life, only reveal all the more our sins and sinfulness. While some among us have sinned more than others, we "all have sinned and come short of the glory of God" (Rom. 3:23).

We have not lived a life like He lived as exemplified in these trials. But the wonderfulness of it all is that He did not come just to live such a life that would show me my sin and condemn me because of my failure to live His righteousness. This is the very heart of the Gospel message. For the Father has made the Son, who knew no sin, to be sin for us that we might be made the righteousness of God in him (II Cor. 5:21). He lived a life I cannot live, and He died a death I cannot die. Through faith in Him, I am the recipient of both.

In the trials not only do we see the perfection of the Son loving completely and totally the Father, but we see how He loved His neighbor in the same way. He was dying for His people Israel and for their sins, as the Old Testament prophets as well as the New Testament verify (Ps. 69:9; Isa. 53:4-6, 8, 11; Matt. 1:21; John 11:50-52 etc.). He was dying for the sins of the whole world (Luke 3:6; John 3:16; Rom. 10:13; Tit. 2:11; II Peter 3:9; I John 2:2). He was also giving Himself for His disciples and for His church (John 15:13; Gal. 1:4; Eph. 5:2, 25; Tit. 2:14; I John 3:16; Rev. 1:5). Yet the wonder of it all is that each of us can make it personal, even as Paul did. Jesus Christ "loved me and gave Himself for me" (Gal. 2:20). It is the Lord of whom the writer of Hebrews says: "Who for the joy that was set before him endured the cross, despising the shame, and is set down at the right hand of the throne of God" (Heb. 12:2). He was seeking "in bringing many sons unto glory" (Heb. 2:10), and so endured all that He suffered through the trials and the cross in order that this might be an accomplished fact. No one else ever loved completely and totally his neighbor as himself. We see this love in the trials and on through the cross that followed as a consequence.

But there is one other aspect of the perfection of the Lord Jesus, and it is a paradox. The perfect Son was made perfect by the things which He suffered. As the writer of Hebrews says, "Though he were a Son, yet learned he obedience by the things which he suffered; and being made perfect, he became the author of eternal salvation unto all them that obey him" (Heb. 5:8-9). The Son learned obedience, and to do so had to experience trials in which He Himself suffered in the will and program of God, i.e., for no other reason than that it was the Father's will. As Adam fell through disobedience, so the Son won salvation and became complete and perfect through obedience. The Father made the Son "perfect through suffering" (Heb. 2:10). He who was perfect deity was brought to full perfection in His humanity. The Lord's humanity was (negatively) sinless, and (positively) perfect. He was all that the Father wanted at every stage of His development as a person, and in His manhood ministry the Lord Jesus exemplified the right attitude and response in everything He was asked to experience. He was made perfect through the experiences and sufferings He endured. In that He Himself hath suffered, being tested, and tried, he is able to come to the aid of us who are tested also (Heb. 2:18). The trials illustrate a significant portion of His suffering which culminated with His cross, and all of this was used by the Father "to make the captain of [our] salvation perfect through suffering" (Heb. 2:10). The trials give us part of the process of the perfection of the Son.

The Sinfulness of Man and His Ways

The finest lace shows its perfection against the blackest background. The purity and perfection of the Lord's person is given to us in Scripture against the blackest background of man's vilest actions. This was man's hour in which the corruption and depravity of the heart of man was demonstrated against the perfect Son of Man.

Man under God has been given authority in two specific areas: (1) religion and (2) government. Since the time of Noah, men have exercised authority over other men either to lead them in the worship of the true God, or away from Him; and either to help establish law, order and justice, or to destroy law, order and justice. In primitive tribes the witch doctor and the chieftain are two separate functions. At the time of Christ, these two functions were combined in the responsibility of the Sanhedrin. In their situation, divine revelation and law, given directly from God Himself, was to govern everything they did. Yet nowhere could be found a greater misuse of power and authority than is demonstrated in the trials of Christ, where every principle or moral decency is violated, to say nothing about precedence and established procedures.

Not only was this true in Israel, but the situation with Herod and Pilate and their political expediency was no better. God did this that the whole world might stand guilty before God in the death of His Son, in order that the Lord might have mercy upon all. What had been established by God for the good of mankind was turned into evil. What He had destined to maintain law and order and give justice, was now used so as to give injustice—in the name of religion and in the name of governmental authority. Here is what we see so vividly portrayed through the entire procedure of the trials.

Still today the same threat exists. The very laws given by God to protect the good and the right, may be turned around to persecute the good and the right, and protect the guilty. Anything resembling what is happening today is purely intuitional. We are seeing the complete breakdown of God's established order based upon the principles of His absolute authority—Scripture. Men claim there are no absolutes, so therefore, anything that the majority says is right (democracy), is right. This philosophy will culminate in that found in the great tribulation when the man of lawlessness will set himself up as the only authority and abolish all other authority. Not only will the Lord Jesus Christ judge him, but His judgment is seen also upon both the religious and the economic Babylons of that time, or the religious and governmental authorities as they have developed at this period. Their wickedness becomes ripe for judgment as they promote and perpetuate just the opposite of what God had intended and instructed them to do as revealed in Scripture.

Man is sinful and vile, and the heart of man deceitful above all things, but never is this so vividly seen as in the trials, and the crucifixion which was the natural outcome. And our Lord said, "Remember the word that I said unto you. The servant is not greater than his lord. If they have persecuted me, they will also persecute you" (John 15:20). As Paul put it, "All that will live godly in Christ Jesus shall suffer persecution" (II Tim. 3:12). In direct proportion as we expose sin like Jesus Christ exposed it, and as we live a godly life and reveal heresy, we likewise will suffer—for the servant is not above his Lord.

The Injustices Done Demand a Day of Justice

Justice was neither given nor received in the entire procedure of the trials, yet God being God, He must be righteous and, therefore, He must clear the innocent and condemn the guilty. Justice must prevail, and so it will. This is the message God proclaimed to all men when He raised Christ from the dead. God highly exalted Him (Phil. 2:9), and so declared His innocence. Paul says that in the resurrection the Father declared to all that Jesus Christ is the Son of God (Rom. 1:4). Peter proclaims this truth over and over in the messages of Acts, as for instance on the Day of Pentecost he said,

"Ye men of Israel, hear these words; Jesus of Nazareth, a man approved of God among you by miracles and wonders and signs, which God did by him in the midst of you . . . Him . . . ye have taken, and by wicked hands have crucified and slain: whom God had raised up, having loosed the pains of death: because it was not possible that he should be holden of it" (Acts 2:22-24).

Why could He not be holden or held to it? Because He was completely innocent, and they were the guilty ones. It is on this basis that Peter urges the whole nation of Israel to repent and publicly do an about face so that this sin might be forgiven them (cp. 2:36-40). The subsequent messages of Peter in Acts present the same truth (cp. 3:13-16, 19, 26; 4:10-12; 5:30-31; 10:38-42).

This is, likewise, Paul's message as the Gospel goes out throughout the Gentile's world. At Athens he testified:

"Forasmuch then as we are the offspring of God, we ought not to think that the Godhead is like unto gold, or silver, or stone, graven by art and man's device. And the times of this ignorance God winked at [overlooked]; but now commandeth all men every where to repent: because he hath appointed a day, in the which he will judge the world in righteousness by that man whom he hath ordained; whereof he hath given assurance unto all men, in that he hath raised him from the dead" (Acts 17:29-31).

Jesus Christ was raised because He was innocent and sinless, but His resurrection was the pledge that all will be judged by Him *in righteousness*, even those who tried Him. He will not give these in that day injustice as He received from them, but they will receive complete and perfect justice. Even in the Old Testament the injuction was the "God shall bring every work into judgment, with every secret thing, whether it be good, or whether it be evil" (Eccl. 12:14). This program has never changed. Progressive revelation has only shown that all judgment is committed to the Son (John 5:22) "who will render to every man according to his deeds" (Rom. 2:6).

No one can honestly read the accounts of these trials without realizing the inequities done, and also realize that there must be, and will be, a future day of accountability when the Righteous and Holy One will be rewarded fully, and the wicked will be judged and punished righteously. The injustices done demand it. For God to be God, it shall come to pass. The day will come when every knee shall bow and confess, "Lord Jesus Christ," to the glory of God the Father (Phil. 2:11).

Jesus Christ, Our Forerunner

The title "Forerunner" is used of the Lord Jesus Christ in Hebrews 6:20 where Jesus is said to be our Forerunner who has entered into the very presence of God. While the term is used of what Jesus Christ is now for us, the concept is seen to apply in all aspects of our Lord's activity. He is our Leader, our Shepherd, our Forerunner. He always goes before and leads the way for His sheep. He only asks us to experience testing or trial that He Himself has already experienced, and been victorious—showing us the way.

This is true in the area of suffering and trials. Not only does the Lord experience these testings first, but He experiences them to a greater extent than that through which He ever asks us to go. No other one suffered in life and time more than what the Lord Jesus Christ did from the Garden of Gethsemane to that of Mount Calvary. And the trials are an integral part of what the Lord experienced.

Whenever we are tested in any area, we can know our Lord has first been tested in this area even to a greater extent. "Wherefore in all things it behooved him to be made like unto his brethren, that he might be a merciful and faithful high priest in things pertaining to God. . . . For in that he himself hath suffered being tempted, he is able to succour them that are tempted" (Heb. 2:17-18). Or as later the same writer says, "For we have not an high priest which cannot be touched with the feeling of our infirmities; but was in all points tempted like as we are, yet without sin" (4:15). The trials, together with the cross that followed, demonstrate the sufferings of our Lord, which were total (in every area), intense, and prolonged. This was men's hour, and whatever men willed to do, he did to the Son of man.

Jesus Christ, Our Example

The fact that the Lord Jesus Christ is the believer's example in suffering is a theme that Scripture itself expounds in great detail. There seems to be various ways in which He is the example for Christians; and although some of these are interrelated, by categorizing them, one can better see the many different lessons that the sufferings Christ endured through the trials and subsequent death teach us.

1. *Christ Did Not Sin in Attitude, nor by Word or Action.* The exhortation is, then, to us that we are to be careful not to sin either by attitude, word or action when we go through unjust trials. First Peter 2:21-23 says: "Christ also suffered for us, leaving us an example, that ye should follow his steps: who did no sin, neither was guile found in his mouth: who, when he was reviled, reviled not again; when he suffered, he threatened not. . . ."

It is very easy for us as believers to allow the old sin nature to take control when we are unjustly accused or wronged. Whenever we have wrong attitudes, it ultimately shows itself in wrong speech and action. The old sin nature is never timid or bashful at such a time. Our concern in such circumstances is never to get under the circumstances and give in to the flesh.

2. *Christ Committed Himself and His Trials to the Father and Trusted in Him.* He becomes our example to do the same when we experience trials and unjustly are called upon to suffer due to no reason in ourselves. It is this truth that Peter goes on to refer to in the same passage previously quoted. "When he suffered, he threatened not; but committed himself to him that judgeth righteously" (I Pet. 2:23).

Such commitment is based upon a knowledge of the character and attributes involved within the Godhead. In the case of the Lord Jesus Christ, He knew that the Father does not and cannot change; He is immutable. Since He is the same, and He was righteous before in all His ways, He commits His present trial, through which He is going, to One who cannot do wrong. What our Lord did all through the trials culminated on the cross. What we cannot understand by sight or insight we must "trust" to the Father. The word signifies *He rolled Himself and His case on the Lord.* The only thing Christ was accused of that had a basis in fact was while He was on the cross. There someone accused Him, not of sin, but of trusting in the Lord (Matt 27:43). The only accusation that they could bring against Him was to ridicule Him for His piety.

It is this very attitude that we are to display. We are to commit ourselves to Him who judges righteously because we judge Him trustworthy. Such a life involves living by faith, in light of what the Word of God presents about the Lord's character and person. The Lord speedily rewards such a life lived before Him. "Wherefore let them that suffer according to the will of God commit the keeping of their souls to him in well doing, as unto a faithful Creator" (I Pet. 4:19).

3. *Christ Was Completely Devoted to the Father and to the Accomplishment of His Will.* It is this that was accomplished in the Garden, and the Lord Jesus, all through the trials, never wavered. What an example for us!

This devotion and dedication is what Paul had more than anything else, and was the reason why he admonished believers to follow him even as he followed Christ (I Cor. 4:16; 11:1; Phil. 3:17; 4:9). He desired to lay hold of the purpose and reason for which the Lord Jesus Christ had laid hold of him (Phil. 3:12), and press toward that mark. At the end of his life, he could say, "I have finished my course" (II Tim. 4:7). Nothing else was dear to Paul. In fact, he so testified of this fact, "But none of these things move me, neither count I my life dear unto myself, so that I might finish my course with joy, and the ministry which I have received of the Lord Jesus" (Acts 20:24).

Scripture recounts, moreover, that this was the whole devotion of the Son on earth. The Lord Jesus told His disciples, "My meat is to do the will of him that sent me and to finish his work" (John 4:34). In His high priestly prayer in John 17, He said to the Father, "I have glorified thee on the earth: I have finished the work which thou gavest me to do" (v. 4). It is in this area also that the Lord is our example, and our whole desire should be to complete those "good works, which God hath before ordained that we should walk in them" (Eph. 2:10).

4. *Christ Loved Even When Others Mistreated Him.* The Lord Jesus in His life fully exemplified His own teaching, and in this becomes an example for us. He had said, "Love your enemies, bless them that curse you, do good to them that hate you, and pray for them which despitefully use you, and persecute you . . . For if ye love them which love you, what reward have ye? do not even the publicans the same? and if ye salute your brethren only, what do ye more than others? do not even the publicans so?" (Matt. 5:44-47).

The Lord's love for His enemies is seen all through the trials and culminates with His words from the cross, "Father, forgive them; for they know not what they do" (Luke 23:34). It was this same attitude exemplified by Stephen when he was being stoned. "And he kneeled down, and cried with a loud voice, Lord, lay not this sin to their charge . . ." (Acts 7:60).

It was because of His love that He did not revile or threaten but rather dealt honestly, firmly and yet in grace. In this He has given us an example that we should follow in His steps.

5. *Christ was Perfected through Suffering.* This truth has already been dealt with, but not from the standpoint that it

is an example for believers; and yet it is. Just as our Lord was made "perfect through sufferings" (Heb. 2:10), so it is true of us. As someone has well expressed it, "God had one Son without sin, but He has no sons without sufferings."

The writer of Hebrews uses this truth as in exhortation to believers when he writes:

"For consider him that endured such contradiction of sinners against himself, lest ye be wearied and faint in your minds. Ye have not yet resisted unto blood [martyrdom] striving against sin. And ye have forgotten the exhortation which speaketh unto you as unto children, My son, despise not thou the chastening of the Lord . . ." (Heb. 12:3-11).

The Lord allows suffering and trials to come upon us in order to mature us, and this is why, James says, we are to reckon it all joy when He brings them upon us (James 1:3-4). Peter, furthermore, ends his first epistle with the truth: "But the God of all grace, who hath called us unto his eternal glory by Christ Jesus, after that ye have suffered a while, make you perfect, stablish, strengthen, settle you" (I Pet. 5:10).

God has called us to suffer. "For unto you it is given in behalf of Christ, not only to believe on him, but also to suffer for his sake" (Phil. 1:29). "For what glory is it, if when ye be buffeted for your faults, ye shall take it patiently? but if, when ye do well, and suffer for it, ye take it patiently, this is acceptable with God. For even hereunto were ye called . . ." (I Pet. 2:20-21; cp. 3:17; 4:13-19).

6. *Christ Exemplifies the Divine Pattern—Suffering Now and Glory Later.* Through the experiences that the Lord went through, God has revealed to us a divine pattern or program that is for all believers and pilgrims on this earth. God's program calls for suffering first, and then glory to follow. Peter tells us, "The prophets . . . testified beforehand the sufferings of Christ and the glory that should follow" (I Pet. 1:11). In just the same way, this is seen as the pattern for believers. The words of Paul repeatedly designate this order. "For I reckon that the sufferings of this present time are not worthy to be compared with the glory which shall be revealed in us" (Rom. 8:18). "For our light affliction, which is but for a moment, worketh for us a far more exceeding and

eternal weight of glory" (II Cor. 4:17). "If we suffer, we shall also reign with him: if we deny him, he also will deny us" (II Tim. 2:12).

Just like the Lord, our glory comes after the suffering and the patient endurance of the present time. Our reward is still in the future.

7. *The Example of Doing Nothing When Anything One Does Would Be Wrong.* So very many times we are caught in the place where anything we do is wrong. There are times when the best thing is to say nothing, and do nothing. This is one of the hardest activities to perform, for the flesh finds it difficult to wait on God. It wants to take matters into its own hands.

Over and over again during the trials the Lord said nothing, so that at times they marveled (Isa. 53:7; Matt. 26:63; 27:14; Mark 15:3; Luke 23:9). As the prophet had said, "He shall not cry, nor lift up, nor cause his voice to be heard in the street" (Isa. 42:2).

He, furthermore, did nothing because this was their hour. Although He made a scourge of small cords and drove out the moneychangers and those who sold in the Temple (John 2:15), and although He walked through the midst of the crowd at Nazareth when they were determined to cast Him over the brow of the hill whereon their city was built (Luke 4:29), yet during all the trials, He was yielded completely to their will. Anything less than this would have been wrong. In His very inactivity and silence, He is our example, so that "he that saith he abideth in Him ought himself also so to walk, even as He walked" (I John 2:6).

The Lord Jesus Christ, then, becomes our example of "patient endurance" under trial. As pilgrims, we are to look beyond the present and immediate situation and keep our eyes upon the future. We are to live this life in light of the next. This is what the Lord did, and He is our example (Heb. 12:1-2).

Fellowship in His Sufferings

There is one other great spiritual truth concerning the trials of the Lord that is of major importance to the believer.

Paul writes in Philippians 3:10, "that I may know him [the Lord Jesus Christ] and the power of his resurrection." We would like to quote this verse and stop there, but Paul does not. He continues, "and the fellowship of his sufferings, being made conformable unto his death." It is this statement that is so significant; but in order to understand what Paul is speaking about, we must look at it in context.

Paul's personality and temperament is seen all through his epistles, but nowhere does it appear stronger than in Philippians, chapter 3. Whatever Paul did, he went into it with his whole heart and soul. His philosophy seemed to be that if something was worth anything, it was worth everything. When he was a Pharisee, Paul's zealousness caused the church to suffer severely. He had, furthermore, much, humanly speaking, in which he might glory, and it is these things that he enlarges upon in 3:4-6. "If any other man thinketh that he hath whereof he might trust in the flesh, I more: Circumcised the eighth day, of the stock of Israel, of the tribe of Benjamin, an Hebrew of the Hebrews, as touching the law, a Pharisee; concerning zeal, persecuting the church; touching the righteousness which is in the law, blameless."

> He could glory in race.
>> He was a Jew, not a Gentile.
> He could glory in customs and traditions.
>> Among the Jews, he was a Hebrew, not a Hellenist.
> He could glory in orthodoxy.
>> Among the Hebrews, he was a Pharisee, not a Sadducee.
> He could glory in activity.
>> Among the Pharisees, he was zealous, not apathetic.
> He could glory in ritual.
>> Among the zealous, he was blameless, not ceremonially unclean.

All of these things would be gain for Paul, had he continued in Pharisaism, for he would have probably been as great, if not greater, than his teacher, Gamaliel.

Yet all of this came to be for nought when the Lord Jesus Christ appeared to Paul, and he did a complete about-face. After the Damascus road experience, these things Paul had prided himself in were no longer what he sought. Now his zeal and all of his efforts were in another direction—an opposite direction.

He writes, "But what things were gain to me, those I counted loss for Christ" (v. 7). In Paul's new life there was no place for self-glory whatever, and if any came in, it was loss for Christ and for His work. All that he had going for him in the past meant nothing now, and was considered by him as nothing.

"Yea doubtless, and I count all things but loss for the excellency of the knowledge of Christ Jesus my Lord: for whom I have suffered the loss of all things, and do count them but dung, that I may win Christ" (v. 8). Paul was pressing just as strongly in his new direction to gain Christ and His approval as he had been to promote self in his life in Pharisaism. Paul was pressing for the top; he was throwing everything into it, and as such was throwing away all that he gloried in before. While formerly it was personal pride, now Paul's only motive was to win the approval of the Lord Jesus Christ. If his Master was pleased, nothing else mattered. If his Master was not pleased, all was loss.

"And he found in him, not having mine own righteousness, which is of the law, but that which is through the faith of Christ, the righteousness which is of God by faith" (v. 9). Paul wants no more legal righteousness which is based upon works done through the flesh. He wants faith righteousness, not only for justification, but for sanctification of life, since the just shall live by faith.

But Paul continues on. His desire now is to go on in Christian experience: "that I may know Him" (v. 10a). This might be translated into English, *come to know Him in experience. My desire,* Paul is saying, *is not just to know about Him, but Him.* You can know about a person without knowing the person himself. You can know about a person by being with someone who knew him; but you can only know someone personally by being with him yourself. Paul said to Timothy, "For I know whom I have believed" (1 Tim.

1:12). We are all too often content to say, "I know *what* I believe."

Besides Paul's desire to know Christ, he wants to know "the power of his resurrection" (v. 10b). The same power that caused the Lord Jesus Christ to rise from the dead, Paul wants in personal experience. The word for power here is *dunamis*. It is the same word for power used in Ephesians 1:19 when Paul prays that the saints might know "what is the exceeding greatness of his power to us-ward who believe" and then explains the standard of that power as being "according to the working of his mighty power which he wrought in Christ, when he raised him from the dead, and set him at his own right hand in the heavenly places, . . ." (1:20). Paul has already taught that we have experienced this power positionally when we came to believe the Gospel, for Romans 1:16 says, "For I am not ashamed of the gospel of Christ: for it is the power of God unto salvation. . . ." For Paul, salvation only commenced the beginning of life for him. His desire was for the personal appropriation of this power in his life continually.

But Paul knew a scriptural principle. No one can experience resurrection with its glory, without first experiencing suffering and death. One cannot be resurrected unless he has first died, and he cannot die who has not suffered death. Thus the only way he can come to know in experience the power of His resurrection is to come to know "the fellowship of his sufferings" (v. 10c).

The church at Philippi was fellowshipping with Paul in the spread of the Gospel (Phil. 1:5). This word "fellowship" signifies "to make common, to have things in common." It signifies sharing something with someone else. Thus it involved partaking of what the other has or does. Because the Philippians were fellowshipping with Paul in financial support, they were sharing with him in the furtherance of the Gospel. A person may fellowship not only financially, but he may fellowship with another in food, ideas, attitudes, and so forth. For instance, Philippians 2:1 speaks of "fellowship of the Spirit." What Paul is referring to in this passage is that each believer shares with every other believer in the same person and ministry of the Holy Spirit that God has given to us, and this being true, Paul wants there to be a unity of mind and direction because of this mutual sharing.

In Philippians 3:10, Paul's desire is to share in the sufferings of Christ for Paul feels that only as he shares in these sufferings that Christ experiences can he truly come to know in experience the Lord Jesus Christ. What, then, does Paul want? He wants to suffer unjustly, and not through any cause within himself. In such a situation, he wants to commit his trial to the Lord, and experience the grace that the Lord alone can give, and so be a positive witness in a negative situation.

What a contrast between Paul and us. The last thing we want to do is suffer, particularly unjustly. But the believers in the early church were different, and perhaps this is why they turned the world up-side down. They rejoiced when they were counted worthy to suffer for the sake of the Lord (Acts 5:41-42; 16:23, 25; I Cor. 4:9-13; II Cor. 6:10; Heb. 10:34; James 1:2ff; I Pet. 4:12-13).

This suffering that Paul wanted to share in, is something he wants perfected in his life to the extent that he is, through this, "being made conformable unto his death." Literally, the word "conformable" signifies "to bring to the same form with some other person or thing." Paul wanted to know the Lord Jesus in personal experience to such an extent that His resurrection power might be his, together with the mutual sharing of Christ's sufferings so that being completely yielded to the will of God and His likeness in meekness and lowliness, he could even die like Jesus Christ died and bear a positive testimony in death.

Paul's ambition is that which not many have had. You cannot throw yourself into anything more than this. Even as he wrote the book of Philippians in Rome, Paul was between life and death (Phil. 1:20) where it could be either one or the other for him. It is not a matter of sharing in Christ's atoning sufferings; Paul knew, even as Peter did, that he could never share in this (cp. John 13:36). Rather, he wants to share in the Lord's unjust sufferings for righteousness sake, for unto such was he called by the Lord (Acts 9:16). These unjust sufferings for the Lord began as a spiritual battle in Gethsemane, and they do not end until Christ's death on the cross. It involves all the sufferings of the trials which the Lord experienced. As Paul suffers in the same manner, he comes to know the Lord Jesus Christ in personal experience. "Therefore," Paul says, "I take pleasure in infirmities, in reproaches, in necessities, in persecutions, in distresses for Christ's sake: for when I am weak, then am I strong" (II Cor. 12:10).

I could leave it at this point, and very few would know that this subject was left incomplete; but let me share a most precious truth found within the Tabernacle and its furniture. Scripture very specifically tells us that the lampstand was one beaten work from a solid piece of pure gold: "all of it shall be one beaten work of pure gold" (Ex. 25:36). Since this article of furniture was to be made exactly as Moses had seen the pattern on the mount, God gave the Holy Spirit to men in order that they might have the ability to make the lampstand exactly as it should be (Ex. 35:30-35). The point to note is that every swing of the hammer against this block of gold was Spirit-directed with the result that in the end it would be an object of perfection.

What is the message that is being conveyed in this? Each article of furniture has definite significance. The pure gold of this lampstand speaks of our Lord Jesus Christ "who, being in the very form of God, thought being on an equality with God not something to hold on to with eager grasp, but made himself of no reputation, and took upon Him the form of a servant" (Phil. 2:6-7, literal translation).

As Christ was in the intrinsic form of God, He took on another entirely different form. The word used indicates that this was not just an outward conformity, but an internal, intrinsic change. However, it needs to be emphasized very clearly that in this voluntary change the Son did in relationship to the Father, He never lost His deity. He still was God all the way through the process. The gold was still gold. Only the gold submitted itself to be beaten—beaten into perfection—the Son submissive to the will of God the Father, whatever that will may be. Christ was before the process perfect deity, absolute holy in His being (i.e., pure gold), yet He was perfected by this experience (Heb. 2:10; 5:8-9; 7:26). This aspect of Christ's perfection is not manifested to the world; it is only seen in the holy place by believers and priests. It needs to be stated also that Christ never became the servant of men; He was the Father's servant—the servant of the Lord. Just as the Spirit was upon certain men that every blow to the block of pure gold would be Spirit-directed and result in what God desired for the lampstand, so everything that was allowed to come upon the Son was Spirit-directed to bring Him to perfection.

The believer needs to realize also that the hammer blows do not have anything to do with the cross-work of Jesus Christ in which He became the altar of God dealing with sin. This is the work of the brazen altar, and signifies what our Lord did upon the cross. This experience Christ went through is not the brazen altar experience, and it is, therefore, not judgment in reference to sin. It is His entire life experience in becoming the servant of the Lord, which involved His submission to go to the cross, but it involved much more (Heb. 2:9-10). This involved all that He experienced by being, at every moment in His life, a slave to God the Father and doing exactly what He alone demanded of Him: completely submissive to His will (Heb. 5:7-8; 10:9).

Christ, Who was in the form of God from all eternity past, had never experienced this until He becomes a servant. As God's servant, He gave Himself completely to every hammer blow that the Father wished Him to receive in His life at the *hand of men*. Thus, this experience was an involvement of His entire life, not just the cross. The beatings or blows He received were not judgment in relation to sin, but it involved His servant submission, and it involved a perfecting of Him even though He was already pure and holy.

There are the cross sufferings of Christ.

There are also the life sufferings of Christ.

> The contrast between the life and death sufferings are brought out in Isaiah 53:4, "Surely he hath borne our griefs and carried our sorrows [life sufferings]: yet we did esteem him stricken, smitten of God, and afflicted [death sufferings]."

The cross sufferings are concerned with sin and its expiation.

The life sufferings have nothing to do with sin's

expiation.

The cross sufferings provided our salvation.

The life sufferings provided His perfection.

The sufferings Christ endured at the hands of God on the cross, bearing our wrath, dying in our place and stead, is the work of the brazen altar.

The sufferings of Christ that He experienced in life at the hands of men as the servant of God, provided nothing in relationship to sin, but perfected Him as God's son, and is the work of making the beautiful lampstand.

The bitter agony of Gethsemane and the trials that followed were the climax of this entire servant ministry of Christ. Few have ever understood this. His agony, His sweat of drops of blood in the Garden never saved anyone. But they are a part—and the climactic part—of the perfection of the servant of the Lord as He prayed, "O my Father, if this cup may not pass away from me, except I drink it, Thy will be done" (Matt. 26:42). The gold that was beaten ultimately became glorified in the very presence of God, but it only was exalted because it was completely yielded to each hammer blow. The suffering Savior is now glorified in heaven itself, but He has been glorified only as a result of His perfect submission as the servant of the Lord.

Christ suffered in His life from three causes. First, in His holy character. He was an infinitely holy person, living in an atmosphere that hated righteousness and manifested that hatred. This is illustrated by Lot, who, being righteous, vexed his righteous soul by the things he saw and heard (II Pet. 2:7-8). The more separated a person is to the Lord and from evil, the more he feels the depths of sin and wickedness about him. Although Lot felt it, living in Sodom, he would not have felt it nearly as great as Abraham would have. The angels, moreover, who visited the city of Sodom, felt it severely, and subsequently they destroyed the city. No one could have felt sin, however, as strongly as the Lord Jesus Christ would have felt it.

Secondly, the Lord suffered in life because of His infinite compassion. He saw completely and accurately, the results that sin had caused, and being the God of love and mercy, must have suffered with mankind with infinite compassion. Yet He could do only that which was the Father's will, and only at specific times when the Father allowed Him to do something about the need around Him.

The feeding of the 5,000 (Luke 9:12; John 6:5).

The feeding of the 4,000 (Matt. 15:32; Mark 8:8).

The raising of the Widow's Son (Luke 7:11).

The healing of one man out of many, at the pool of Bethseda (John 5).

Many healings on one day (Mark 1:32-34; Luke 4:40).

The Lord suffered, thirdly, because of His omniscient anticipation. This seems to be the only explanation for the suffering He experienced in the Garden. He knew all that He was going to suffer on the cross even before He came to the cross itself. The Lord Jesus was not shrinking from physical death itself, but from the spiritual death that would take place between the Father and the Holy Spirit when He would be made sin. He was experiencing the experience before it was actual.

Even though Christ suffered much at the hands of men during His life, nevertheless no man was able to do anything that the Father had not willed and the Holy Spirit permitted. We know this (1) from the doctrine of election (Acts 2:23); (2) from the perfect obedience of the Son to the will of the Father (John 8:29); (3) from the fact that the Spirit was given to Him without measure (John 3:34); (4) from the fact that angels had charge concerning Him (Matt. 4:6; Ps. 91:11); and (5) from the fact that no man laid hands on Him until His time had come to go to the cross (John 7:30; 8:20; 12:23, 27; 13:1; 17:1). Man only laid hands on Him during the one day of the trials and crucifixion. Following His death on the cross only believers touched Him. Thus, the things that happened to Christ during His life were *all under the control of God.*

God takes time to make and perfect His servants, and this stands in contrast to man's ways. He took eighty years with Moses before God was ready to use him. He took a number of years with David, having him chased all over the country by Saul before the Lord brought David to the throne. Remember, then, this beaten work from one solid talent of pure gold took days to make. It stands in vivid contrast with another gold object, the "golden calf" which Aaron made, for that idol was cast from a mold (Ex. 32:4).

But this is only a part of the truth that the Spirit of God has for us. The lampstand itself consisted of three main parts: (1) the base, of which nothing is stated but which was an absolute necessity in order that the structure would be stationary; (2) the central shaft or lampstand; and (3) the branches. The base and the central shaft are treated as a unit, called "the candlestick" or better, "the lampstand." The branches are said to come out of the lampstand (Ex. 25:32-33), and the lampstand is definitely referred to as the central shaft (Ex. 25:34).

All of the tabernacle and its furniture represent things spiritual, as they will be found in heaven. This is why all Moses saw had to be made exactly, and he could not change anything. The base and central shaft of the lampstand give to us a vivid illustration of the person of our Lord Jesus Christ, while the six branches, which come out of the central shaft and are connected with it, portray the relationship the church enjoys inseparately joined with the Lord Jesus Christ and partaking of both His sufferings and His glory. But let us develop this point by point.

The word translated "shaft" is rendered "thigh" in Genesis 24:2, and "loins" in Genesis 46:26. As the children of Israel came from the loins of Jacob, so came the branches from this *shaft*. It gave them their being. They came from it and have its same life, nature and beauty. As this is true of the branches from the lampstand, so it is true of the church, which comes from Christ. She possesses His life and is adorned with His beauty. "He that sanctifieth and they who are sanctified are all *of one*" (Heb. 2:11).

Since the six branches were not artifically joined to the central shaft, they could never be severed from it. They may be compared to a body of many members, all having the same nature and life, and united by a common bond to the living Head. Because the lampstand is all one beaten work, the branches are just as secure, therefore, as the central shaft: they are eternally secure (John 10:29; Romans 8:38-39). Moreover, since the six branches spring out from the shaft, three on either side, no branch could say of any other branch, "I have no need of you" (cp. I Cor. 12:12-27).

By nature the branches are six, the number of man and imperfection. By nature we are the children of wrath, "but God who is rich in mercy, for his great love wherewith he loved us, even when we were dead in sins, hath quickened us together with Christ . . . and hath raised us up together, and made us sit together in heavenly places in Christ Jesus; that in the ages to come he might shew the exceeding riches of his grace in his kindness toward us through Christ Jesus" (Eph. 2:4-7). Being united with Christ we reach perfection.

We are so connected with Christ that we have an intrinsic relationship to Him which can never be separated. This union with Him is brought out in Scripture by the use of seven figures, each of which makes a definite contribution to our total understanding of our complete relationship with Christ.

1.   The Last Adam and the New Creation.

As Adam is the head of a race in which all partake of his nature and originate from his being, so Christ is the head of a new race or creation in which all partake of His nature and originate from His being (I Cor. 15:45, 47; II Cor. 5:17; Gal. 6:15; Rom. 5:12-21).

2.   The Head and the Body of Christ.

The head gives direction and gives life to the body (I Cor. 12:12-27; Col. 1:18; Eph. 1:22-23).

3.   The Shepherd and the Sheep.

There is no relationship between the hireling and the sheep, but there is between the true shepherd and his sheep. He gives his life for them (Luke 15:3-7; John 10:1-28; 21:16-17; I Pet. 5:1-4; Heb. 13:20).

4.   The Vine and the Branches.

It is impossible to tell where the vine ends and the branch begins (John 15:1-11).

5.   The Chief Corner Stone and the Stones of the Building.

In the ancient construction of buildings, everything was done in relationship to the chief corner stone (Eph. 2:20; I Pet. 2:4-8).

6.   The High Priest and the Royal Priesthood.

As the priests all came from the same family, being

related to the High Priest, so we are all related to Christ and are descendants from Him who is both King and Priest. We, therefore, are a royal priesthood (Hebrews; I Pet. 2:5, 9; Rev. 1:6).

7. The Bridegroom and the Bride.

This looks more to the future than to the present, but it shows the relationship of those who become one flesh (John 3:29; Eph. 5:25-33; Rev. 19:6-8).

A good number of other minor expressions are used in Scripture as well as statements like John 17:20-22 which reads, "Neither pray I for these alone, but for them also which shall believe on me through their word; that they all may be one; as thou, Father, art in me, and I in thee, that they also may be one in us .... And the glory which thou gavest me I have given them."

The central branch of the golden lampstand was the chiefest of them all. It is for this reason called of itself "the candlestick," or the "the lampstand." It alone had four sets of almond clusters of bowls, knops and flowers rather than three sets as was the case in each of the branches. The reason for this is that Christ is the head of His church. Christ must "in all things . . . have the preeminence" (Col. 1:18). Truly He is the "chiefest among ten thousand . . . yea, He is altogether lovely" (Song of Sol. 5:10, 16). It is His nature, furthermore, to be "in the midst" (Luke 2:46; John 19:18; Matt. 18:20; Luke 24:36; John 20:19, 26; Rev. 1:13; 2:1; Rev. 5:6).

While Christ was made like unto His brethren (Heb. 2:17; Rom. 8:29), yet Christ was never to be forever like us (i.e., the incarnation was not the end of the process, but only the initial step); but we are to be made forever like Him (i.e., like He is in His final position with a glorified body in heaven) (Rom. 8:30; I John 3:2).

The Lord Jesus is the head of the church; we are the members, one *in* Christ, and one *with* Christ. Just as He was made into this beautiful and exquisite lampstand because He was completely submissive to the Father's will in everything, so we are also to suffer with Him because we are obedient to our heavenly Father's will. This suffering in no way adds anything to our salvation. Christ did that *in toto* on the cross.

This suffering completes the lampstand, making it a glorious article which will be glorified in God's presence forever.

Paul was one who was specifically called upon to suffer greatly for the Lord (Acts 9:16; I Cor. 4:9-13; II Cor. 11:23-28). He suffered because he was the Lord's bondservant (Eph. 4:1). In his suffering for the church, Paul states that he was filling up the sufferings of Christ for His body—the church. "Who now rejoice in my sufferings for you, and fill up that which is behind of the afflictions of Christ in my flesh for his body's sake, which is the church" (Col. 1:24).

This at first seems a strange statement in the epistle that speaks of the fulness of Christ. Yet it is not, when we understand that the sufferings of Christ may be divided into (1) that which we can share in, and (2) that which cannot be shared with anyone. In the sufferings of Christ which provided our eternal salvation, we have no part in whatever; in the sufferings of Christ as the servant of the Lord, we have the privilege of sharing with Him because we are inseparably connected with Him as a branch of the lampstand. When the process of suffering with Him is all over, we will be glorified together with Him in God's presence for all eternity.

The Scriptures are full on this subject, yet very few believers have ever entered into the significance of this truth. Let us first give the Scripture, and then relate it to the making of the lampstand from one lump of pure gold—Jesus Christ being the central shaft while we are the branches.

"And if children, then heirs; heirs of God, and joint-heirs with Christ; if so be that we suffer with him, that we may be also glorified together" (Rom. 8:17). The same gold made the central lampstand and the branches. It was one beaten work inseparably related in both suffering and in glory. As we have suffered with Him, so we will be glorified in heaven together with Him.

"For I reckon that the sufferings of this present time are not worthy to be compared with the glory which shall be revealed in us" (Rom. 8:18). We shall have the same glory as Christ does because of our relationship to Him. When the process of beating is over, and we are glorified with Christ, we will wonder why we complained at all.

"As it is written, For thy sake we are killed all the day long; we are accounted as sheep for the slaughter" (Rom. 8:36). We receive the hammer blows continually in time because we are "the Lord's." It would, in many ways, be much easier to die for the Lord than to live for Him— completely submissive to His will.

"And whether one member suffers all the members suffer with it; or one member be honoured, all the members rejoice with it" (I Cor. 12:26). This is seen vividly in the one-piece golden lampstand where every branch is related to every other branch through Christ the stem. This relationship is not a forced one, but an intrinsic one. Truly, "God has tempered the body together" (I Cor. 12:24).

"For as the sufferings of Christ abound in us, so our consolation also aboundeth by Christ. And whether we be afflicted, it is for your consolation and salvation, which is effectual in the enduring of the same sufferings which we also suffer: or whether we be comforted, it is for your consolation and salvation. And our hope of you is stedfast, knowing, that as ye are partakers of the sufferings, so shall ye be also of the consolation" (II Cor. 1:5-7). The statement is sufficient of itself. Those with Paul were suffering but also receiving comfort from the Lord. So also those at Corinth were suffering, and they will also be partakers of the same comfort. Every believer has a place in the sufferings of Christ in order that he might be glorified with the Lord in the lampstand.

"For which cause we faint not; but though our outward man perish, yet the inward man is renewed day by day. For our light affliction, which is but for a moment, worketh for us a far more exceeding and eternal weight of glory" (II Cor. 4:16-17). God gives us grace each day to bear the blows of the hammer He directs at us in order that someday we will not only be "in Christ" but will be absolutely beautiful in Christ.

"For unto you it is given in the behalf of Christ, not only to believe on him, but also to suffer for his sake" (Phil. 1:29). Believing in the Lord Jesus Christ takes care of the brazen altar experience in which we come to the cross where the Lord bore our sins. We do not go through this experience, for Christ suffered and died in our place. But we do have the privilege of suffering with Him, and this is the lampstand experience.

"That I may know him, and the power of his resurrection, and the fellowship of his sufferings, being made conformable unto his death" (Phil. 3:10). We have now come around again to this verse and its truth. While we cannot enter into the death experience with Christ which paid our eternal salvation, we can enter into the servant aspect of His life which led Him to go even to the death experience of the cross. This is what Paul wants to experience in his life. He wants to be just as yielded as the Lord Jesus Christ was when He "became obedient unto death, even the death of the cross" (Phil. 2:8).

"Who now rejoice in my sufferings for you, and fill up that which is behind of the afflictions of Christ in my flesh for his body's sake, which is the church" (Col. 1:24). The lampstand is still in the process of being pounded out today. His body, the church, is still receiving the hammer blows. Christ has already received all of His blows and is glorified. The branches are receiving their's now in time. Some day this work will be over, and the Lord will take His body home with Him in heaven. But until we are ready to be glorified in God's presence forever, there is suffering in the body down here on earth.

"If we suffer, we shall also reign with Him" (II Tim. 2:12). We have a part in the golden lampstand.

"Yea, and all that will live godly in Christ Jesus shall suffer persecution" (II Tim. 3:12). You cannot live for the Lord down here without receiving the blows of the hammer from men.

"For in that he himself hath suffered being tempted, he is able to succour them that are tempted" (Heb. 2:18). Compare this verse with II Corinthians 1:5-7 for our consolation from the Lord.

"Remember them that are in bonds, as bound with them; and them which suffer adversity, as being yourselves also in the body" (Heb. 13:3). This again reveals our intrinsic relationship, branch with branch, through Christ the central stem (cp. I Cor. 12:26).

First Peter 2:20-23 contains much about suffering. "For what glory is it, if, when ye be buffeted for your faults [i.e., you sin and are buffeted for it], ye shall take it patiently? but if, when ye do well and suffer for it, ye take it patiently, this is acceptable with God." The servant of the Lord who does well and suffered for it, is the servant who is receiving blows that will glorify him before God forever. "For even hereunto were ye called: because Christ also suffered for us, leaving us an example, that ye should follow his steps." We cannot follow Christ in His death for sin, but we can follow Him in suffering. We were all called to suffer. "Who did no sin, neither was guile found in his mouth." He was the true servant of the Lord without sin, always doing those things which please the Father. "Who, when he was reviled, reviled not again; when he suffered, he threatened not; but committed himself to him that judgeth righteously." He was pure gold submitting himself to every blow of the hammer because He knew that no blow could ever fall which was not His Father's will for Him to receive, and that the Father was always righteous in what He allowed. How do we measure up as servants, and how do we feel about the blows we are receiving?

First Peter 4:12-16 is another extended passage. "Beloved, think it not strange concerning the fiery trials which is to try you, as though some strange thing happened unto you." Fiery trials are the norm for believers in order to conform them into the very image of Christ glorified. "But rejoice, inasmuch as ye are partakers of Christ's suffering that, when his glory shall be revealed, ye may be glad also with exceeding joy." It is hard now; but it is only glory by and by. "If ye be reproached for the name of Christ, happy are ye; for the spirit of glory and of God resteth upon you: on their part he is evil spoken of, but on your part he is glorified." The Holy Spirit of God, which is glory itself, is upon us, bearing the burden of each blow and making us, even now, more into the image of Christ. "But let none of you suffer as a murderer, or as a thief, or as an evildoer, or as a busybody in other men's matters. Yet if any man suffer as a Christian, let him not be ashamed; but let him glorify God on this behalf." Suffering as a Christian should make us shine. It should increase the light, not dull it.

"But the God of all grace, who hath called us unto his eternal glory by Christ Jesus, after that ye have suffered a while, make you perfect, stablish, strengthen, settle you" (I Pet. 5:10). This verse, with its truth concerning the golden lampstand, leaves me in awe. Just to think that we who are by nature children of wrath become pure gold by being partakers of His divine nature, and we are called by God into His eternal glory through being united with the Lord Jesus Christ. Thus we have been given Christ's nature of glory (pure gold), and made into His very image of exceeding eternal glory (lampstand). Now we are suffering for awhile in time, but then perfect, i.e., complete in all our individual parts. The hammer blows upon the branches will all be over, even as they are upon the central shaft. Hallelujah, what a Savior!

So we see that the same process used to fashion the central shaft was used to fashion the branches. In like manner, we become conformed to the likeness of Christ by partaking of the sufferings of Christ. God permits suffering to come into our lives just so we may be conformed to the image of Christ. By sufferings, by tribulation, by persecution, by trials, we are progressively beaten into the very image of Christ's perfection. The blows may be of many kinds—financial, physical, spiritual, mental, social—but they only come because God permitted them to fall upon us, and we may trust Him, that they are for our good, and will ultimately result in our glory.

May we "consider him that endured such contradiction of sinners against himself, lest ye be wearied and faint in your minds. Ye have not yet resisted unto blood, striving against sin" (Heb. 12:3-4).

Chapter 16

The Day
Christ Died

John says they would not enter in "lest they should be defiled; but that they might eat the passover" (John 18:28). The mention of eating the Passover has presented a real problem. How was it that Christ and His disciples had already eaten the Passover, but the leaders of Israel had not? "Some doubt exists as to whether the Last Supper was the paschal meal or not. According to the Synoptic Gospels, it was (Lk. 22:7; Matt. 26:17; Mk. 14:12); while according to John, the Passover was to be eaten some time following the Last Supper (Jn. 18:28)" (*The International Standard Bible Encyclopaedia*, IV. 2258). Dr. Robertson phrases the question another way: "To put this question in another form, it would be, On what day of the month was Jesus crucified? For the crucifixion occurred on the same Jewish day as the eating of the meal recorded by all four evangelists" (*A Harmony of the Gospel*, p. 279). Adam Clarke quotes Bouilleau as saying, "If I be not mistaken, this question will never be thoroughly understood." Then he adds himself, "It would be presumptuous to say, Christ *did eat* the passover this last year of his ministry: it would be as hazardous to say *He did not* eat it . . ." (*Clarke Commentary*, V. 267).

To show further something of the problem, let us briefly present some of the solutions offered.

(1) "When the Passover fell on Friday Night, the Pharisees ate the meal on Thursday and the Sadducees on Friday, and that Jesus followed the custom of the Pharisees" (Chwolson, 1904, quoted by *I.S.B.E.*, IV, 2258).

(2) "It is a common opinion that our Lord ate the passover some hours before the Jews ate it; for the Jews, according to custom, ate theirs at the end of the fourteenth day, but Christ ate his the preceding evening, which was the beginning of the same sixth day, or Friday; the Jews begin their day at sun-setting, we at midnight. Thus, Christ ate the passover on the same day with the Jews, but not on the same hour. Christ kept this passover the beginning of the fourteenth day, the precise day and hour in which the Jews had eaten their first passover in Egypt" (*Clarke Commentary*, V. 248).

(3) "The disciples followed the true φασις, or appearance of the new moon, confirmed by sufficient witnesses, he and his disciples ate the passover on that day; but the Jews, following the pertinacious decree of the San-hedrin, did not eat it till the day following" (Dr. Cudworth, quoted, by *Clarke Commentary*, V. 265).

(4) "Our Lord did not eat what is commonly called the passover this year, but another, of a mystical kind" (Toinard, quoted by *Clarke Commentary*, V. 266).

(5) " . . . Jesus ate the passover meal at the regular time about 6 P.M. beginning at 15 Nisan. The passover lamb was slain on the afternoon of 14 Nisan and the meal eaten at sunset the beginning of 15 Nisan" (A. T. Robertson, *Word Pictures in the New Testament*, I, 207). " . . . in John 18:28 it is probable that the passover feast, referred to as the passover meal (the last supper) had already been observed" (Ibid.).

(6) A slight variation of the above is given by Sir Robert Anderson. He holds that Jesus ate the Passover meal at the regular time after being killed the afternoon of the 14th of Nisan. But that the eating at night of the 15th of Nisan was reckoned still the 14th and that at sunrise the day was the 15th of Nisan, and it was the Feast Day.

Edersheim makes an important contribution to this problem when he states, " . . . the term Pesach, or 'Passover,' was applied not only to the Paschal Lamb, but to all the Passover sacrifices, especially to what was called the Chagigah, or festive offering (from Chag, or Chagag, to bring the festive sacrifice usual at each of the three Great Feasts). According to the express rule (Chag. I.3) the Chagigah was brought on the first festive Paschal Day. It was offered immediately after the morning-service, and eaten on that day—probably some time before the evening, when, as we shall by-and-by see, another ceremony claimed public attention. We can therefore quite understand that, not on the eve of the Passover, but on the first Paschal day, the Sanhedrists would avoid incurring a defilement which, lasting till the evening would not only have involved them in the inconvenience of Levitical defilement on the first festive day, but have actually prevented their offering their offering on that day the Passover, festive sacrifice, or Chagigah. . . . There would have been no reason to fear 'defilement' on the morning of the Paschal Sacrifice; but entrance into the Praetorium on the morning of the first Passover-day would have rendered it impossible for them to offer the Chagigah, which is also designated by the term Pesach" (*The Life and Times of Jesus the Messiah*, II, 568).

Jeremias agrees when he says, "It is true that the paschal sacrifices (hagigah) which were eaten during the seven days of the feast (Nisan 15-21) sometimes were called pesah in accordance with Deut. 16:2 and II Chron. 35:7, so that John 18:28 could be referred to as Nisan 15. The meaning then would be that the members of the Sanhedrin did not enter the praetorium lest they be defiled and so prevented from eating the paschal sacrifice (hagigah)" (*The Eucharistic Words of Jesus*, pp. 20-21). (Notice that what Edersheim spells Chagigah, Jeremias gives as hagigah, yet this refers to the same offering.)

Jeremias, however, questions this interpretation, feeling that the Gentile Christians to whom John wrote would not have so understood the phrase in this way. While this may be true, it is difficult, from our vantage point now, to understand just how they would have understood it. Because of the teaching of John and others, the Christian community may have had far more understanding than we give them credit for. Moreover, John may not have wanted to go into a detailed explanation that would have been required by the use of any other word then simply "the passover." John would have been technically right, as anyone who knew the totality of the Jewish customs could have explained.

After listing the other positions, Jeremias proclaims, "None of these attempts at harmonization therefore is convincing; the situation still is quite simply that the synoptic and Johannine datings of the Last Supper sharply contradict one another, and that means that the question remains an open one: Was the Last Supper of Jesus a passover meal or not?" (Ibid. p. 26).

Personally, I feel that Edersheim's explanation is a valid one, for John uses the word "passover" ten times in his Gospel, and each time he seems to refer not to the paschal supper, but to the passover feast of the next day (2:13, 23; 6:4; 11:55; 12:1; 13:1; 18:28, 39; 19:14). So the phrase, "eat the passover," can refer to the celebration of the passover festival. There need be no contradiction whatever between John and the Synoptics.

However, the date proposed by various ones as Robertson and Edersheim for killing and eating the passover and the unleavened bread that follows is quite out of harmony with the days of the month on which these occasions fell when they were instituted in the Old Testament. While Pharisaism and Rabbinism had, through their traditions, nullified much of the Old Testament Scriptures at the time of Christ, it had not as yet affected the date or time when the passover lambs were slain at the Temple. The passover lambs were killed "between the evenings" at the going down of the sun (Deut. 16:6; Ex. 12:6, 18; Lev. 23:5; Num. 9:3, 5). Edersheim comments in regard to "between the two evenings" as follows: "There can be no question that, in the time of Christ, it was understood to refer to the interval between the commencement of the sun's decline and what was reckoned as the hour of his final disappearance (about 6 P.M.)" (*Life and Times of Jesus the Messiah*, II, 490). The lambs could be sacrificed only one place, which was Jerusalem at the Temple

(Deut. 16:6). Since there were thousands of lambs to be slain there, these began to be killed just as soon as the sun permitted—about 3 P.M. With all the courses of priests present, the offerer would kill his lamb, and the priest would catch the blood in a golden bowl which was then sprinkled before the altar. The lamb was prepared by being roasted, and with the three-fold blast of the silver trumpets at about 6 P.M. the pascha had commenced.

With this, Josephus agrees when he says, " . . .[the] feast which is called the Passover, when they slay their sacrifices, from the ninth hour [3 P.M.] till the eleventh [5 P.M.] . . ." (*Wars of the Jews*, VI, 9, 3). That the night on which the lambs were eaten was the 14th of Nisan and not the 15th is clearly stated by Josephus also. "In the month. . . , called Nisan, and is the beginning of our year, on the fourteenth day of the lunar month, when the sun is in Aries, (for in this month it was that we were delivered from bondage under the Egyptians,) the law ordained that we should every year slay that sacrifice which I before told you we slew when we came out of Egypt, and which we called the Passover; and so we do celebrate this passover in companies, leaving nothing of what we sacrifice till the day [break] following. The feast of unleavened bread succeeds that of the passover, and falls on the fifteenth day of the month, and continues seven days . . ." (*Antiquities of the Jews*, III, 10, 5).

The pascha, then, was eaten during the night, but no later than the middle of the night. The night for eating the pascha was the 14th of Nisan, for it could not have been the 15th, which was a high or sabbath day; and therefore the killing of the lambs commenced "between the evenings" of the 13th and 14th, or at some time after 3 P.M. on the 13th of Nisan. If the lamb was not slain until the afternoon of the 14th, as Robertson and Edersheim as well as others contend, then it would have been the night of the 15th on which they were eaten, and this is just not the case. The Chagigah was eaten then on the daylight period of the 14th of Nisan, or the first day of the feast.

No leaven was permitted in the Israelite's dwelling at this time. The cleansing of all leaven had taken place the

night of the 13th, and the burning on the morning of the
13th of Nisan. An Israelite would not enter into a Gentile's
dwelling lest he be defiled by leaven in that Gentile's home.
At sunset on the 15th of Nisan was the beginning of the
Feast of Unleavened Bread. This was a high day, and as such,
no work of any kind was permitted. The 15th of Nisan was
the day that Israel came out of Egypt (Num. 33:3; Ex.
12:17; 13:3). The 15th being a high day or Sabbath day, the
day before was the preparation. Christ was killed on the
preparation, which was the 14th day of Nisan, and His body
was taken down from the cross and buried before the
Sabbath began. He had kept the Passover with His disciples as
was His desire (Luke 22:15). On the day of preparation
things could be bought (John 13:29; Mark 15:46). Yet a
person could be defiled by a wrong use of the day (Ex.
12:15-20). A person even before this time had to be clean,
and had to remain clean (Num. 9:6-11; II Chron. 30:15-20;
John 18:28; Compare this with John 15:3).

Thus there is no conflict in Scripture if, as Edersheim
holds, the Chagigah is offered on the first day of the feast,
and this day is the 14th of Nisan and not the high or Sabbath
day of the 15th.